CERDIC

CERDIC

MYSTERIOUS DARK AGE KING WHO FOUNDED ENGLAND

PAUL HARPER

Pen & Sword
MILITARY
AN IMPRINT OF PEN & SWORD BOOKS LTD.
YORKSHIRE – PHILADELPHIA

First published in Great Britain in 2024 by
PEN AND SWORD MILITARY
An imprint of
Pen & Sword Books Limited
Yorkshire – Philadelphia

ISBN 978 1 39903 728 0

A CIP catalogue record for this book is available from the British Library.

Typeset in Times New Roman 11/14 by
SJmagic DESIGN SERVICES, India.
Printed and bound in the UK by CPI Group (UK) Ltd.

Pen & Sword Books Limited incorporates the imprints of Atlas, Archaeology, Aviation, Discovery, Family History, Fiction, History, Maritime, Military, Military Classics, Politics, Select, Transport, True Crime, Air World, Frontline Publishing, Leo Cooper, Remember When, Seaforth Publishing, The Praetorian Press, Wharncliffe Local History, Wharncliffe Transport, Wharncliffe True Crime and White Owl.

For a complete list of Pen & Sword titles please contact
PEN & SWORD BOOKS LIMITED
George House, Units 12 & 13, Beevor Street, Off Pontefract Road,
Barnsley, South Yorkshire, S71 1HN, England
E-mail: enquiries@pen-and-sword.co.uk
Website: www.pen-and-sword.co.uk

or

PEN AND SWORD BOOKS
1950 Lawrence Rd, Havertown, PA 19083, USA
E-mail: uspen-and-sword@casematepublishers.com
Website: www.penandswordbooks.com

FSC
www.fsc.org
MIX
Paper | Supporting responsible forestry
FSC® C013604

Contents

Civitas of Britain in 410 (Rupert Matthews)

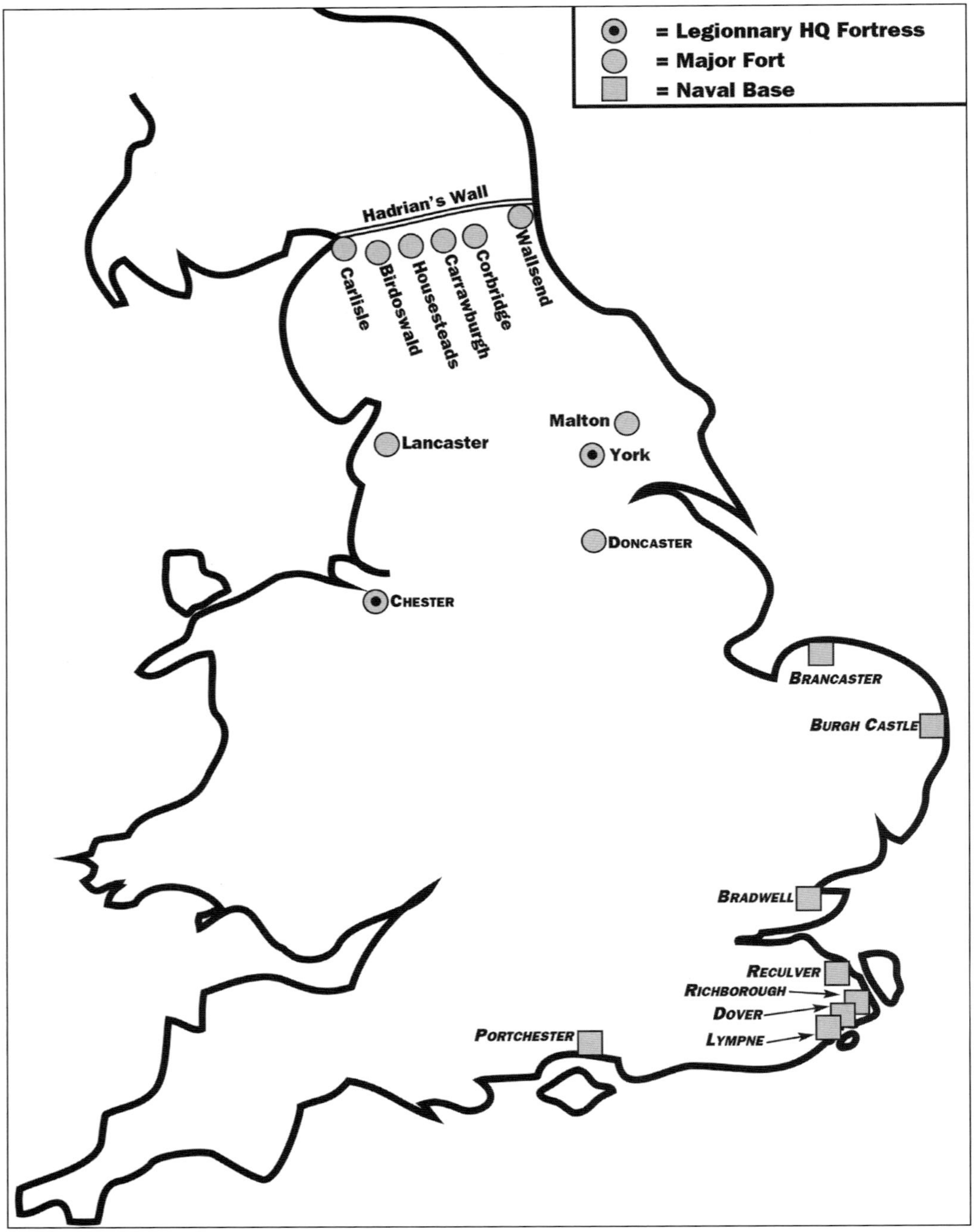

The Roman military in Britain in 410 (Rupert Matthews)

Britain as described by Gildas c.530s (Rupert Matthews)

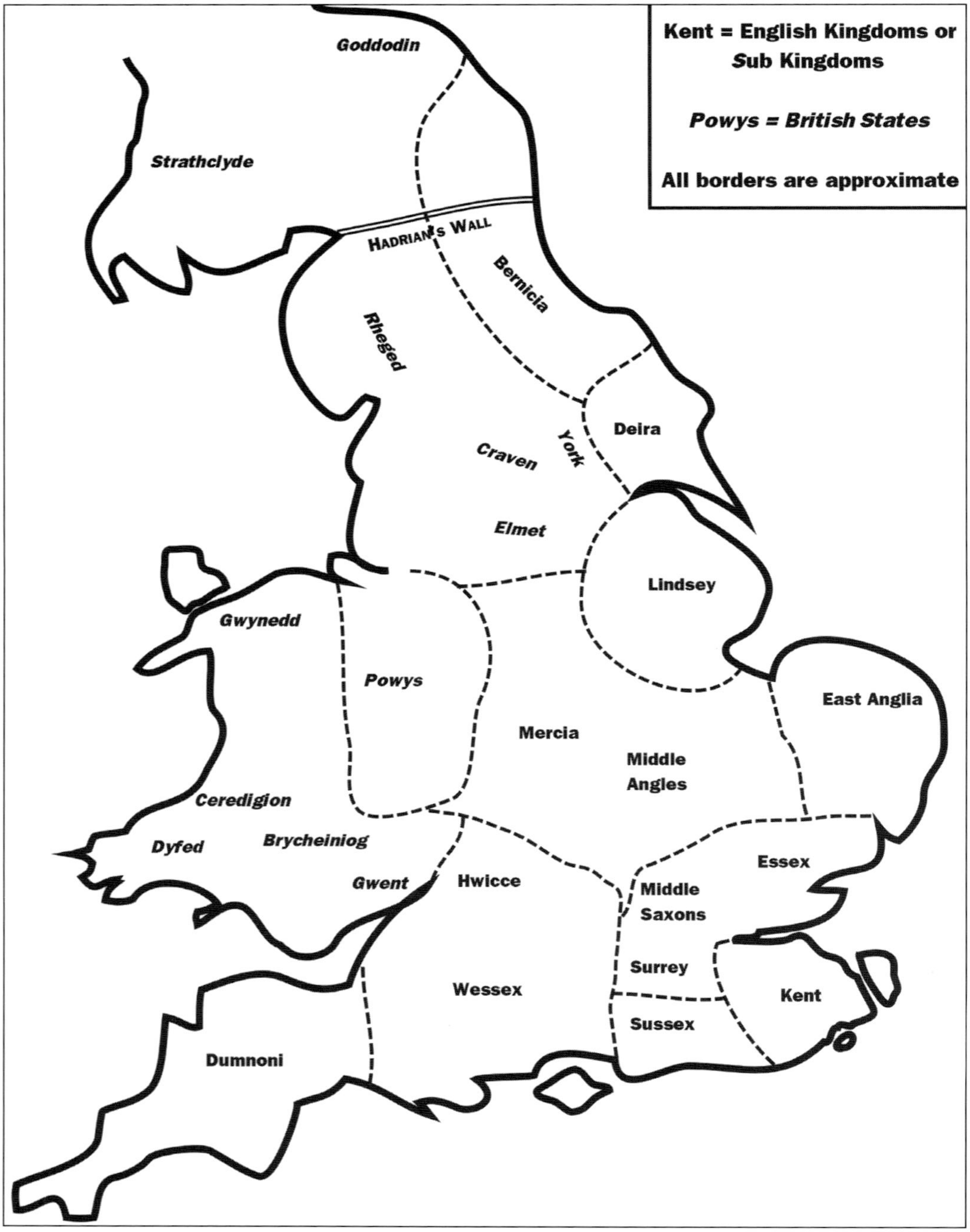

Britain in c.600 (Rupert Matthews)

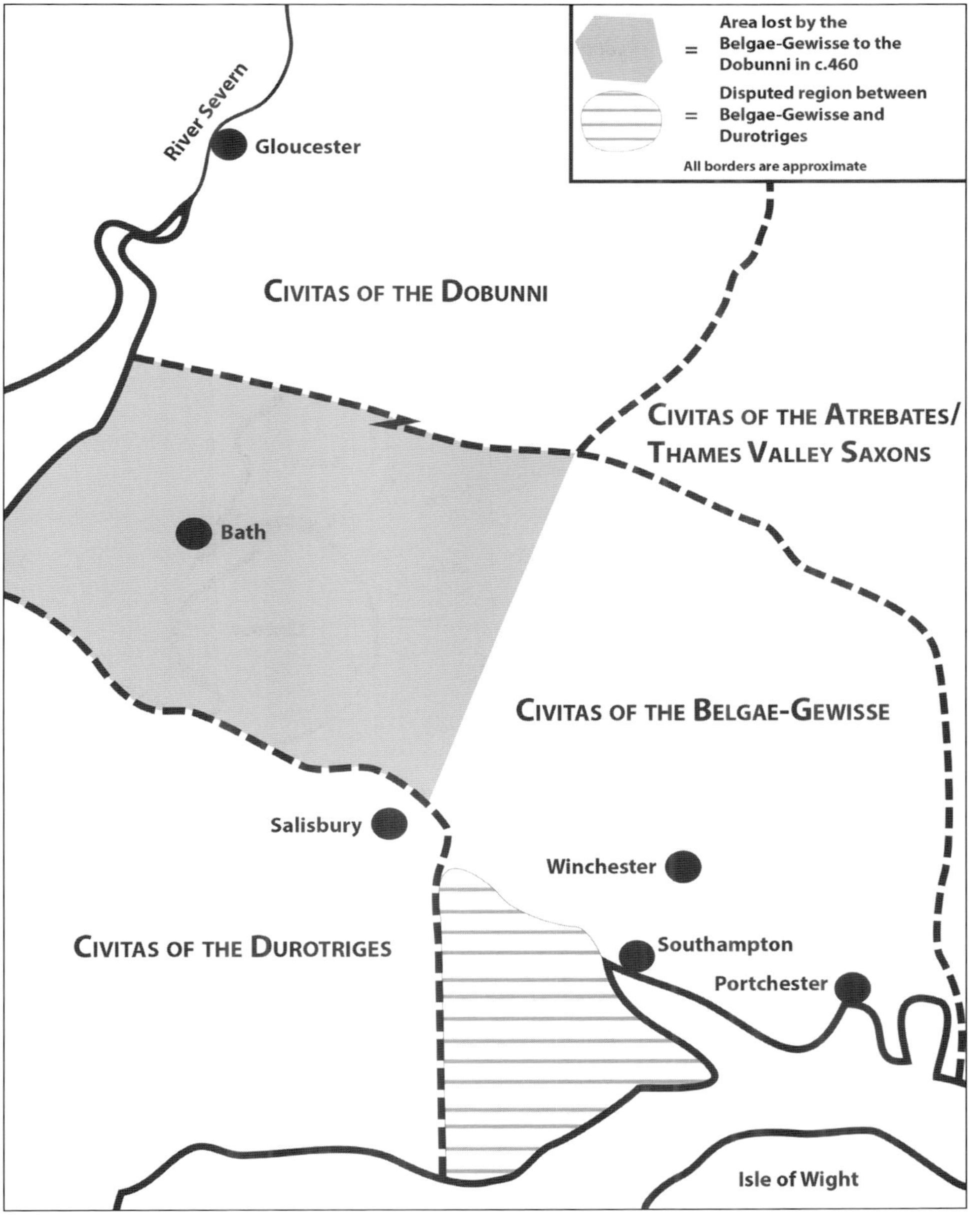

The civitas of the Belgae-Gewisse c. 520 (Rupert Matthews/Paul Harper)

Preface

The warband gathered on the shores of the Isle of Wight just before sunset in preparation. Surprising their enemy in the early hours was crucial to their success. In near darkness, they dragged their huge clinker-built vessels, so-called because the edges of the hull planks overlap, across the pebble beach at Cowes for the short journey over the Solent.

As the raiding party, which was around 300 strong, edged closer to the shoreline, they mulled over the impending confrontation and consequences. They sought to rule from this day forward without recognizing any superior authority. Securing this coastline would make or break the entire plan. This row was just a few miles but may have felt like an eternity with the extreme risks lying ahead.

Warriors would have travelled in a vessel matching the seventh-century Gredstedbro or the Nydam from 300 years earlier, which were both found in modern-day Denmark and shared a very similar design. These largely oak-built rowing ships, which also shared similarities to later Viking ships with masts, could be between 70ft to 80ft long.[1]

The Gredstedbro, first uncovered in the Kongeå (King's River) in South Jutland, featured a nailed frame and a flat keel so it could navigate smaller rivers and showed signs of being regularly dragged to shore. It had the same keel, scarf and stern as the famous Sutton Hoo burial ship.

The Nydam Boat, the oldest Germanic deep-sea vessel and dated to between AD 310 and 320, was found in a sacred bog of the same name, which has thrown up spears, arrows, swords, brooches and other artefacts that were chucked in as ritual offerings.

Each side of the Nydam has five clinker-built oak strakes, which are joined with iron clench nails, while the hull is tied to frames and attached to the keel plank.[2] With space for forty-five men including thirty rowers, the Nydam was thought to have been a large military transport vessel that was perfect for navigating dangerous coasts.[3] A similar vessel would have

Cerdic's forces landed in a vessel resembling the Nydam boat, which was discovered in a bog in southern Denmark (Anneli Karlsson/Sjöhistoriska Museet)

transported the warband for the trip from the Isle of Wight, which some knew would be their last.

Most of the warband would have been armed with spears and several javelins and a sax, a large dagger or knife, which gives the Saxons their name. Many of the boat's crew would have looked fearsome[4] with descriptions of military attire at the time including white sheaths for knives, gilded armour built to scale, animal skin coats and iron-splinted armour for the limbs known as a chain mail, made up of hundreds of interlocking and riveted tiny rings. Each of the men would also have a shield made from leather-covered lime with a large iron.

Rich warriors and generals may have been armed with swords, which often had so-called 'life stones', a form of religious totem, attached to their scabbards and were often handed down from generation to generation. The main weapon of choice was the spear, which was used for throwing, occasionally thrusting and lateral cutting.

As the ships made landfall on the south-east coast, each man slowly edged out over the side and stepped onto the shingle, pulling the vessel along with them.

Their leader, who they knew as Cerdic, was the last to leave the ship. Pausing on the shore, he glanced back at the Isle of Wight one last time and thought of his bride and son. The next few hours would decide all their futures. Little did Cerdic realize what happened next would also shape the course of British history.

As a journalist, I've always loved investigations and the unexplained, and no era has gripped me as much as the early Anglo-Saxon period after the Roman troops departed, which has always remained shrouded in mystery to a degree because of the few contemporary sources.

View from Stansore Point near Lepe showing the short distance to the Isle of Wight

At the centre of this mysterious era is Cerdic, one of Britain's most enigmatic figures. Incredibly, little is known for certain about Cerdic, including even his actual name, even though his descendants on paper include the current royal family. I have always found this truly fascinating.

Our knowledge rests on the *Anglo-Saxon Chronicle* written down hundreds of years later, which cannot be taken at face value and often poses more questions than it resolves.

The findings in this book will offer a new theory on how Cerdic forged the powerful kingdom of Wessex, which evolved into England, based on extensive archaeological findings and academic studies.

This investigation begins in Winchester, which became the capital of Wessex. Examining its fate in the early medieval period – along with other key regions such as the Isle of Wight and Upper Thames – is crucial to understanding how Cerdic rose to power.

Other chapters will also explore the dramatic impact of significant migration from the North Sea and investigate the few available records, such as the questionable account in the *Anglo-Saxon Chronicle*, and an infamous text by the monk Gildas.

One of my most enlightening discoveries has been learning how a decade of climate disasters shaped a new Anglo-Saxon world. A comprehensive study has found that Cerdic is likely to have reigned during this very period.

One by one, mysteries connected to his reign, including the identity of his missing son Creoda, the location of every bloody battle, the shadowy group known as the Gewisse and the links to a famous elegy for a heroic warrior, will be investigated.

Myths and folklore connected to Cerdic, including his possible identity as a Welsh king and warfare against the legendary Arthur, are also probed but left until near the end as simply the most confusing aspect.

When I started work on this book, my focus quickly shifted to a vague but intriguing reference to the possible burial site of Cerdic in an ancient royal charter issued by the son of Alfred the Great. What followed was something of a treasure hunt.

Hundreds of barrows once covered the landscape of Britain in which people buried their loved ones and leaders under, often in prominent locations on the edge of kingdoms to claim the land and connect with the mythological past. Aerial photography has revealed traces of these barrows even if they have been extensively ploughed over and the results are displayed in an online database mapping the many historical finds across England. Investigations took me to a small hill and a site known as 'Ceardices Beorg', i.e. Cerdic's Barrow. The discovery could solve one of Britain's great historical mysteries. The story of Cerdic, England's founder.

Chapter 1

Winchester

But Alfred up against them bare and gripped the ground and grasped the air. Staggered, and strove to stand, he broke them with a broken sword. A little towards the sea, and for one hour of panting peace, ringed with a roar that would not cease.

The Ballad of the White Horse, G.K. Chesterton, 1911

The Westgate was one of the six ancient medieval entrances to the former walled town of Winchester. Heading through the Westgate's massive arch leads to the current high street, which was rammed on the Saturday before Christmas, even amid the train strikes.

The statue of Alfred the Great, who famously defeated the Vikings, stands at the bottom of Winchester High Street

Alfred the Great's statue loomed large at the bottom of the high street just past the crowded market, but my first destination was slightly beyond this unmissable monument to Winchester's most renowned resident.

Here, I found the last trace of the thick Roman walls, which encircled the town and enclosed a circumference of 2 miles, in a small section next to the River Itchen, which features a small, gated holding cell. Winchester's famous walls were otherwise demolished several hundreds of years ago after falling into disrepair and with the risk of a potential collapse becoming a danger for pedestrians.

The Westgate at the top of Winchester High Street is one of only two fortified gateways still standing

With the surrounding slopes and the walled perimeter, you quickly begin to understand why Winchester was turned into a Roman fortress and the heart of the Anglo-Saxon kingdom of Wessex.

When stepping out of the station in Winchester, I had a sense of instant familiarity with the successive small slopes reminiscent of the urban parts of my home county of Devon, which is famed for its dramatic rolling hills. This unique landscape is a product of Winchester's position at the end of the western chalk ridge of the South Downs, a remarkable hilltop, which can be followed on a 100-mile trail to the iconic white cliffs of Beachy Head in East Sussex.

Even before Rome's troops and officials arrived and turned Winchester into a thriving market town, tribes took full advantage of the ringed chalk slopes in the surrounds, and the natural protection they offered, by creating a large fort at St Catherine's Hill and earthworks suggest another stronghold in the south at Oliver's Battery.

Bronze Age people buried their dead on Magdalen Hill Down to the east, where three of the circular barrows are still of considerable size,[1] with steep-sided circular mounds and diameters ranging from 52ft to 65ft and standing between 5ft to 11ft high on different sides. They remain an

A small cell next to the River Avon is all that remains of Winchester's Roman wall, which encircled the town

impressive site just yards from the public entrance on a slope overlooking Winchester to the west and Twyford to the southeast. This cemetery, which includes five barrows in total, is thought to date to the Late Neolithic and Bronze Age.

Britain has long been a tribal island. Throughout this book, you will find repeated references to dykes, often called the 'Devil's Ditch' or 'Grim Ditch', along with hill forts and barrows. Tribes proudly marked the extent of their territory with massive ditches, buried their loved ones in unmissable mounds on prominent hills and lived in large forts surrounded by imposing ramparts so they could see danger for miles around.

The next stop in Winchester was another of the many hillsides steeped in history just a short walk from the high street in the shape of St Giles Hill, which overlooks the town from 50m above. I've been particularly interested in suggestions that St Giles Hill was a burial ground when Cerdic reigned and the level of occupation in the town is shrouded in mystery.

An existing churchyard cemetery can still be found close to the grassed open area at the top. St Giles Hill featured furnished and unfurnished burials dated to before the seventh century, which were uncovered around 100 years ago. These included a skeleton with a dagger and a knife, another

Three of the five round barrows on Magdalen Hill on the outskirts of Winchester, where Bronze Age tribes used to bury their dead

man buried with a sword and a further six burials, which included two spearheads, two iron ferrules (a type of ring to reinforce a shaft) and a twisted silver ring.

Just over twenty years ago, more objects were unearthed in a house extension, including a bronze sword pommel, amber and glass beads, two shield bosses, an iron buckle, a key, a knife and a spearhead. These likely originated from graves and hint at the existence of an undiscovered burial site nearby.[2]

The Historic Environment Records (HERs) database details the thousands of ancient barrows, trackways and settlements across the land in each county, many of which are no longer or only partially visible on the ground. According to the records, a potential early Anglo-Saxon cemetery may have been located at the back of the grassed area of St Giles Hill, where three graves were discovered in 1898, one of which is thought to have been an Anglo-Saxon chieftain.[3]

At the bottom of the park is Chesil Street, which is noteworthy because one of the main post-Roman burial grounds on the Isle of Wight is also called Chessell Down. These may both derive from the Old English word *ciest* meaning 'chest' or 'coffin', combined with *hyll*, meaning 'hill'.[4]

As I trudged up St Giles Hill on one of the several winding paths, I bumped into a friendly couple walking their dog who told me how just below the hill was once a clearing and a spot where people were hanged.

Locally, there had indeed once been a place known as Gallows Hill, where crowds of people would morbidly watch the hangings conducted by Winchester Prison, which dates to the thirteenth century in some form and was once located in the high street area.[5] History can be found everywhere you turn in this eastern corner of Winchester.

Tree-covered paths lead up St Giles Hill, and it proved worth the hike with the impressive panoramic views from the vantage point. As I reached the summit, the sunset had begun to the west providing a dazzling backdrop. It is not hard to see why this historically appears to have been such a popular burial location for the townsfolk.

Clearly visible in the foreground were the spires of the spectacularly long Winchester Cathedral, while to the south stands Winchester College, where the old Roman wall can be made out around the college. In the foreground, Charles II's late-seventeenth century castle loomed large. St Giles Hill's grass summit was the former setting for an annual medieval fair, which became one of the most popular in Europe.

Winchester from the stunning viewing point at St Giles Hill where burials dated to around the time of Cerdic's reign were discovered

Winchester's past has been comprehensively documented from Roman times, but its fate during the early Anglo-Saxon period, as with so many other towns and villages, has proved much less transparent.

Cerdic's battles revolved around Hampshire and so the question is understanding how Winchester figured in this emerging kingdom despite the lack of archaeological evidence and signs of life inside the walls for 200 years from the mid-fifth century.

Burial sites just outside Winchester have, however, hinted at what was happening during this mysterious age after throwing up several artefacts. One such cemetery was discovered by chance during the Second World War when the laying of water pipes for an American military camp at Worthy Park in Kingsworthy, around 3 miles further up the River Itchen from Winchester, led to the discovery of an Angel-Saxon burial site.[6]

Worthy Park was excavated by the scholar Sonia Chadwick Hawkes in the early 1960s, but her resulting report remained unpublished until after her death in 1999. Findings reveal the cemetery contained some ninety-four inhumation graves and a further forty-six cremations within an area of 900 square metres, which most likely served a nearby settlement at Abbots Worthy, of around forty people and eleven households, for two centuries.

Hawkes believed it could have contained double the number of graves if the full site had been excavated. Her investigation revealed how from the late-fifth century inhabitants were using an Anglo-Saxon inspired culture evidenced by their grave goods.

The practice became widespread across eastern England at around this point when in late Roman times people were generally buried without accompanying items and burials with weapons were banned.

Human tragedies were obvious at Worthy Park where the graves reveal a tight-knit community, which honoured its dead with compassion. These forgotten heroes farmed the land, raised families and survived against the odds. Inhabitants built their own timber-framed houses and outbuildings, maintained their livestock, such as cows, pigs and sheep, produced their own clothes and consumed almost everything they produced.

Investigations showed life would have been extremely physical for those at Worthy Park; many were lucky to live into middle age and the brutal reality of life is often reflected in their skeletons. Widespread occurrence of arthritis in graves in post-Roman Britain is testament to hard physical labour. A snapshot survey found thirty-eight of forty-three individuals (88.3 per cent) examined at Worthy Park displayed signs of the condition.

Sunken-featured buildings (SFBs) such as this one at West Stow Anglo-Saxon Village were popular throughout eastern England in the early medieval period (West Stow Anglo-Saxon Village)

Some of the discoveries were heartbreaking. One tragic woman, aged between 21 and 25, had died in childbirth, with the foetus placed between her thighs and its leg bone still resting next to her pelvis and a layer of chalk rubble covering its body. The woman was buried with an earring in the form of a bead on a copper alloy ring found next to her skull. Another child who died aged just 15 to 18 months was laid to rest with a pot and bead. One woman displayed a curvature of the spine, which showed she was a hunchback, and was found with a tin-coated bronze pin, iron tweezers suspended from a ring and an iron knife. Grave goods were objects that had personal meaning and they would be needed in the afterlife.

Life was tragically short in comparison to modern standards. The average age of death in a sample of thirty men was 36.4, while it was 38 years for the same number of women. Of the 104 burials, fifty-eight were confirmed as dying before 40, including thirty-two before the age of 16 years old. This is in keeping with six other sites at Jarrow, Monkwearmouth, Thetford, Caerwent, Caistor-on-Sea and North Elmham, where the range varied from 31.6 to 40.3 for men and 30.4 to 42.2 for women.

Excavations found the people of Worthy Park had a good intake of meat in their diet based on their strong jaws that indicated 'plenty of meat which had to be well chewed', according to Hawkes' report. Cambridge University research found the diet during the early medieval period was largely vegetable and cereal-based, with low amounts of protein, mirroring a modern-day vegan diet.[7] Families grew various vegetables and lived off daily servings of bread, sometimes with cheese and meat, along with a typical leak and grain pottage. Food was either boiled or roasted in pots

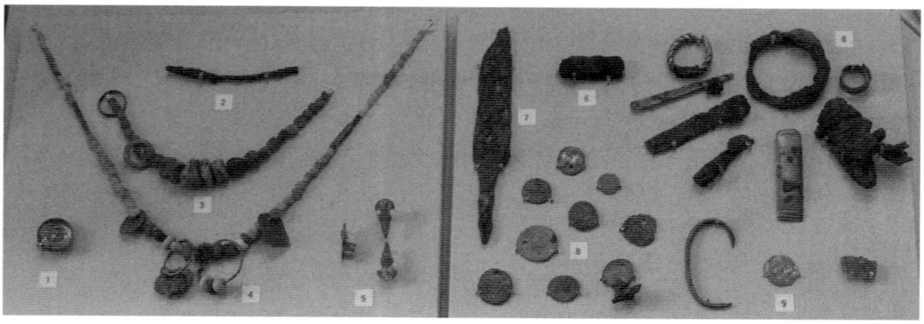

Finds from the Anglo-Saxon burial site at Worthy Park, including a string of amber beads, button brooch and an iron all-purpose knife (Winchester City Museum)

or cauldrons over open fires. Livestock were kept for a range of purposes as well as consumption, such as sheep for wool and cows for milk, while animal bones created belt ends, knife handles and pins. Hides were used for leather and sinew (tendon tissue) from animals, particularly deer, made sewing thread.[8]

Research at West Stow, the site of a reconstructed Anglo-Saxon village, which would have mirrored Worthy Park, revealed cattle, pigs, sheep and goats were eaten regularly but not every day. Meat was more abundant during the autumn when young animals were killed to avoid having to provide fodder over winter. Beer was the staple drink, but mead with honey and wine was also popular on special occasions such as feasts, which were a regular occurrence with food roasted on a central hearth.

Worthy Park had a mixed community in terms of status. One of those buried, seemingly of higher rank, lay in a wooden coffin with multi-coloured glass beads and rings, an iron belt plate, a knife, a gilt bronze button brooch and up to seventeen Roman coins.

Several coins featured Emperor Valentinian I who ruled between 364 and 375 around the time of the Great Barbarian Conspiracy in 367, when Saxon, Pict and Irish forces in cahoots ransacked the country. In response, a military force was seemingly stationed at Winchester, and the man buried at Worthy Park may have descended from a soldier with the coins passed down through generations Traditionally, in an age filled with superstition, people were buried with coins so they could be used to pay gatekeepers in the underworld.[9]

Another man, aged between 30 and 40, was also buried in a wooden coffin with an iron knife and shield.

Unlike other contemporary sites, the instances of weapon injuries are described as 'very slender' and one minor wound may have resulted from a 'sleazy brawl with a carver, cleaver or garden hoe'. Several adult males were buried with weapons, which in a barbarian society was associated with being freemen and heads of their respective households, but despite the prevalence of weapons, it appears these men were not involved in regular warfare and their existence seems to be largely peaceful.

Despite the lack of obvious war scars, Worthy Park men displayed signs of intense physical exertions and their well-developed muscles hinted at their possible trades. One man had 'powerful muscle markings' throughout his body and could have been a labourer ready to help with various tasks, while another possessed strong leg muscles and powerful forearms,

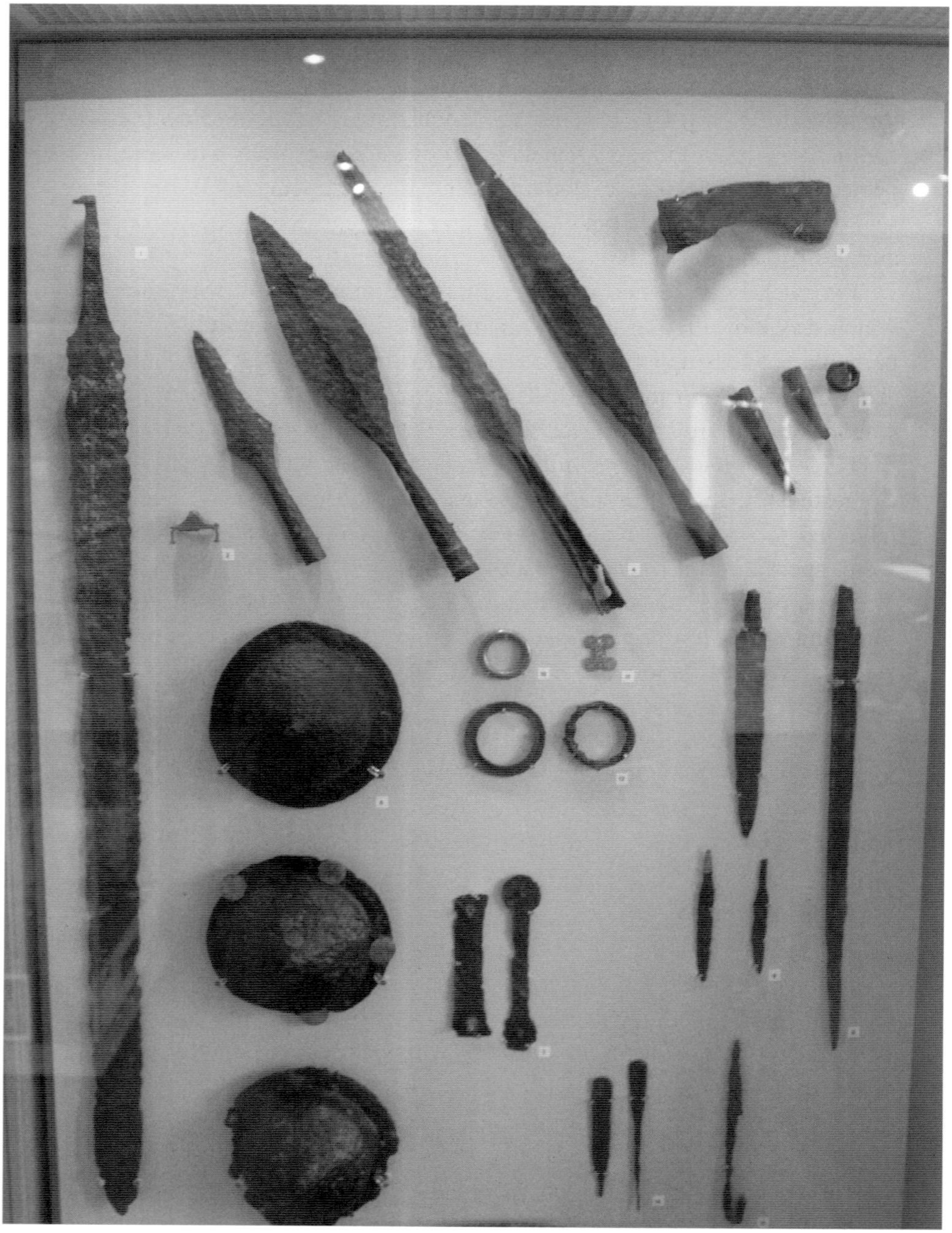

Sword, spear heads and shield bosses found in Winchester and the surrounding area from the early medieval period (Winchester City Museum)

which implied he was a specialized ploughman with his shoulder arthritis indicative of such a role.

The occupant of another grave was suspected to be a blacksmith given his powerfully built forearms did not match his less-developed lower limbs, and a possible lumberjack was also discovered. This man had seemingly been 'swinging his life to fell trees and then dragging or lifting heavy sections of their boles (trunks)' based on his exaggerated shoulder muscles and the arthritis in his shoulders.

Two males had particularly strong muscles in an area of their forearms, which was indicative of a life at the plough. Another man did not possess particularly strong upper or arm muscles, but extremely strong legs, which hint at a lifetime walking across the country perhaps as a shepherd, accompanying wagons or as a 'drover' who led livestock between seasonal pastures.

Three men had spears while two had spears as well as shields, which suggested 'modest affluence'. Weapons training from an early age would have led to strongly developed muscles, but it is thought such activities were 'sporadic' and warfare even less so.

Signs of osteoarthritis in the elbows could equally have resulted from throwing spears on regular hunts, the report noted. Freemen of warrior status at Worthy Park appeared to have laboured in the woods and fields and carried out specialist tasks for their neighbours.

Taken together, the burials suggest the men of the household gained manual trades to provide for their loved ones and neighbours who must have rewarded their efforts. Sites such as Worthy Park, small communities of around a dozen families, were typical in post-Roman Britain as towns were largely abandoned for smaller rural settlements, including the reoccupation of old Iron Age forts.

Another burial site using an Anglo-Saxon inspired culture has been found a little over 2 miles east of Worthy Park during the laying of a Southern Gas pipeline through the field next to Itchen Abbas Primary School.[10] It is believed to be a long-running cemetery, which could date to the late-Roman and early Anglo-Saxon period, with an estimate of 300 to 600 graves. One grave appears to be of a young boy, without grave goods, who was wrapped in a shroud indicating a Christian burial.

The burials were east to west with the feet to the east and head to the west, which was custom as it was believed Jesus would return from the east. The pagan tradition would also place bodies facing the east because this is where the sun would rise.

There were no coffins or grave goods associated with the burial, aside from one man found with an iron spearhead, knife or dagger and bronze belt fittings. According to Historic Environment Records, there could have been 'hundreds of burials' at another undiscovered location nearby.

Long before the Anglo-Saxons and the Romans, the region of Hampshire had faced another invasion from Gaul (largely modern-day Belgium and France). Writing in the Gallic Wars, Julius Caesar praised the Belgae as the 'most courageous' tribe in Gaul.[11] Caesar said the Belgae were 'continually at war with Germans across the Rhine' but seemingly shut off from the wider world as they were 'farthest removed from civilization and least visited by merchants'.

Increasing pressure from Roman expansion, which culminated in the conquest of Gaul of 54–58 BC, must have led to their migration across the channel.

The legendary Roman general revealed the Belgae settled in the 'maritime regions' of Britain and that they 'came to raid and stayed to sow'.

Mystery surrounds the exact territory of the Belgae, but it is thought they inhabited central and southern Hampshire, including the area around the Solent, within the region of the Atrebates, another Belgic tribe. More than eighty silver and gold Iron Age coins have been attributed to a group known as the Belgae, according to numismatic expert Chris Rudd.[12]

After the Roman invasion of Britain, the Atrebates district was split into three civitas, with the Belgae centred on Winchester, the Regni in Chichester and the Atrebates in Silchester. Civitas were administrative areas based on tribal territories where the British civilians governed themselves under the supervision of Roman authorities based in London.

The Regni and Atrebates civitas roughly correspond to Sussex and Berkshire respectively, while it is striking on maps of Iron Age coin finds how Hampshire closely mirrors the Belgae territory before the Romans arrived.

I have found it fascinating how Iron Age divisions appear to have determined many of the Roman civitas, later Anglo-Saxon kingdoms and present-day county authorities. Ancient boundaries that separated Iron Age tribes were seemingly brought back into use after Rome's troops left with new authorities often burying their dead in the barrows or huge ditches on their neighbour's doorstep.

The Belgae's boundaries appear to have closely mirrored Hampshire but not extended as far north as Silchester, which was a post Romano-British stronghold until the mid-sixth century when it was abandoned.

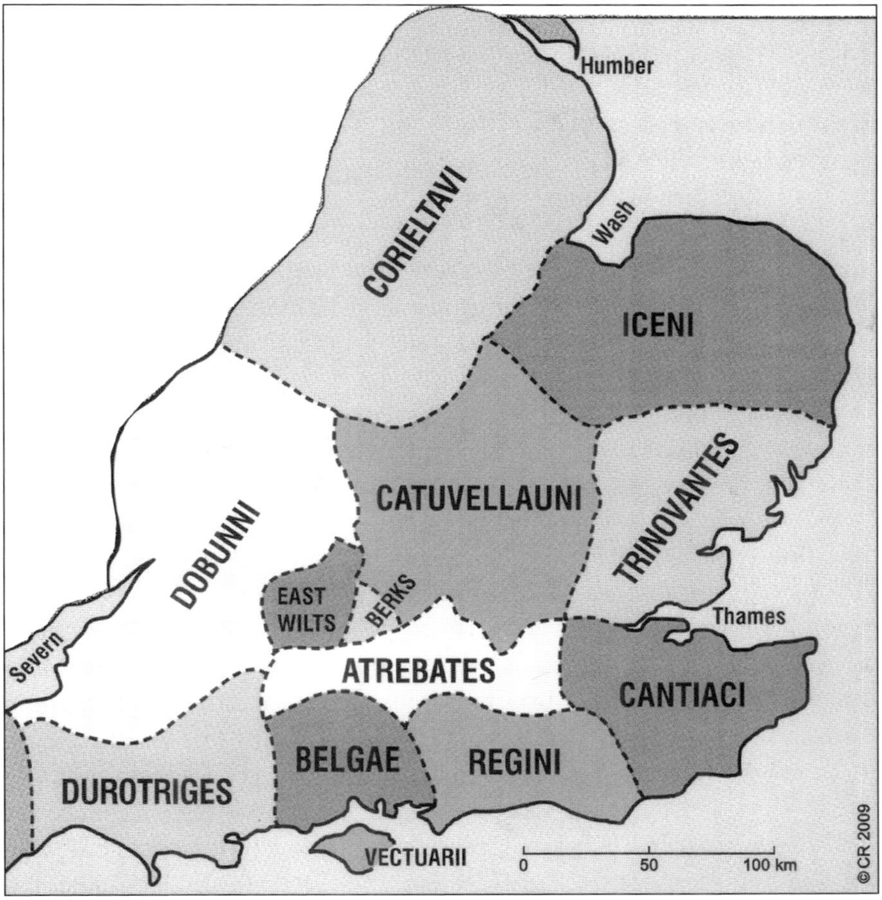

Iron Age tribal regions based on coin finds, which show some striking similarities with modern-day counties (©CR 2009 – Chris Rudd)

Alton, around 17 miles north-east of Winchester, was occupied during Cerdic's reign and produced one of the most remarkable finds of the early Anglo-Saxon period. Iron Age Belgae coins have been found in the town, which is also likely to have been the site of a lost pottery-producing estate known as Vindomis. This estate, meaning 'mansion of the wine country', had some 2,500 residents.[13]

More than 100 graves, dated to between the fifth and seventh centuries, were unearthed at a burial in Mount Pleasant Road in Alton near a spring, which is the source of the River Wey. Finds were dated to between 425 and 525 but include some from the early-seventh century. The most spectacular discovery was unearthed in the grave of a man aged 28, who was buried with a sword and showed signs of disease in his mouth and shins.[14] This was a jewelled silver-gilt buckle, which belongs to a Kentish design from the late-sixth to early-seventh centuries, and featured gold plates and filigree, and garnet decoration. It included a large strap hole and was positioned under his forearm with the sword laid diagonally across the pelvis and legs, possibly suspended from a belt. At each side of the triangular plate is a bird's head with a curving beak and garnet body. The exquisite item suggested the man was a leading local chieftain.[15]

The River Blackwater running north between Aldershot and Swallowfield forms part of the Hampshire boundaries with Berkshire and Surrey and was likely a long-running border. Around sixty-one buildings dated to the sixth and seventh centuries were uncovered in Chalton, which lies on the current Hampshire–Sussex border.[16]

In the south, the huge Bokerley Dyke separated the Belgae civitas from the Durotriges, which evolved into Dorset but largely remained outside of Wessex influence or control until the mid-to-late seventh century. There is some suggestion the territory of the Durotriges had extended as far

Silver gilt buckle, worn on the hips or waist and dated to the late-sixth and seventh centuries, which was found in Alton (Hampshire Cultural Trust)

as Southampton Water and included the New Forest before the Roman conquest and was contested after the troops departed.[17] Given three battles were placed between Charford and Old Sarum in the sixth century, both around 12 miles from the dyke, this suggests conflict between Cerdic and a warlord in the Durotriges territory, which revolved around control of coastal trade around the Solent.

A similar dyke to Bokerley, possibly marking the advance of the Belgae in the Iron Age, can be found near the Wiltshire border on the outskirts of Andover. This area is the focus of the investigation into a potential burial site for Cerdic in later chapters.

At the heart of the Belgae civitas in Roman times was its capital Winchester, known in Latin as Venta Belgarum, which translates as the 'marketplace of the Belgae'. The word *venta* was also found in the Roman civitas Venta Silurum (Caerwent) and Venta Icenorum (Caistor St Edmund near Norwich) and is associated with open-air markets along with the slaughter and sacrifice of cattle and sheep.[18]

Winchester's ritual nature was revealed during excavations of deep pits in Lower Brook Street near a known temple, which unearthed a wooden statue and cones representing fertility in Celtic and Roman culture.[19] This wooden figure is believed to date from the second century and symbolizes the horse goddess Epona or a priestess of her cult.

The word Belgae derives from the Celtic *belg*, meaning to 'swell with anger' but could also equate to the 'the proud ones', which would be in keeping with other bombastic titles given to Iron Age tribes in Britain.[20]

During Roman and Anglo-Saxon times, Winchester could rival and even eclipse London as one of the most vibrant and powerful places in what became England. With a surface area of 144 acres, it was the fifth largest Roman town featuring the standard street grid pattern, with Roman civic amenities, such as a forum, baths, a market building, temples, an aqueduct and a theatre. The town is thought to have included a factory, where people produced woollen cloth, sourced from the rich surrounding farmlands, for the military as an imperial tax.[21] In the late-fourth century, Winchester evolved from a walled town into a 'major military centre' with the addition of twenty external bastions and possibly became a base for the late-Roman field army, according to a report edited by Professor Martin Biddle, who led the excavations of Winchester, and historian Derek Keene.

Most of Rome's troops were largely withdrawn from Britain by the usurper Constantine III in 407, following previous removals six years earlier and under Magnus Maximus in 388. The sixth-century Greek historian Zosimos wrote in his account of the Roman Empire, called the *Historia Nova*, that in 409 the 'Britons took up arms, and braving danger for their own independence, freed the cities from the barbarians threatening them'. Evidence suggests the Roman army may have returned for three years from 418 and heavily taxed the local population to pay for upgrading forts and other works.[22]

The *Anglo-Saxon Chronicle* also refers to how the Romans were 'collecting treasures' in 418, some of which they 'hid in the earth' or took back to Gaul. Some seventy-eight treasure hordes of gold, silver and precious metals have been found dated to the fifth century, and it is believed these were buried by Roman elites to avoid taxation and to collect in the future when they left with the army for Gaul.[23] The Roman army and many of the wealthy civilians would never return to Britain.

Urban life in Winchester and across large parts of England is believed to have collapsed by 420, having been in terminal decline for the previous sixty or so years. Only the forum in Winchester, a huge structure measuring about 360ft by 330ft with walls 3ft 3in thick survived until much later. The south gate collapsed and was bordered up with a blocking wall.[24]

Mass production, local commerce and heavy coin use, with the last Roman coins dated to the early-fifth century, all faltered, people stopped being buried in coffins because of the lack of nails and many of an estimated 2,000 villas dotted around the land were abandoned as the western empire crumbled.[25]

Excavations of Winchester in the 1970s found little evidence of continued settlement for around 250 years after the Roman troops departed from Winchester, aside from the intriguing discovery of pottery shards in Lower Brook Street, including a Frankish biochemical urn, which hinted at a lost settlement as the rubbish was spread over a wide area.[26] According to the study by Professor Biddle and Keene, this was the first sign of occupation in the walled town, which seems required by the 'remarkable cluster of sixth-century cemeteries outside the walls' including Worthy Park.

Given the obvious decline of Winchester, which later became the capital of Wessex, it is puzzling how Cerdic gained any authority in the first place. When civilians were no longer burdened with the demands from Roman officials, why did they turn to another seemingly more local empire. The answer may be found in an early-medieval system in which towns and parishes evolved as productive territories, where farms would render goods and services to a central place known as a vill headed by a powerful lord who in the early Anglo-Saxon times offered protection.

Many evolved from the remnants of Roman forts such as at Birdoswald where descendants of the late-Roman stronghold and with a strong military tradition built a huge timber hall and lived off the supplies from farming families in the hinterland who they in turn protected. Excavator Tony Willmott said the 'only change' in the early-fifth century was that troops of the fort were 'no longer paid by a central authority'.[27]

Outside Birdoswald Fort on the remarkable Hadrian's Wall, which stretched for 73 miles across northern England

This system would have been based on a principle known as *iugum* in Latin, *feorm* in Old English and *treth* in Brythonic, in which taxes were raised in the form of consumable and perishable goods, such as ale, honey, meat and cheese, along with grain, wool, linen and timber.[28] A lord's role may have included settling local disputes, carrying out raids during bleak winters and providing access to legal status, marriage alliance and feasting.

Evidence of a flourishing post-Roman settlement, which evolved from the previous military centre at Winchester mirroring Birdoswald, has not been found, but there have been numerous finds that 'tell a different story' of abandonment, according to the report by Professor Biddle and Keene.[29] These discoveries reveal 'a concentration of Anglo-Saxon settlements, cemeteries and isolated finds within a radius of 5km (3 miles) – an hour's walk from Venta (Winchester)'.

According to Professor Biddle and Keene, the town continued to be an area where 'some form of authority was exercised. This included perhaps certain rights of control and taxation over surrounding territories inherited from the late Roman period.' This was a system known as *fiscus*, which included all the earnings and possessions of the former Roman Empire and would make sense of the decision by King Cenwalh of Wessex to build the Old Minster church in Winchester, possibly between 660 and 663, when the king appointed Wine as the first bishop of Winchester. From this period, the town again began to flourish and served as the seat of Wessex kings. The report by Professor Biddle and Keene noted:

> *'If something like this (fiscus) had happened with the former Roman town of Venta, it would explain both the clustering of early Anglo-Saxon sites in the valley above and below Winchester and the otherwise apparently inexplicable decision to build a church and establish a bishopric inside a walled area which looks today at first sight to have been virtually deserted.'*

The report added that the absence of evidence showing organized life at Winchester continuing in post-Roman Britain was in 'large part' due to the lack of archaeological studies of the south-east quarter of the walled town, including the current cathedral site.

There have been further finds around Winchester, including at Winnall just outside the old Roman walled town and around a mile east of St Giles Hill. Railway workers constructing the Southampton to Newbury line in

1884 at Easton Lane came across several possible sixth-century shallow graves based on a newspaper report from the time, but sadly all that survives are three shield bosses. A second cemetery contained some forty-five burials dated to the late-seventh century.[30]

Another large Anglo-Saxon burial site[31] was uncovered at Twyford, roughly 3 miles south of Winchester, with graves dated to Cerdic's sixth-century reign. Twyford place names are found throughout Anglo-Saxon England because it describes a point where two shallow areas of a river converge. The cemetery, discovered during work on building new classrooms for Twyford School in 2007, revealed eighteen burial pits but represent only a part of a much larger burial ground, which cannot be established because of heavy landscaping to the immediate east. The graves suggested this settlement had been a 'local, rural population enjoying a fairly good standard of living' with little difference in health, status or origins, according to a Hampshire Field Club report:

> *'The community appears to have been rural, largely participating in agricultural activities as evidenced by skeletal indicators of heavy labour. Some individuals were also probably engaged in craft activities, such as textile or leather working, as indicated by excessive and specific wear to the teeth.'*

The field club report stated Twyford would have been 'heavily influenced' by a new political elite which led to the 'widespread adoption of aspects of Anglo-Saxon material culture, including burial practice.'

These settlements such as Twyford, Worthy Park and Itchen Abbas, along with Winnall and St Giles Hill, could have been similar in size and scale. They reveal a rural community close to Winchester, within a few miles around the Itchen Valley, when Cerdic reigned. It is thus possible to imagine an authority headed by the chief magistrate Cerdic that had an administrative base in Winchester and had evolved or taken over the previous Roman one.

Cerdic's ancestry was most probably linked to a post-Roman ruler who led a local militia in the early-fifth century – the kind described by Zosimos and most likely drawn from leftover auxiliary troops – which guarded civilians at a time of upheaval and threats from barbarian tribes. This ruler may have been a prominent civic or military official in the dying days of the Roman administration, capable of mustering and managing a force in the former Belgae civitas.

Barbarian law codes dated to the late-fifth century from the continent, *The Codex Euriciaus* (*The Code of Euric*), describe freemen beneath the noble class called *bucellari* who acted as military escorts, ensured efficient tax collection and could transfer their allegiances between lords, who were recruited by councils or leading families.[32] Paramilitary post-Roman burials with quoit brooch and zoomorphic buckles in Dorchester, Winchester and Mucking could relate to such *bucellari* contingents who, as with Birdoswald, included many local descendants of previous Roman soldiers.

As new authorities headed by powerful lords and warbands, such as Cerdic's, emerged from the ashes of Roman towns and systems, the east coast of Britain was experiencing significant transformation with the influx of new migrants from across the North Sea. These newcomers would become known collectively as the Anglo-Saxons. Their arrival would change the face of Britain.

Chapter 2

The Anglo-Saxons

For the Saxon is the most ferocious of all foes. He comes on you without warning; when you expect his attack he makes away. Resistance only moves him to contempt; a rash opponent is soon down. If he pursues he overtakes; if he flies himself, he is never caught. Shipwrecks to him are no terror, but only so much training. His is no mere acquaintance with the perils of the sea; he knows them as he knows himself.

Sollius Apollinaris Sidonius, 480

Hadleigh Castle's romantic ruins are a short distance from the pretty fishing village of Old Leigh in Essex, which boasts cobbled streets, craft shops and hearty boozers with fantastic names, such as Ye Olde Smack and the Crooked Billet. A setting resembling a classic Cornish coastal village, such as Looe, Falmouth or St Ives, but just an hour away by train from central London. You can while away the afternoon sampling the famed Rossi ice creams, or my guilty pleasure was its cheese sauce on chunky chips, and then gaze out across the estuary at the tiny boats often stuck in the mud during a receding tide and the sight of neighbouring Kent in clear weather.

Heading east along a narrow bank path at the edge of Old Leigh takes you to a promenade, beginning from Chalkwell, and leading all the way to the lively seaside city of Southend 2 miles away, with its amusements and arcades. Packed beaches, gatherings on the grass verges and barbecues that continue long into the evening are common throughout the summer all along this route, which is perhaps even more enjoyable in the winter when the number of day trippers falls, and you can better appreciate the stunning views.

Walking west towards the Leigh on Sea station, you'll come to hugely popular cockle sheds and fish merchants, which enjoy a booming

Snapshot of Old Leigh with boats stuck in the mud during low tide

Coastal village of Old Leigh with its cobbled streets and old pubs

trade selling fresh catches from the estuary. Beyond the station lies the picturesque ruins of Hadleigh Castle, which is unmissable on the hill on the train journey from Fenchurch Street in London.

The castle was first built during the tumultuous early-thirteenth century reign of King John, which ended in the Magna Carta. Most of the structure was dismantled for its stone in the late-sixteenth century, but it was once a treasured place of Edward III and featured an orchard outside the entrance and surrounding parkland.[1] To this day, it remains a popular tourist haunt and site for an afternoon picnic for families, with kids running around and enjoying pretend sword fights underneath and around the massive arch. Standing next to the huge shell of the former south tower, you get all encompassing views across the marshes and the Thames Estuary before it joins the North Sea, traditionally associated with the Anglo-Saxons.

At the edge of the River Thames, you begin considering all the adventurers and invaders who entered at this point as perhaps civilians watched their arrival from sites such as Hadleigh. As these Germanic migrants rowed along the shores of Britannia, now stripped of Rome's military presence,

Overlooking the beach and promenade at Chalkwell, which leads to and from Old Leigh

the lands around the estuary would have made for a great place to settle for trade, access to water and fertile soils for farming.

North Sea adventurers would have edged slowly along the many creeks from the estuary looking for land to call their new home, either by invitation from some existing warlord who wanted to defend his territory or perhaps this region was largely deserted after inhabitants left with the Romans or moved further inland without their protection.[2]

There was undoubtedly a powerful new Anglo-Saxon kingdom known as 'Essex', derived from its old English name of *East Saexe* meaning 'East Saxons', which started appearing prominently in records of the early-seventh century. It appears to be based on the territory of the Trinovantes civitas formed from the pre-Roman tribal region.[3] As with other neighbouring kingdoms, its evolution into an Anglo-Saxon realm is shrouded in mystery to a degree due to the lack of contemporary records. That was until twenty years ago when evidence emerged spectacularly around 2 miles from Hadleigh Castle.

In 2003, workers in Prittlewell on the outskirts of Southend stumbled upon what was quickly heralded the 'most exciting Anglo-Saxon archaeological discovery' of the past sixty years since the iconic ship burial at Sutton Hoo, which is located 65 miles further along the east coast.[4] While now only detectable with a plaque in the ground, the site overlooking the adjacent Priory Park had turned up a fascinating window into late-sixth century Britain. This

Hadleigh Castle was first built in the late-twelfth century during the troublesome reign of King John, which led to the Magna Carta

Hadleigh Castle's massive south tower with the River Thames in the background

was the final resting place of the 'Prittlewell Prince' aka the 'King of Bling'.[5] When widening the road, the workers had chanced upon a large square pit filled with timber lining. Within a day, the now cordoned off parcel of land threw up yet more artefacts. Archaeologists unearthed a beautiful copper-alloy hanging bowl, a glass bowl from Asian minor, an iron folding stool, a solid gold belt buckle, two Frankish gold coins, a sword and shield, a lyre musical instrument and a Byzantine flagon drinking container.

Far removed from the 'Dark Age', the term for the centuries after the Western Roman Empire crumbled now shunned by scholars, this had clearly been a cultured individual with extensive trading links to the wider world. Exotic items had been placed in a wooden chamber buried under a sandy mound, some were hung on its walls and clearly suggested the person laid to rest so regally had been a king or prince.

In 2019, the Museum of London Archaeology concluded that based on radiocarbon dating the person died between 575 and 605 and was most likely Saexa, the brother of Sæberht the first recorded Christian king of Essex, but his body had long since dissolved due to the acidity of the soil.[6] The enterprising pub nearby is called the 'Saxon King'.

Later, I was intrigued to learn another barrow burial had been excavated in 1924 dated to more than 600 hundred years earlier, just 30 miles away from Prittlewell, near Colchester, known as the Lexden Tumulus. This shared obvious similarities as a wooden plank chamber grave, under a sandy mound, which measured around 70ft in diameter and at least 5ft in height, with items laid around the occupant including a folding stool to match the iron one at Prittlewell.

Incredible finds included at least seventeen amphorae containers with Italian wine, a chain mail suit with thousands of interlocking iron rings each about 5mm across, copper alloy figurines of a boar and a cupid, a bronze table, a silver medallion created from a coin featuring Augustus, fragments of a horn, burnt human remains and most intriguingly a Late Bronze Age axe.[7] This is known as a 'palstave' and was at least 900 years old when it was deposited in the ground, which suggests it had passed through more generations than we could possibly conceive. This truly incredible find had also been 'mutilated with a gouge down the side' and wrapped in a cloth.

The occupant was at first linked to Cunobelinus, who ruled central and eastern England territories of the Trinovantes and Catuvellauni tribe, until just before the conquest of Rome in 43. Cunobelinus is thought to descend from Cassivellaunus who resisted the original Roman invasion of Britain

The small burial mound of the Prittlewell Prince at the site of its famous discovery during road works more than twenty years ago

by Julius Caesar in 55 BC. Notably Caratacus, the son of Cunobelinus, would fight the Roman conquest for more than a decade, and this Essex dynasty proved a long-running thorn in the side of imperial ambitions.

A more recent assessment suggests the burial dates 15–10 BC[8] and is the tomb of Addedomaros, a king of the Trinovantes.[9] However, Philip Crummy, from the Colchester Archaeological Trust, believes the occupant is most likely to have been Cunobelinus' father Tasciovanus who died around 9 BC but is known to have minted coins from Colchester in the decade before his death.[10]

Artist impressions of the burial arrangement show the undeniable likeness between the chamber burials in Prittlewell and Lexden. Historian and archaeologist Francis Pryor, in his book *Britain AD*, said the 'remarkable' similar items and themes at both Lexden and Prittlewell showed the 'tradition of barrow burials had not died out in Roman times in eastern England' but 'doubtless diehard Anglo-Saxonists would dismiss the evidence'. Complexities in Roman Britain are frequently lost in a polarized argument, as hinted by the phrase 'Anglo-Saxonists' focused on ethnicity rather than identity.

The debate and popular theory have been shaped by the few contemporary records, such as Gildas (to be explored in the next chapter), which speak of the new arrivals in almost apocalyptic terms. One early account from Roman poet and politician Sollius Apollinaris Sidonius describes how Saxon pirates threw captured slaves into the sea as part of a sacrifice to their gods:

> *'When the Saxons are setting sail from the continent and are about to drag their firm-holding anchors from an enemy's shore, it is their usage, thus homeward bound, to abandon every tenth captive to the slow agony of a watery end, casting lots with perfect equity among the doomed crowd in execution of this iniquitous sentence of death.*
>
> *'This custom is all the more deplorable in that it is prompted by honest superstition. These men are bound by vows which have to be paid in victims, they conceive it a religious act to perpetrate this horrible slaughter, and to take anguish from the prisoner in place of ransom; this polluting sacrilege is in their eyes an absolving sacrifice. I am full of anxiety and apprehension about these dangers.'*

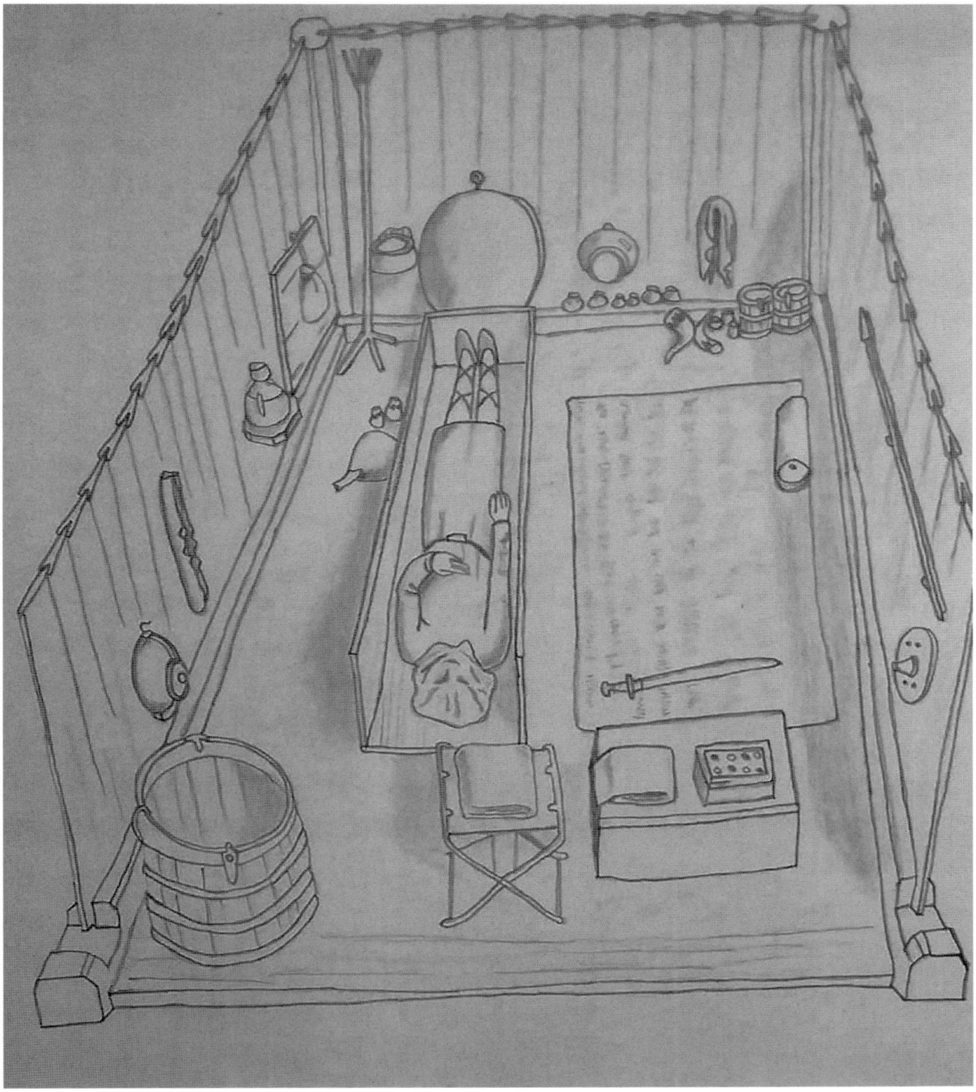

Opposite: Artist's impression of the prince or king burial in Lexden near Colchester in Essex dated to a few decades before the Roman invasion (Laurent Cusolito – based on original illustration by Stephen Crummy in City of Victory published by Colchester Archaeological Trust)

Above: The Prittlewell Prince chamber, dated from 575 to 605, shared obvious similarities with the Lexden burial created just over 600 years earlier (Laurent Cusolito – based on original illustration by Faith Vardy/MOLA)

Notably, pirates made their boats from animal skins stitched together and every man was both captain and crew, hinting at a much simpler existence. And this is more reflective of the North Sea settlers who arrived in the 200 years after the Romans departed with estimates ranging widely from as low as 10,000 to 200,000 among around two million inhabitants of Britain.[11] Newcomers were often simply farmers not brutal pirates hell-bent on pillaging and conquering but just looking for a better life because rising sea levels were flooding their coastal homelands.

The concept of a 'hide' of land, which became the default method for working out how much a kingdom or settlement had to pay to keep their

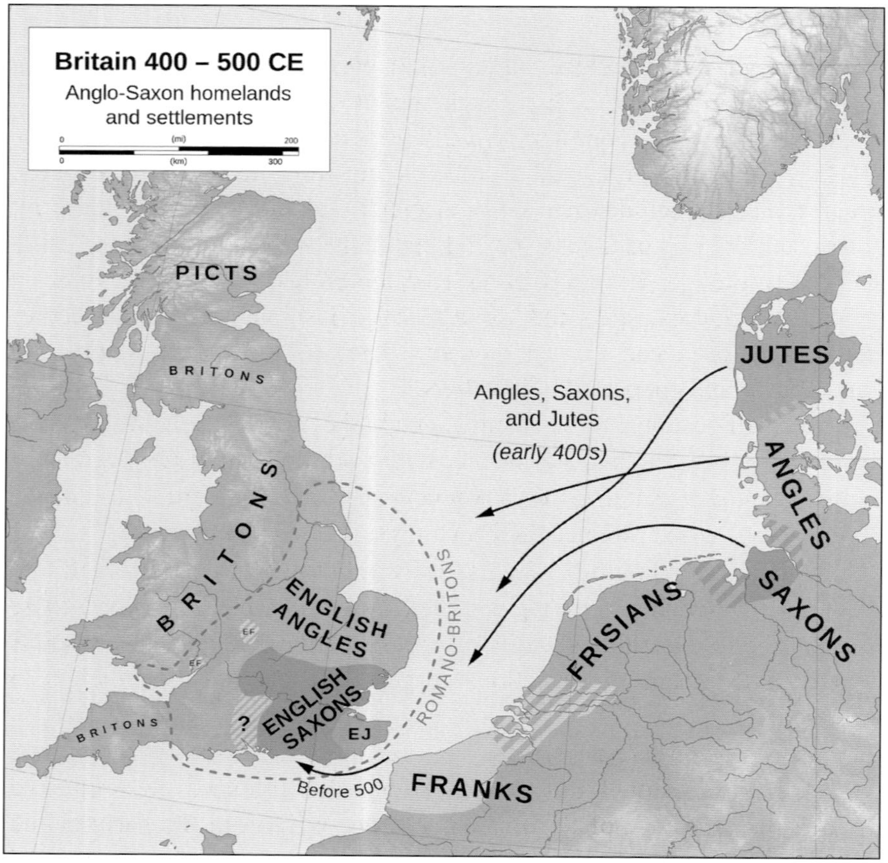

Anglo-Saxon homelands and settlements in Britain between 400 and 500 (mbartelsm/CC BY-SA 3.0)

lords and kings happy, was believed to be derived from the Germanic word *hiwisc*, implying a married couple.[12]

Kin groups quickly set themselves up as independent farmers with dependents, including slaves who helped work the land. Some of the enslaved were believed to be hard-up Britons. Evidence has, however, shown many of the small family groups lived next to Romano-British peasants on now abandoned villa estates or on farmland close to Roman roads and they were even buried alongside each other in many instances.

Many Britons slipped back into an Iron Age material culture and were largely confined to the countryside. Even at the height of the western Roman Empire in the second century less than 20 per cent of the population occupied towns, and this number plunged further as urban life collapsed.[13]

One Anglo-Saxon village exhibition at West Stow in Suffolk reveals a fascinating window into life on such settlements.[14] West Stow contained around seventy of the common *grubenhauser* or sunken-featured buildings (SFBs), covering a period of over 200 years from the mid-fifth century, which typically included two posts at either end, a gabled roof and a pit underneath flooring used for storage. Inhabitants at West Stow herded cattle and sheep, ploughed the gravel soils of the valley, fenced their flock in pens, made pottery, spun and wove textiles, fashioned pins and needles from bones, produced buckets to carry water, forged their weapons and traded beads and copper alloy jewellery.[15]

These self-sustaining communities made the most of their own textiles for clothing, bedding and furnishing, with each household turning one of the *grubenhauser* cottages into a weaving shed where a vertical loom was set up so they could produce their own rugs, dresses and blankets.

Large extended families with slaves lived in small settlements featuring buildings for sleeping, weaving and their own hall. Only two swords were found at West Stow, thought to be for community leaders buried as warriors for the afterlife, and all indications suggest they spent most of their time farming.[16]

One of the most respected sources for the early medieval period was the Northumbrian monk and scholar Bede, who produced the influential Ecclesiastical History of the English People. Writing in the early-eighth century, Bede remarks how the migrants came from 'three powerful Germanic people, the Saxons, Angles and Jutes', who came to be known collectively as the 'Anglo-Saxons'; a phrase only coined in the eighth

Small halls such as this one at the West Stow Anglo-Saxon village would have been focal points of family settlements (West Stow Anglo-Saxon Village)

century by Latin writers to distinguish the groups in Britain from those on the continent. Anglen in northern Germany, the homeland of the Angles, 'remained deserted to the present day', according to Bede.

A DNA study of 460 ancient north-western Europeans, including 278 individuals from England, taken from skeletons across thirty-seven different sites in England, Ireland, the Netherlands, Germany and Denmark found people had been migrating on a 'large-scale' from the North Sea since the early medieval period.[17]

Researchers found up to 76 per cent of those analyzed from eastern England from the early-medieval period had ancestors from the North Sea zone, which varied in different regions. This figure is as high as 47 per cent for south-eastern, eastern, and central England, especially Sussex, the East Midlands and East Anglia. The increase was closely related to the early-medieval and present-day inhabitants of Germany and Denmark, a connection highlighted in previous studies linking the material culture and burials in early Anglo-Saxon England with Elbe-Wesser, named after two rivers in a northern Germany region, which includes Hamburg.

Analysis revealed no difference between the number of men and women arriving in England, suggesting that an invasion by an army of men was not responsible for the changes in genetic ancestry.

There is some evidence of integration between the groups, with men of all backgrounds equally likely to be buried with grave goods, which indicates higher status. The extent of separation between groups is unclear as some Europeans were buried separately from Britons, while women descended from European arrivals were more likely to be buried with grave goods, again reflecting their social standing.

The DNA was compared to published genetic data from more than 4,000 ancient individuals, who lived between 200 and 1300, and just over 10,000 present-day Europeans. The North Sea ancestry region covered from northern Netherlands to the southernmost tip of Sweden, with a large proportion of individuals connected to Lower Saxony. Alongside the significant North Sea migration, there had also been notable continuous arrivals from France on a smaller scale from the post-Roman period, evidenced by Frankish material culture in Sussex and Kent. Migrations appear to be part of a 'continuous movement of people from across the North Sea to Britain from the later Roman period into the 11th century', the study concluded.

The cemetery at Spong Hill in Norfolk, which featured more than 2,200 cremations and fifty-seven inhumations, is a most notable distinctive early-Germanic burial site.[18] Similar ones around the Wash estuary between Norfolk and Lincolnshire may have housed the first wave of North Sea migrants in the fifth century.

Many of the North Sea settlers would have been pagans who engaged in rituals and worshipped gods such as Woden, Thor and Tyr, along with other supernatural forces. Pagans at Spong Hill cremated their dead on funeral pyres and their ashes were placed in decorated urns, handmade and not fired in kilns, which were buried along with smaller undecorated pots containing animal bones, such as sheep, cattle and pig.[19]

Some 227 horses were cremated at Spong Hill, most likely the whole animal, a practice typically associated with wealthy male burials. The famous 'Spong Man', a three-dimensional humanoid figure on the lid of one urn, was among the finds.

Three cremation urns also included rare runic inscriptions (letters from various early alphabets used by Germanic peoples dating back as far as possibly the first century) and a stamped term *alu*, which has a literal

The incredible Spong Man humanoid figure discovered in an early Anglo-Saxon grave on display at the Norwich Castle Museum and Art Gallery (CC BY-SA 4.0/Norwich Castle Museum and Art Gallery)

meaning of 'ale' but could represent magic or the possible ecstatic mental state from drinking during a ritual.[20]

Most objects featuring runic inscriptions, such as urns, drinking vases, coins, buckles and weapons, have been found in Scandinavia but around 200 were unearthed in eastern England at places such as Spong Hill, Pensthorpe and Grimston in Norfolk, Lovenden Croft in Lincolnshire and a few have been uncovered in Kent, the Upper Thames and on the Isle of Wight.[21]

During the sixth century, a distinct new pattern emerged with a shift away from cremation to burials with grave goods, which became increasingly more elaborate because communities were now adopting regional identities that were reflected in their fashions and burials.

In east Kent, where large cemeteries were found at Saltwood, Ozengell and Sarre, the clothing and burial practices were closely associated with the material culture of Jutish tribes from Scandinavia and the post-Roman kingdom of Francia.[22] Meanwhile, west Kent retained closer links to north Saxony.

Women in east Kent became distinctive with clothing and items based on popular Frankish fashions, wearing belted skirts and short jackets, garnet-set pins in the shape of rosettes or little brooches fashioned in the shape of birds.[23] They were also fond of Scandinavian square-headed brooches and gold wafer-thin pendants, which featured beasts and faces. Many of these fashion accessories, while influenced by Frankish tastes, were in fact made in Kent and altered slightly to suit regional tastes.

In northern England, women began sewing metal clasps onto the end of their sleeves to hook cuffs together indicating they were now wearing long-sleeved undergarments. These clasps were popular among well-heeled women in western Norway originally, but they quickly became a must have for wealthier women in regions of the Angles such as Yorkshire, Lincolnshire and Norfolk.

Likewise in Mercia, largely based on the modern-day Midlands, the brooches, costumes and even accent afflictions, singled them out from other regions associated with Anglian settlers, such as Northumberland and Kent.

People were, in effect, creating a regional British identity while celebrating their North Sea homelands in their clothing and customs. In turn, this material culture was readily adopted by Brittonic neighbours along the east coast who abandoned their previous Roman inspired tastes.

There was also an increasing gap between the rich and poor not evident in the previous century. This was reflected in the burials as tribes and local warlords bullied their neighbours into submission and grew ever more powerful with more territory from which they demanded tribute. The lavish burials, including the famous uncovered sites at Prittlewell, Sutton Hoo and Taplow, were a celebration of their new prestige.

One of the largest Anglo-Saxon burial sites in east Kent was found at Buckland in Dover, which contained some 260 graves dated to the sixth century.[24] Just over two thirds included grave goods for the afterlife and a significant number were richly furnished, including seven men with a sword, which indicates they were freemen of higher social status, one of whom was believed to be a leader equipped also with a spear, bronze studded belt and scales. Rich women were identified by their fine brooches, coloured glass and amber beads, of which more than 2,000 were discovered. The brooches were used as clothes fasteners and found near the cheek, chest and lower body. Buckland was the home of 'a peaceful, well-established local community which included some individuals of fairly high status', according to a report on the cemetery by the leading British archaeologist Vera Evison.

One woman's skeleton was found in an 'extraordinary position' with her upper body downwards and the skull facing upwards. Her right arm was under the body with the hand over the shoulder; the left was bent at the elbow with the forearm under the pelvis. The left leg was extended with the right leg bent up underneath. It is believed the woman was buried alive and the extreme position was caused by her attempting to free herself. She was also found with a bracelet near her head instead of being on her forearm. Tragically, this was also due to her trying to escape the grave. The woman also wore a necklace, which featured garnet and silver gift pendants with a cruciform design, thought to be of Christian significance.

Construction of the HS2 railway line in Wendover, Buckinghamshire, led to the discovery of a large Anglo-Saxon burial site dated to the fifth and sixth centuries.[25] Excavations uncovered 138 graves, with 141 inhumation and five cremation burials, with finds dated to the Roman, Iron Age, Bronze Age and Neolithic periods. More than 2,000 beads were discovered at Wendover, as well as eighty-nine brooches, forty buckles and fifty-one knives. Discoveries included a unique sixth-century ceramic window urn with reused Roman glass fired into the bottom, while another ceramic bead had been made from reused Roman pottery.

In one gruesome burial, a man aged between 17 and 24 years old was found with a sharp iron object embedded in his spine. It is believed the weapon blow had been delivered from the front. Another woman discovered with various goods, including an ornate glass bowl made of pale green glass, which could be an heirloom from the Roman era, was believed to be wealthier than other inhabitants.

Many burials were found with two brooches on their collarbone to hold up garments such as a cloak or peplos, a body-length garment worn by women, and the brooches vary in style from disk types made with gilt or coin brooches made from silver coins. One design was a miniature version of the famous square-head brooch uncovered at Chessell Down on the Isle of Wight. Some items uncovered could have been imported from across Europe, such as amber beads, and various metals and raw materials were used to make the artefacts. Two glass cone beakers were uncovered intact, mirroring vessels made in Northern France, although they were being produced in England at the time.

Wendover was representative of how communities in large parts of eastern and central England were evolving in post-Roman Britain as they began using an Anglo-Saxon material culture, which was reflected in their dress and burial practices.

At West Heslerton, an organized large Anglo-Saxon settlement sustained for 200 years from the fifth century featured dozens of the *grubenhauser* timber-post structures typically associated with Germanic people. However, an examination of tooth enamel from those buried with continental grave goods, such as Scandinavian wrist clasps and northern German

Anglo-Saxon decorative glass beads uncovered during HS2's archaeological excavation of a burial ground in Wendover (HS2 Limited)

A ceramic bead, made from reused Roman pottery, uncovered during HS2's excavation in Wendover (HS2 Limited)

A set of copper alloy small square-headed brooches, decorated with gold gilt, from the fifth or sixth century, uncovered during HS2's archaeological work in Wendover (HS2 Limited)

bucket pendants, had surprising results. It turns out most inhabitants had predominantly local strontium markers, and the site was founded by local people whose ancestors grew up nearby.[26]

Investigations with the same method at Eastbourne in East Sussex produced the same results, with only one of nineteen individuals buried between 375 and 600 from continental Europe.[27]

Widespread displacement of people and new settlements directly related to an invasion of incomers from across the North Sea has been largely missing from archaeological investigations in areas deemed Anglo-Saxon heartlands. Heavily excavated sites such as West Heslerton and Mucking show continued use from the Iron Age and through the early medieval period, albeit with marked changes in material culture and buildings in post-Roman Britain. Field farming layouts have largely displayed the same continuity.

By the seventh century, most of lowland Britain, including the Midlands, East Anglia, Lincolnshire, London and York, were now speaking Old English as their first language.[28] It is believed, however, that the main language in these regions had been Late Latin and not Brittonic at the onset of the Anglo-Saxon migration in the fifth century. This begins to explain in part the distinct lack of Brittonic words in Old English, which is often attributed to a lack of interaction and almost apartheid takeover by Anglo-Saxon elites.

Hundreds of Latin loanwords can be found in Old English, which were a product of military contact and trade between Romans and Germanic tribes from the first century. Old English words borrowed from Latin include ones for plants, animals, household items, building materials, commercial and military terms.[29] Examples show in order Latin, Old English and modern English in brackets:

piperis, piper (pepper)
radicem, rædic (radish)
cattus, catt(e) (cat)
cāseus, cyse (cheese)
vinus, win (wine)
candeō, candel (candle)
cocina, cycene (kitchen)
vallum, weall (wall)
balteus, belt (belt)
campus, camp (field, battle)
strātus, strœt (road)
mīlia, mil (mile)
pondō, pund (pound)

Additional loanwords were borrowed during the fifth and sixth centuries amid the Anglo-Saxon migration, and then from the seventh century when a new educated clergy drew from classical Latin for military and legal terms, musical and religious words, and wild animals. This includes:

cōnsul, consul (consul)
versus, fers (verse)
chorus, chor (chorus)
delphīnus, delfin (dolphin)
leopardus, pard (leopard)
altare, alter (altar)
clēricus, cleric (clergyman)
daemōn, the demon (demon)
paradīsus, paradis (paradise)

The names point to a new contact language between two sets of people evolving into the common Germanic language of Old English, with borrowings from Latin and British. It shows there was a common ground between the North Sea migrants and Romano-British inhabitants and points to how a new language emerged.

The dominance of English place names across England and even Wales to a degree was a product of the landscape being renamed in the ninth century when most people spoke Middle English. Those localities dating from the fifth and sixth centuries suggest peaceful co-existence between Britons and English-speaking settlers given many Latin names, such as Portus Adurni (Portchester); the scene of one of the first battles in early Wessex.[30] Many of the great natural landscape features of the island retained their original British names, such as the Thames, Severn, Malvern Hills and the Pennines.

There is also the widespread occurrence across central and southern England of further place names with pre-Latin and Latin words, such as many containing 'unt' and 'font'.[31] For example, Boarhunt in Hampshire, Chadshunt in Stratford-on-Avon and Cheshunt in Herefordshire, which are thought to derive from the Latin word *Fontana*, meaning 'spring, place where the water rises'. Likewise, an Eccles-on-Sea can be found in Norfolk from the Latin word *Ecclesia*, which stands for church, as does possibly Eccles in Kent. It is thought the name recognized British sites of religious Christian observance.[32]

Meanwhile, place names of 'comb(e)', from the Welsh word *cym* meaning deep valley, are typically associated with the south-west, where in places such as North Devon they can be found one after the other along the coast in Woolacombe, Ilfracombe and Combe Martin. They are also found further afield in Sacombe in Herefordshire, where St Catherine's Church dating back 1,000 years sits above a valley.

Amid this mass migration and cultural change, it is fascinating to note how the regional differences in the late-sixth century are almost in evidence in the present day, based on a massive Oxford University study. The research identified seventeen distinct genetic clusters in the UK from a sample of DNA from 2,000 people compared with 6,000 Europeans, which placed on a map remarkably mirrored the seventh-century divide between culturally Anglo-Saxon and British-speaking kingdoms, including Wales and Scotland.[33]

This divide was, in turn, based on the Roman civitas created around tribal regions. There was no mythical Celtic group of people and results threw up remarkable differences between places such as Devon and Cornwall and north and south Wales.

Neither did the Anglo-Saxons wipe out the natives with their contribution estimated to be at least 20 per cent of the gene pool in England as a whole. There had clearly been a steady stream of migration from Europe for thousands of years.

The Prittlewell Prince was laid to rest in a wooden chamber with lavish goods at a spot now overlooking the modern-day Priory Park

Prittlewell more than hints at this more complicated picture as it appears traditions dating back to Lexden were incorporated. A clue can be found in how it is suspected the body had been laid in the coffin by Christians with tiny white Latin crosses placed over his eyes before being buried by pagans. Kings descended from the North Sea settlers may have enlisted Romano-Britons in helping with the burial as they forged connections with the landscape and previous dynasties. They could even have aligned through intermarriage with a British tribe or power block who could trace their roots all the way back to Lexden.

Ultimately, this speaks of many areas where different cultures were sharing ideas and legends, living side by side in harmony rather than perpetual warfare and eventually formed a new society still rooted in the past.

When England did officially come into being in the ninth century under Aethelstan (the grandson of Alfred the Great), who was first to be described in a 927 charter as *Rex Angloroum* in Latin meaning 'King of the English', these complexities had long faded into memory. A poem marking Aethelstan's victory at Brunanburh over the kings of Scotland, Dublin and Strathclyde recalled:[34]

> *'Never, before this, were more men in this island slain by the sword's edge – as books and aged sages confirm – since Angles and Saxons sailed here from the east, sought the Britons over the wide seas, since those warsmiths hammered the Welsh, and earls, eager for glory, overran the land.'*

Cerdic was chief among these warsmiths in the account provided by the *Anglo-Saxon Chronicle*, having sailed over with his son Cynric and conquering all those who stood in his path. This was the story that influenced our understanding of England's foundation for more than 1,000 years. The story was far more complex but every bit as monumental.

Chapter 3

Gildas and the *Anglo-Saxon Chronicle*

Foederati Rebellion, Wessex's British Origins

> *A new race succeeded, who were ignorant of this troublesome time, and had only experience of the present prosperity, all the laws of truth and justice were so shaken and subverted, that not so much as a vestige or remembrance of these virtues remained among the above-named orders of men, except among a very few who, compared with the great multitude which were daily rushing headlong down to hell.*
>
> On the Ruin and Conquest of Britain, Gildas, sixth century

Gildas

In 2018, the British Museum staged a huge exhibition, with around 180 treasures, which told the story of the Anglo-Saxon period.[1] Exhibits included the earliest surviving English charter, the oldest original letter written in England from the Bishop of London in the eighth century, famous Old English poetry manuscripts, such as *Beowulf*, and decorated manuscripts from St Augustine and Lindisfarne gospels.

Stunning artefacts such as the Alfred Jewel and a gold buckle from the Sutton Hoo ship burial were among a plethora of fascinating grave finds, literature, jewellery, weapons and clothing, which captured this most incredible age of British history.

One striking item was a gold coin minted by ninth-century ruler King Offa of Mercia, perhaps the most famous Anglo-Saxon king before Alfred the Great. This coin featured the Arabic inscription 'No God But Allah' and had been minted along with hundreds of gold dinars featuring his name and the Islamic declaration of faith as a product of trading with modern day Spain, then under Muslim rule.[2]

I remember attending the event when working as a journalist and being taken by one artefact on display, not an immaculate sword, an intrinsically engineered brooch or anything that looked visually impressive, but an extremely old medieval annal. One resembling a hefty bound book dug out from the corners of a dusty cellar, covered in cobwebs. Pages of the manuscript were damaged in a fire in Westminster, which damaged numerous other rare annals held in a private collection by Sir Robert Cotton, while ink on the parchment pages had now considerably faded but was still decipherable.[3]

Despite going to walk away, I kept returning to this book, completely transfixed as I knew the magnitude of these words, which shaped so much of what is known about the early Anglo-Saxon period. For this was a copy of Gildas' *On The Ruin of Britain and Conquest of Britain*, believed to be dated to the tenth century. While intended not as a historical record, with little in the way of names and places, this polemic verse, which covered several hundred pages, provided in a small section one of the few contemporary accounts of Britain after the western empire collapsed.

Writing in classical Latin, the monk Gildas described how a council led by a 'proud tyrant' first invited Saxon mercenaries to fight off tribes of Picts (originating from modern-day Scotland) and Scots (from Ireland), which 'sealed its doom by inviting in among them like wolves into the sheepfold, the fierce and impious Saxons, a race hateful both to God and men'.

Gildas then refers to 'foederati', which were a feature of the Roman empire and were typically Germanic tribes bound by treaty who provided military assistance to Rome often in exchange for land or supplies. These foederati arrived in 'three ships of wars' and settled on the eastern side of the island, and Gildas says they soon called for 'a larger company of her wolfish offspring'.

According to Gildas, the barbarian soldiers were given 'plentiful' provisions of food, which 'stopped their doggish mouths', but the Saxons were unhappy with their supplies and threatened to 'break the treaty and plunder the whole island. In a short time, they follow up their threats with deeds.'

Leaders of the foederati who first arrived were later identified as Hengist and Horsa, the traditional founders of Kent, and the tyrant who invited them as Vortigern by the eight-century monk Bede in his famous work of about AD 731 – *Ecclesiastical History of the English People*.

A vivid picture of the widespread destruction is revealed by Gildas, which 'spread from sea to sea' as the Saxons ransacked 'neighbouring towns and lands' with their carnage dipping its 'red and savage tongue in the western ocean'.

> *'All the husbandmen routed, together with their bishops, priests, and people, whilst the sword gleamed, and the flames crackled around them on every side. 'Lamentable to behold, in the midst of the streets lay the tops of lofty towers, tumbled to the ground, stones of high walls, holy altars, fragments of human bodies, covered with livid clots of coagulated blood, looking as if they had been squeezed together in a press; and with no chance of being buried, save in the ruins of the houses, or in the ravening bellies of wild beasts and birds.'*

Many people fled to the mountains, while the remainder were 'murdered in great numbers; others, constrained by famine, came and yielded themselves to be slaves forever to their foes, running the risk of being instantly slain, which truly was the greatest favour that could be offered them.'

Amid the turmoil, Gildas praises a leader called Ambrosius Aurelianus whose parents he said 'wore the purple', a sign of significant wealth or authority in Roman times, but they had died during the conflict. It is Ambrosius who helps the Britons 'regain their strength'.

Defeated Britons were saved from 'utter destruction' as they took up arms under Ambrosius and 'provoke to battle their cruel conquerors, and by the goodness of our Lord obtain the victory'. Gildas describes a decisive British victory at Badon after back-and-forth military success, which has been perennially associated with King Arthur.

Despite the triumph, Gildas appears to suggest a partition of the eastern side of the island after a 'grievous divorce with the barbarians', which remained in the hands of the Saxons, preventing people from visiting the 'shrine of the martyrs', believed to be St Albans in modern-day Hertfordshire.

British kings are then subject to Gildas' wrath and likened to biblical beasts for adultery, civil warfare, greed and dishonesty, and the arrival of the Saxons was punishment from God for such sins.

Frustratingly, Cerdic's name is nowhere to be found in the writings of Gildas, but his absence could be crucial in placing his reign in a specific time frame. The narrative of Cerdic as an invading Saxon contradicts Gildas who appears to describe the time from 495 to 534 when Cerdic reigned as one of peace.

Victory at Badon had ushered in a golden age where citizens lived lawfully and happily, and this peace was shattered when a new generation was born who were ignorant of the hardship their ancestors endured.

> *'For as well the remembrance of such a terrible desolation of the island, as also of the unexpected recovery of the same, remained in the minds of those who were eyewitnesses of the wonderful events of both, and in regard thereof, kings, public magistrates, and private persons, with priests and clergymen, did all and every one of them live orderly according to their several vocations.*
>
> *'But when these had departed out of this world, and a new race succeeded, who were ignorant of this troublesome time, and had only experience of the present prosperity, all the laws of truth and justice were so shaken and subverted, that not so much as a vestige or remembrance of these virtues remained among the above-named orders of men, except among a very few who, compared with the great multitude which were daily rushing headlong down to hell, are accounted so small a number, that our reverend mother, the church, scarcely beholds them.'*

This golden age is precisely when Cerdic is supposedly terrorizing local inhabitants and building a massive new kingdom. Badon's actual date has been intensely debated by scholars and will probably continue to be thrashed out for many years to come. Estimates range from as far back as the early-fifth century, while consensus places it between 495 and 514, as the later date given in the Annales Cambriae. What is confusing is how this period covers three landings and same-day conflicts – in 495, 501 and 514 – related to the kingdom that became Wessex.

Shedding further light, Gildas wrote Badon had taken place in the year of his own birth forty-four years ago: 'And this commences, a fact I know, as the forty-fourth year, with one month now elapsed, it is also the year of my birth.' His damning account of post-Roman Britain must have been written before 547 when one of the five kings he condemns, Maelgwn Gwynedd, who he brands the 'dragon of the island', is said to have died from a 'great mortality'.[4]

So, when exactly did Gildas write his legendary account of post-Roman Britain? Well, according to Irish annals, Gildas died in Brittany in 570 and so was most likely writing at some point between 530 and 540, which would place the Battle of Badon between the years 490 and 500. This is a date that seems favourable.

In an academic study, David Woods from University College Cork noted how Gildas refers in Chapter 93 to a 'dense cloud and black night' that 'looms over the whole island', conceivably a reference to the extreme weather event in 536, but he does not mention the subsequent documented famine this event caused in Britain and Ireland the following year.[5] Therefore, historian Andrew Breeze argues he was writing in the summer of 536, which would mean Badon occurring in 493 with Gildas' precise reduction of the forty-fourth year with one month elapsed, i.e. forty-three years and one month.[6]

As it happens, this is roughly the same date Bede provided for Badon but based on the battle occurring forty-four years after the first Saxon confederates arrived in 449 during the joint reign of Marcian and Valentinian III, who were eastern and western Roman emperors respectively. It is just two years before Cerdic and Cynric supposedly arrived.

Notably, another king condemned by Gildas known as Vortipor, the 'tyrant of the Demetae', died in 540 according to royal ancestry records, which would support the date of 536. It is worth considering because, as the next chapter will reveal, the extreme weather event was remarkably well documented, and you would perhaps expect Gildas to dedicate more attention to the dramatic reduction in sunlight. However, the text is notoriously thin on specific details and a date in the 530s based on all available evidence seems the most logical.

Moreover, in a separate text the Chronica Majora, the scholar Bede places Ambrosius in the time of Zeno (the eastern Roman emperor) between 474 and 491, which would coincide with a long period of warfare before Badon at the end of the fifth century.

Triumphantly, Gildas describes Badon as a decisive victory in the Saxon confederate war, claiming it was the 'last almost, though not the least, slaughter of our cruel foes'. After lamenting the decline of cities in post-Roman Britain, he mentions how the 'foreign' wars with the Saxons had ended, which would seem unlikely if the dates and context of the early Wessex battles were accurate: 'And yet neither to this day are the cities of our country inhabited as before, but being forsaken and overthrown, still lie desolate; our foreign wars having ceased, but our civil troubles still remaining.'

If Cerdic was a Briton, he must be part of the 'civil troubles' battling against rival kingdoms and would be singled out by Gildas alongside the other kings. As a British ruler aligned with the Germanic confederates, this surely would have been an unforgivable crime in Gildas' world, and if Cerdic had been a Germanic invader, then the 'foreign wars' would not be over.

Chroniclers were likely more informed about sixth-century dates than it appears and may have fixed the date of Cerdic's landing immediately after Badon. Historian Marc Morris points out how the *Anglo-Saxon Chronicle* is 'tolerably accurate' for fifth-century dates when it comes to popes, bishops and emperors.[7]

Perhaps the chroniclers wanted an earlier start date for Cerdic's reign and battle sequence or it was not available in oral tradition. Therefore, what better date than after Badon, which they knew as a great victory in Welsh tradition but the last significant triumph before Lloegyr (the Welsh name for England) was lost to the Saxons. They filled a void in Anglo-Saxon encroachment and successes after Badon in the peaceful generation mentioned by Gildas. On closer inspection, the early chronicle entries provide just cause to believe they have been deliberately altered.

Britons and the Anglo-Saxons

The chronicle is thrown into doubt because the name Cerdic is almost certainly British rather than Germanic, which seems strange for an apparent North Sea invader. Cerdic was an Old English version of popular names such as Caradoc, Ceretic and Caraticos from the language referred to as Brittonic; the ancient language before it branched off into Welsh, Cornish, Breton, Cumbric and possibly Pictish. This name is thought to derive from that of the British king Caratacus, who led the resistance against the Roman invasion in the first century.

Caratacus' grandfather may have been the occupant of the spectacular burial in Lexden, Essex, which as discussed in the previous chapter shared fascinating similarities with the chamber burial unearthed just 30 miles away on the outskirts of Southend in 2003.

A chieftain of the Catuvellauni tribe, which ruled in much of what is now south-east and central England, Caratacus led a guerrilla war against the Roman army for more than a decade before he was betrayed by

Cartimandua, queen of the Brigantes, who handed him over in chains. His capture effectively pacified the region between the River Humber and River Severn until Boudicca's uprising a decade later.

Yet, this is far from the last we heard of this legendary Briton who gave a passionate and iconic speech, recorded by the historian Tacitus in the Roman senate, which persuaded Emperor Claudius to spare him, extolling how without rivals such as himself the Roman army would never have achieved the same greatness.[8] He boasted of having 'horses, men, arms and wealth' and asked if 'everyone should accept (Roman) slavery?'

> *'If I were now being handed over as one who had surrendered immediately, neither my fortune nor your glory would have achieved brilliance. It is also true that in my case any reprisal will be followed by oblivion. On the other hand, if you preserve me safe and sound, I shall be an eternal example of your clemency.'*

Fortunately for Caratacus, the magnificent speech, which of course could be a complete invention but captured the essence of events, had the desired effect and won his freedom. Moreover, it ensured that along with Boudicca he would become immortalized as a hero of the Britons.

You would presume a pagan Germanic warrior invading and conquering lands from British peoples, as Cerdic is described in the chronicle, would not just happen to share a name possibly derived from one of the island's native heroes? The fact one early Anglo-Saxon king has a Brittonic sounding name may not be as significant as first thought. For example, the sixth-century Christian king Tewdrig, who was mortally wounded defending Gwent from a Saxon invasion (linked to Cerdic's descendant Ceawlin), according to legend has a name that could easily be a variant of the Germanic Theodoric.[9] The big difference, however, is Cerdic and nearly all his descendant kings until the eighth century had names that could include a Brittonic element, including his recorded son.

Cynric

Cynric's name has been linked to the Brittonic name Cunorix, which means 'hound king', because *cun* ('hound') and the suffix *rex* is a Brittonic derivation of the Latin word *rix* ('king'). It could also mean 'warrior' as well as 'hound'.

The *cun* element, which was pronounced 'cune' in Brittonic, was common among the ancestors of the great fifth-century post-Roman warlord Cunedda, who removed invading Irish tribes in north Wales and founded the dynasty of Gwynedd.[10]

Notably, one of Cunedda's sons was called Ceredig and gave his name to Ceredigion in West Wales, although he is described as beginning to rule seventy years before Cerdic landed. Some writers have attempted to associate Cerdic with the Ceredig from Wales, but this seems unlikely.

Another Ceredig is remembered in a famous bardic praise poem *Y Gododdin* commemorating British-speaking warriors who died apparently fighting northern Anglian foes in the late-sixth or early-seventh century. Heralded as a 'beloved leader, a rampaging hero in the fight' who 'held the front like a true man', it is assumed he was killed along with most of his ill-fated comrades.[11]

The name Cunorix was found on a monument uncovered in 1967 during excavations in Wroxeter, formerly the great Roman city of Viriconium.[12] Later moved outside the city walls from a more prominent position in the centre, the tombstone included an inscription 'Cunorix macus Maquicoline' interpreted as 'Cunorix son of Maqui Coline'. The use of the word 'Macus', a Latinized version of the Gaelic word 'Mac' which means the 'son of', indicates Cunorix was of Irish descent.[13]

There was a substantial influx of Irish migration on the western coast of Britain after the departure of Roman troops, which mirrored the Germanic migration on the eastern shores. Elites in southern Ireland during the fourth century began memorializing their dead by inscription stones in a script known as Ogham.[14] These began appearing in western Britain during the fifth century, alongside Irish place names, in regions such as Pembrokeshire, Cardiganshire, Devon and Cornwall, which demonstrated Irish elites were settling and making their presence felt.

Clearly, Cunorix was a significant ruler with Irish descent who either ruled around Wroxeter, perhaps as a sub-king of Gwynedd, or was allied with kings in the region who commemorated him.

Both Cerdic and Cynric then share the same names as memorable British and Irish rulers, but this was just the start of a pattern in the naming of early Wessex rulers.

Ceawlin

The warring king Ceawlin, Cerdic's recorded grandson, has a Brittonic etymology and is said to be recorded in Welsh genealogies as Kollen or Collen, but this is based on dubious and conflicting ancestry records.[15]

According to Bede, he was the second Anglo-Saxon king to hold the infamous title of 'Bretwalda', which is believed to have signified overlordship of southern English kingdoms up to the River Humber. When listing the Bretwaldas, Bede notably remarks 'Celin, king of the West-Saxons, who, in their own language, is called Ceaulin'. Perhaps Bede was hinting at the ancestry of Ceawlin as he did not make this distinction with language for any other Bretwalda. In a crucial remark, Bede also describes how the West Saxons were also known as the Gewisse.

Another early Wessex royal Cedda (Chad or Cad), whose father Cuthwine was the son of Ceawlin, had a Brittonic name with the root *cad* meaning 'battle' from the Old Welsh version *cat*.[16] He shares the name with a prominent seventh-century churchman St Chad of Mercia, who became the abbot of several monasteries.

Cynegils

Wessex ruler Cynegils, the son of Ceol who had followed Ceawlin, ascended the throne in 611 and reigned for thirty-one years.

While Cynegils is not typically thought to have a Brittonic name, it does include the element *cyn,* derived from *cun*, meaning 'hound' in Brittonic, which as previously mentioned is linked to Cerdic's supposed son Cynric.

The word *cyn* began appearing on inscriptions from the seventh century and is found among Welsh rulers from the early medieval period. One includes Cynddylan, a possible king of the post-Roman kingdom of Powys, who was remembered in a famous tribute poem – the *Elegy for Cynddylan* – and fought alongside the legendary Mercian warlord Penda at the battle of Maserfield in 642; the year of Cynegils' death.

Meanwhile, the word *cyne* means 'royal and ruler' in Old English and features among several Mercian and Wessex kings, princes and princesses up until the late-eighth century.[17]

Cenwalh

Brittonic elements continued among descendants of Cerdic in the seventh century in the case of Cenwalh of Wessex who followed Cynegils and ruled initially from 642 to 645 before he was driven out of his kingdom by Penda. After three years in exile, Cenwalh returned to his kingdom in safety and ruled until his own death in 672.

Intriguingly, the *wealh* or *walh* part of the name was the Old English term for 'Welshman', 'foreigner' and 'slave'.[18] It appears frequently in Anglo-Saxon texts and even among the names of seventh-century rulers in neighbouring Mercia. One of Penda's sons, according to Kent annals, was called Merewalh.[19] This is said to mean 'Glorious foreigner' or 'Glorious Welshman', which seems an odd title in the scheme of things.

Many of the early Mercian kings, like their counterparts in Wessex, bore names with more obvious Brittonic elements until Penda's reign, who notably aligned with Welsh kingdoms against Northumberland.[20]

At the point of Cenwalh's reign, we can begin to have much greater confidence in records as the spread of Christianity among the English-speaking peoples led to greater literacy and documenting of events by monks. Described as the most talented historian of his age, Bede, writing in 729, recalled how when Cenwalh returned to power he was furious that Frankish Bishop Agilbert in Dorchester on Thames did not speak Old English:

> *'At length the king, who understood none but the language of the Saxons, grown weary of that bishop's barbarous tongue, brought into the province another bishop of his own nation, whose name was Wini, who had been ordained in France; and dividing his province into two dioceses, appointed this last his episcopal see in the city of Winchester, by the Saxons called Wintancestir.'*

Caedwalla

The last Wessex king to have a British name was Caedwalla, grandson of Cedda, and his reign was perhaps the most significant since Ceawlin around 100 years before.

Caedwalla bore the same name as Gwynedd ruler Cadwallon ap Cadfan, who conquered Northumberland in alliance with Penda and ruled the region for a year before his death at the hands of Oswald in 634. Unsurprisingly, Bede, who was based in Northumberland and aligned to its royal dynasty, is scathing in his recollection of Cadwallon (Cadwalla) and how he treated the English-speaking peoples:

> *'Cadwalla, though he bore the name and professed himself a Christian, was so barbarous in his disposition and behaviour, that he neither spared the female sex, nor the innocent age of children, but with savage cruelty put them to tormenting deaths, ravaging all their country for a long time, and resolving to cut off all the race of the English within the borders of Britain.'*

Considering an almost certainly English-speaking king of the West Saxons had an anglicized version of his name around fifty years later, the accuracy of this damning statement is hard to accept. Ironically, Cadwallon's downfall was in part due to his own so-called countrymen and not the English.

Dal Riata warriors on the island of Iona had offered refuge to Oswald and his family years earlier when his father, Aethelfrith, had been killed in a battle against suspected Sutton Hoo occupant Raedwald and his dynastic rival Edwin. The young prince was a threat to his uncle Edwin who assumed the throne. These same Dal Riata warriors then joined Oswald in battle against Cadwallon, while the Brittonic kingdom of Rheged gave Oswald shelter, provisions and horses.[21] Oswald's brother, Oswiu, was married to a Rheged princess, Rieinmelth, and her people seem to have favoured Oswald over Cadwallon.

Britons who had grown tired of the occupying army, even if they were fellow Britons, most likely tipped off Oswald.[22] This enabled the Northumberland king to launch a surprise early morning attack near Hadrian's Wall, bringing Cadwallon's occupation to an end.

Caedwalla of the West Saxons reigned between 685 and 688 and conquered the Isle of Wight, Surrey and Kent before he abdicated and headed to Rome to be baptized, where he died from wounds suffered during his Isle of Wight conquest. Nearly 1,000 years later, Bede's account of his life was confirmed when the tombstone of Caedwalla was discovered during building work on St Peter's Basilica in Rome in the 1670s.

Another later ruler of Gwynedd, called Cadwaladr, died from an instance of the plague in 664 and was described as 'the last King of Britain' by

Geoffrey of Monmouth, who conflated the story of his life with the Wessex king and described him as heading to Rome to be baptized before his death.

The Laws of King Ine, who succeeded Caedwalla, indicate many British-speaking people were living in the kingdom as late as the eighth century. Some scholars claim the laws reveal an almost apartheid structure, where the Britons were an inferior class.

It mentions six classes of *wealhs* or *willisc* ('Welsh, Britons') and confirms the lower status of the 'natives', while a couple of clauses imply Germanic and native populations lived close together. Roman civilians are referred to as *Rumwalas* in the heroic Germanic poem *Widsith,* which is related to *wealhs*, so the term is not specific to Britons.[23]

Susan Oosthuizen, a professor of medieval archaeology at the University of Cambridge, highlighted in *The Emergence of the English* how the Laws of King Ine were based on long-standing customary Romano-British laws and how just nine (7 per cent) of the 119 law codes mention people called *willisc* or *Englisc*, which suggests politics, society and economy was not structured on ethnicity. These clauses included *wergilds*, which were compensation for crimes against a person, and ones that made it easier to accuse a *williscne* slave compared to an *Engliscne* slave. The nine clauses, Professor Oosthuizen argues, either implied the *Engliscne* were of higher status, they were intended to deter discrimination against the *Engliscne* or in the case of the *williscne* simply based on long-standing Roman traditions. It is believed the Laws of Ine were originally written in Latin and then translated into Old English around 150 years later during Alfred the Great's reign.

Conflict between the British and English-speaking people during the seventh century was not nearly as black and white as it would be painted 200 years later, as allegiances were sometimes forged on a regionalized level as evidenced by Penda, the Mercian, who consistently fought alongside Welsh kingdoms.

When the late ninth-century writers of the chronicle discovered references to Cerdic from oral traditions or lists of kings passed down through generations, he could not be treated as anything other than an English king because the people of England had by that point been almost completely anglicized.

In comparison, notably, the kingdom of Northumberland, which emerged in a post-Roman Britain stronghold known as the 'Old North', features distinctly English-sounding named early kings. Kent and Sussex, in the regions of Iron Age tribes the Cantii and the Regni respectively, again had more obvious English-sounding rulers.

Arguably, the very fact the name Cerdic appears in the early history of Wessex must be overwhelming proof of his existence as surely the chroniclers would not have chosen a Brittonic name for their founder.

Research and archaeological studies have shown how this era saw three patterns emerging: one of significant migration from across the North Sea, which by the seventh century led to elite English-speaking settlements; an 'Anglo-Saxon' inspired culture developing across eastern England, no doubt influenced by their new neighbours and trade from this region; and the west clinging to the previous Romano-British customs.

What complicates matters is those buried with Germanic grave goods were not, as tooth enamel studies of excavated skeletons have shown, necessarily from distant shores, and neither could the new English elite be classed as foreigners in a land where their ancestors may have arrived up to a 100 years earlier.

In short, who was 'native', 'Briton' and 'Saxon' was a murky subject, and probably one based on language rather than ancestry, but even then, many people were bilingual.

When the chronicle was composed in the late-ninth century, everyone was 'Anglo-Saxon', give or take some clusters of modern-day Cumbria, parts of the west country (including Cornwall), Wales and Scotland. The picture was much simpler and the regional nuances less apparent or wilfully ignored, the process of cultural transformation was brushed over for one of displacement. Tales of fire and sword and ethnic dominance prevailed because the more complicated version was a little less inspiring, not understood or simply forgotten. US-based history professor Philip Jenkins, who has a first-class honours degree in Anglo-Saxon, Norse and Celtic Studies from Cambridge University, explains: 'The story of Wessex is a classic example of how the very mixed society of post-Roman Britain became Anglo Saxon, that is English and German speaking, to the point of forgetting that it was ever anything else. The process took some generations, but it was thorough. Britain became England.'[24]

Historian John Morris, in his 1973 work *The Age of Arthur*, is under no doubt Cerdic was British:

> *'A ruler with a British name, with no ancient tradition of English forebears or English descendants, is plainly British.*

> *Though he was the earliest ruler of the future Wessex whom the later English knew, the claim of ninth century Wessex kings to suzerainty over all the English could not be built upon the authority of a British king. He had to be treated as an Englishman.'*

Evidence clearly suggests a strong Brythonic element in early Wessex, which began with Cerdic, whose name commemorates a famous Briton and scourge of the Romans. As Wessex grew in power from the reign of Ceawlin, their kings were anglicized, but they paid homage to their British ancestry. Realizing Cerdic had British heritage along with most of his successors for the next 150 years and was almost certainly based in the region he apparently invaded changes the whole nature of the story.

Chapter 4

Gildas and the *Anglo-Saxon Chronicle*

Dating Cerdic's Reign, the Shadowy Creoda

Deeply troubled by poor literacy among his fellow countrymen, Alfred the Great, the King of Wessex, believed the Viking invasions, which preceded the educational decline, were a 'punishment for the moral failings

The statue in Winchester High Street honouring one of Britain's most revered monarchs, Alfred the Great

of the English people'.[25] In wide-sweeping education reforms, Alfred ordered a collection of annals written in Old English in different times and places between the late-ninth and mid-twelfth century, which provide a chronological list of events, battles and kings in each kingdom. These became known as the *Anglo-Saxon Chronicle* and first revealed the story of Cerdic's reign. Composed anonymously, it is believed they were written by clergymen at main religious sites and grew out of the original chronicle created at Alfred's court in Winchester in 893.

Chroniclers hoped to unite divided realms against the common Northman enemy by documenting how the founders of each Anglo-Saxon kingdom were either brothers or father and son, who nearly all descended from a shared ancestry of mythical Germanic heroes and pagan gods, such Woden, and had arrived in small groups of ships and began conquering the natives.

Monks who composed the chronicle at the behest of King Alfred were seemingly aware something different was happening in Wessex because notably the entry for 519 describes Cerdic and Cynric as having 'undertook the rule of the West Saxon kingdom'. This phrase, which in Old English is *rice onfengun*, is not found anywhere else, and the usual one is *feng to rice* when a ruler inherits a kingdom. When Ida, a near contemporary of Cerdic founded Bernicia in 547, one half of which became Northumberland, the phrase *feng to rice* was used.[26]

Both Cerdic and Cynric are described as 'ealdormen' in the first 495 entry. In the ninth century, this would refer to an individual who led in battle, presided over courts and levied taxation on behalf of a king, which seems odd. Therefore, Cerdic and Cynric are described as having authority over a region they are supposedly invading.

In *The English Settlements*, John Myres suspected the unusual term implied Cerdic was possibly the 'head of a partly British noble family', which had authority to defend the region in the post-Roman period and so would be the equivalent of an 'ealdorman' in ninth-century terminology. He speculated the Cerdic ruling dynasty had established blood relationships with Saxon and Jutish settlers, something implied by Isle of Wight founders Stuf and Wihtgar being described as his nephews and Jutish settlers having been based on the island as early as the late-fifth century.

Once the effective post-Roman authority had faded, Myers believes Cerdic launched his bid for power, either during the foederati rebellion, which was outlined in dramatic terms by Gildas, or some forty years later when the generation of peace following Badon had ended. According to

Myres, the Cerdicing ruling family 'might have taken matters into its own hands' and eliminated competing British chieftains, such as the mysterious Natanleod, so it could 'begin to reign without recognising in future any superior authority'.

A simple scan of Cerdic's ancestry reveals it is clearly a literary invention beyond his grandfather, with descent from Elesa, Elsa, Gewis, Wye, Frewin, Frithgar, Balday and Woden. Including Gewis as a mythological figure explains the name for the Gewisse, while Woden is the chief god of Germanic mythology, who rulers of all the Anglo-Saxon kingdoms claimed their right to rule through descent, asides from Essex, which attached itself to the Saxon god Seaxnēat.

Another peculiarity in the Wessex entries is a theme in the dating of the various battles. Most medieval annals recorded events on an Easter cycle, also known as the 'Metonic Cycle', which was approximately nineteen years after which time the phases of the moon reoccur at the same time of the year. This formed the basis of Greek and Hebrew calendars and was used to calculate the dates of Easter. It is suspected the Easter cycle was applied to Wessex early entries because chroniclers would unlikely have dates from oral traditions of battles, and there are gaps of nineteen years between various battles and landings with entries in 495–514 and 508–27.

A separate West Saxon Genealogical List of King Alfred, which serves as a preface to Manuscript A of the *Anglo-Saxon Chronicle*, places the landing of Cerdic a year earlier in 494 and claims that he took over the kingdom six years later and reigned for sixteen years.[27] Again, the pattern is repeated as the date of 500 is nineteen years before Cerdic took over the kingdom according to the *Anglo-Saxon Chronicle*.

Late-tenth century West Saxon chronicler Aethelweard, who was a descendant of Alfred the Great's brother Aethelred I, provided the same version as the West Saxon Genealogical List.

To complicate matters further, some chroniclers would begin a new year from March or 25 December, while others used the traditional Roman date of 1 January.[28] The pattern in dating could be linked to how dates were calculated at the time.

In 525, an eastern-Roman monk known as Dionysius Exiguus produced an Easter table over a ninety-five-year term between 532 and 626, which included five nineteen-year Easter cycles and was adopted across large parts of the western world. For example, the date of the Paschal Moon, the first full moon after the spring equinox that determines the date of Easter, would fall in 532 on 5 April, which was repeated in 551 and 570 and so on. Dionysius invented the Anno Domini (AD) dating method, derived from a Latin word *anno*, meaning 'in the year of the Lord', which remains in place in the modern day and calculates dates from the birth of Christ. Bede's later Easter table was inspired by Dionysius' version.

Some academics believe Cerdic's story has been retold over two Easter cycles, which seems a real possibility as a later chapter will explore.[29] Dates of battles would have been altered using the same nineteen-year cycle.

The question remains whether the chronicle timeline for Wessex and Cerdic has been backdated, and the most comprehensive study of the West Saxon Genealogical List so far came to this exact conclusion.[30]

Dating Cerdic's reign

Scholar David Dumville, now an emeritus professor at the University of Aberdeen, examined the Wessex dynasty between Cerdic and Alfred, and his analysis has proved vital in understanding Cerdic's actual timeframe and the shadowy figure of Creoda. Crucially, it has also placed Cerdic at a different point in time, one of great strife and suggested more plausible reigns of subsequent kings.

Professor Dumville analyzed the three main sources for the kings of Wessex, which are the West Saxon Genealogical Regnal List of the Cerdic dynasty, the *Anglo-Saxon Chronicle* and the West Saxon royal genealogies, which display the family interrelationships and the right to rule. Included in the study are the twelfth-century Annals of St Neots and the tenth-century Latin version of the *Anglo-Saxon Chronicle* composed by Aethelweard.

Nine versions of the Genealogical Regnal List survive, which date between the ninth and twelfth century and three were attached to the *Anglo-Saxon Chronicle*. In all these records, the ancestry of ten kings showed a clear line of descent from Cerdic with Professor Dumville noting in his study: 'The right of each king to rule is thus explicitly stated: it is plain that in the view of the text's compiler descent from Cerdic was the crucial legitimising factor.' In total, the study covered the reign lengths of the twenty-two West Saxons kings from Cerdic to Aethelred, who was king between 865 and 871 before his brother Alfred. According to the list, which appears to derive from an unmanipulated original source because barring a few translation errors the reigns are consistent for all kings, Cerdic reigned sixteen years in five versions, six in one and thirteen in another, while one version has been damaged and a final one is abbreviated. The six and thirteen are thought to be scribal errors with the Roman numeral dates.

All the chronicle texts studied during the research agree on an arrival date for Cerdic and Cynric of 494/95. Such a scenario is, however, unlikely because the chronicle clearly records Cerdic and Cynric as beginning to reign as kings in Wessex in 519.

Other academics, such as Frank Stenton, have noticed duplicate entries in the foundation of Wessex, which is referenced in the research:

- 494/95 and 514 – arrival of West Saxons
- 500/501 and 519 – taking of land and kingdom
- 508 and 527 – battle with Britons
- 516 and 534 – end of Cerdic's reign; Cynric king

It is obvious Cerdic's grandson Ceawlin is the subject of the biggest discrepancy in the Genealogical Regnal List, with his reign either lasting seven or seventeen years. However, Professor Dumville believes his revised seven-year reign of Ceawlin between 581 and 588 was accurate, and this 'short, glorious and violent end' would have been fitting, but it must have been considered too brief and was, therefore, extended to thirty-plus years. A late date is further supported by how Ceawlin's forces battled Aethelbert of Kent in 568, but it was another twenty-one years before the Kentish king is said to have reigned from 589 until 616. As Aethelbert allowed Augustine and his missionaries into his kingdom, he is someone who can be more securely dated.

The study by Professor Dumville highlighted missing periods. For example, the Genealogical Regnal List claims that the West Saxons took the kingdom in 500, which was 396 years before the accession of King Alfred in 871, but it should have been 371 years.

The total reign of all kings between 500 and 871 including the different dates for Cerdic, Cynric and Ceawlin would still be either thirty-seven or twenty-six years less than the required figure of 371 years. The Wessex king-lists are considered questionable up until the point Cynegils was converted to Christianity in 635 and subsequently died in 641 or 642.

It appears Cerdic's reign began 104 years before 641 or 642 when you subtract the most likely length of time kings before this date ruled: Cerdic (sixteen years); Cynric (twenty-seven years); Ceawlin (seven years); Ceol (six years); Ceolwulf (seventeen years); and Cynegils (thirty-one years). Adding the lengths of all these reigns together, you get 104 years.

Summing up, Professor Dumville found Cerdic's reign should be placed in 538, which would mean it was backdated twice by nineteen years from its original date of 500, a logical conclusion given the clear gaps of nineteen years between various entries. The new reign list for the Wessex kings, suggested by Professor Dumville, is as follows:

- Arrival 532
- Cerdic 538–54
- Cynric 554–81
- Ceawlin 581–88

Creoda

While not impossible, Cynric's twenty-seven year reign also seems unlikely. One obvious issue in Cerdic's story is the improbable long lifespan of his son Cynric, who seemingly arrived at the end of the fifth century as a young man and lived well into his 80s after fighting numerous battles. This traditional account was clearly simply not true. Chroniclers claim Cynric reportedly landed alongside Cerdic in 495 and reigned as King of Wessex following his father's death in 534 until 560, which seems completely implausible.

Cynric is recorded winning a battle against the Britons who were 'put to flight' at Searobyrig, or Old Sarum, near Salisbury in 552, before fighting the Britons at Beranburh, identified as Barbury Castle, alongside his recorded son Ceawlin four years later.

This account would fit with a logical westward expansion of Cerdic's kingdom, but it would mean accepting Cynric died conceivably in his late 70s or early 80s when most people did not live long into their 30s. This fact alone throws the chronicle into question given the length between the first and last documented battles of Cerdic, Cynric and Ceawlin was thirty-five, sixty-one and thirty-six years respectively. Moreover, such battle-hardened warriors were surely most at risk of an early demise given the brutal nature of warfare. These were not kings who waited safely from afar surrounded by guards and looked on as their field army tore into the enemy. Instead, they were leading cavalry charges picking off those unfortunate enough to have become separated from the mass of the shield wall. The average age of death for fifty-nine Roman emperors between 193 and 476 was 46 years, with an age range between 19 and 80 years, highlighting how even the most powerful were unlikely to reach the half century in this era of history.[31]

Anyone who has visited Old Sarum would know this must have been a spectacular defensive fortress surrounded by a huge rampart dating back to the Iron Age, which is still an impressive sight to behold. Scaling the massive ditches and banks against an opposing force would have been a monumental challenge for anyone, let alone someone in their late 70s as Cynric would have been according to the historical record.

Based on the chronicle, there was a gap of twenty-five years between Cerdic's final battle on the mainland at Cerdicesleaga in 527, placed around Odstock Copse near Salisbury,[32] and Cynric's first confrontation at Old Sarum in 552, which is less than 5 miles away from the woods.

A simple explanation for Cynric's very questionable period of rule lies with the mysterious Creoda, who is listed in some West Saxon genealogical lists as his father and the son of Cerdic but clearly seems to have been erased from the *Anglo-Saxon Chronicle* story of early Wessex kings. Creoda appears in all but one version of Alfred the Great's father Aethelwulf's pedigree in the Genealogical Regnal List and in the Anglian collection of genealogies. Logically, it is safe to conclude the result of Creoda seemingly being erased from history may have influenced the dubiously dated kingships of Ceawlin and Cynric.

As a result, Professor Dumville believes the *Anglo-Saxon Chronicle* compilers created the origin story of Cerdic and Cynric as the kingdom's founders to make up the gap left by Creoda's removal, which he believes they found 'embarrassing'. He concludes: 'A short-lived campaign began, to expel Creoda from the received Cerdicing pedigree. The precise motive remains obscure. That motive must, however, have been powerful.'

It was common throughout the chronicle for Wessex defeats to be glossed over. In this case, they appear to have glossed over Cerdic's son. The reason for Creoda's removal could lie with Wessex's great rival Mercia. One Anglian king's list dated to the eighth century records a Creoda as the first king of Mercia around 200 years earlier and he is said to have built a fortress at Tamworth, which became the capital of the kingdom.

There is also a Creoda who is the father of Pybba but named a son of Cynewald in the Abingdon versions of the *Anglo-Saxon Chronicle* in the genealogy for Penda. No information survives relating to Cynewald besides a link with the village of Killamarsh in Derbyshire listed as 'Chinewoldemaresc' in the Domesday Book and 'Kinewaldesmers' in a thirteenth-century charter roll, which is said to mean 'Cynewald's Marsh'.[33] The name itself could be a title along the lines of 'strong ruler', as *cyne* is the Old English for 'royal, ruler' and *wald* stems from the same Proto-Indo European word equalling 'strong, powerful, command'.

Chronicler Henry of Huntingdon, writing in the twelfth century, also describes Creoda as a Mercian king who died in 593 when Cerdic's grandson Ceawlin perished alongside a Crida.

Known as the last 'great Anglo-Saxon pagan warrior king' as all his successors embraced the Christian faith, Penda was recorded in Mercian genealogies as the son of Pybba, who was the documented son of Creoda.

In the first conflict of Mercia, Penda defeated the Wessex kings Cynegils and Cwichelm at Cirencester in 628 and captured the former Dobunni civitas now ruled by the Hwicce, which had been won by Ceawlin around fifty years earlier before an apparent civil war. The territory included the towns of Bath, Cirencester and Gloucester.

The entry six years before the Dobunni victory in 571 features a Cuthwulf (also named Cutha in one manuscript) who took four towns in the previous Catuvellauni civitas, namely Liggeanburh (Limbury, Bedfordshire), Aeglesburh (Aylesbury, Buckinghamshire), Bensingtun (Benson, Oxfordshire) and Egonesham (Eynsham, Oxfordshire). Described as Ceawlin's brother, Cuthwulf died in the same year after he captured the towns, which along with the Dobunni territory later became a central part of the Mercian realm.

This led me to start considering whether the Creoda of Mercia and Wessex along with the Crida, who died in 593, was in fact the same person. As sources regarding Mercia's foundations are even scarcer than Wessex, this seemed tenuous at best. Then I discovered some remarkable findings by Dr Graham Jones of the University of Oxford, which revealed the strong possibility as stated of the Mercian royal kings beginning with Creoda followed by a Pybba and his son Penda.[34]

The word Creoda itself is thought to be associated with a Welsh and Cornish word *cred* meaning 'faith', borrowed from the Latin word *credo*, while Penda includes the Brittonic element *pen* equalling 'chief, head, prince' and most famously features in the name of King Arthur's legendary father Uther Pendragon.

Pybba could derive from the Welsh root word *pybyr* meaning 'staunch, strong'. The new Mercian empire allied with Welsh counterparts against the

Northumbrians in its early wars and was the most powerful Anglo-Saxon realm up until Ecgberht's victory in 825. Its capital became Tamworth in the Midlands around 30 miles away from the River Trent, where Anglian tribes had settled throughout the sixth century.

While Creoda has seemingly been airbrushed from Wessex history, the landscape remembered the existence of a ruler of this name. The study found thirteen place names ultimately derived from Creoda, along with a further thirteen containing elements from Pybba, eleven associated with Penda and fourteen tied to his son Peada. Most sites would fall within the heart of the old Mercian kingdom in Gloucestershire, along with Wiltshire, Worcestershire, Hertfordshire, Buckinghamshire and Oxfordshire.

Jones found a 'correlation' with ancient royal estates and that a 'significant proportion' were found at military strategic places such as Criddi's Hoh, derived from 'Criddi' and associated with Creoda, meaning 'spur of land', in Elmley near Cropthorne in Worcestershire.

One reference to Pybba in the *Anglo-Saxon Chronicle* calls him 'Pyqba (son of) Cryding', while he is commonly referred to as Pybba in later translations. Such an individual is thought genuine and according to the *Historia Brittonum* had no less than 12 children, including the famed Penda, who in the seventh-century Welsh praise-poem *Marwnad Cynddylan* for a Powy king of the same name was heralded the 'son of Pyd'.

Places linked to Creoda include a Credenhill in Hertfordshire, named 'Cradenhille' in the 1086 Domesday Book, which features a large Iron Age hill fort and is just north of the large former Romano-British town of Magnis at Kenchester.[35] In the same county lies a Cradley, recorded as 'Credelaie' in the Domesday Book, which could translate as 'Creoda's clearing'.

Elsewhere, the study highlights a Curbridge in Oxon noted as 'Crydan bridgce', meaning 'Creoda's bridge' in a late-tenth century charter, and a Long Crendon in Buckinghamshire, which was recorded as 'Credendona' ('Creoda's Hill') in 1086 and is opposite the River Thame.[36] Notably, it shares a border with Ickford, i.e. 'the ford of Icca', thought to commemorate the name of Icel, the supposed semi-legendary Mercian dynasty founder but probably so named because it leads to the ancient Ickenfield trackway. The most telling discovery was of a 'Creodan hyll', translating as 'Creoda's hill', situated in Alton Priors in Wiltshire, which was mentioned in a charter dated to 825 and issued by the Wessex king Ecgberht, who was the grandfather of Alfred the Great.[37] In the charter, Ecgberht granted fifteen hides to Saint Peter and Paul Church in Winchester in the same year that he defeated Beornwulf of Mercia at the Battle of Ellandun at Wroughton near Swindon and ended the supremacy of the neighbouring kingdom.

Creoda's Hill itself is thought to be the current Golden Ball Hill near the Knap Hill neolithic camp, seemingly guarding a point of the historic Ridgeway trackway, and in the charter, the land boundary is moved to the hill from the nearby East Wansdyke, a huge ditch, which will be covered at length in a later chapter.

Jones also references a 'Criodan treow', translating as 'Crioda's tree' in another charter of 825 by Ecgberht and possibly associated with the location of the Battle of Ellandun, which occurred around 10 miles away from Creoda's Hill in Alton Priors.[38]

Most significantly the Golden Ball Hill (Creoda's Hill) is only a half a mile from a neolithic long barrow known as Adam's Grave, where Cerdic's grandson Ceawlin was defeated in 592 following an apparent civil war among Wessex rulers.

Ceol (Ceolric), son of Cynric's son Cuthwine, ascended the throne and is possibly referenced in the charter with a landmark called 'Ceolra cumbes', which contains the Old English word *cumb* – from the Brittonic *cym* for 'valley'.

The East Wansdyke at Tan Hill near Adam's Grave, where Gewisse kings fought in a civil war

Chroniclers speak of 'great slaughter' at Adam's Grave and how 'Ceawlin was driven out' before he died a year later alongside the Crida associated with Creoda.

In the research, Jones notes Cerdic's son Creoda 'may be identical' with the Crida who died along with Ceawlin and Cwichelm.

All these events, the slaughter at Adam's Grave near a Creoda's Hill and the death of Ceawlin and a Crida (Creoda), whose recorded grandson Penda defeated Wessex kings around thirty years later, must be related and suggest Creoda's removal from the chronicle was because of his role in Mercia's foundation. Penda's victory, which led to overlordship of the large former Dobunni civitas for nearly 200 years, seemingly caused such bitterness that Creoda was all but erased from history when it was first composed by Alfred the Great's monks in 893.

Later in his reign, Penda drove out the next Wessex ruler, Cenwalh, who remained exiled for three years. As one of the most famous Anglo-Saxon kings, Penda's reign from 626 to 655 can be accepted with more confidence as record taking improved considerably from the seventh century with the

The site of Adam's Grave where Ceawlin was 'driven out after great slaughter' (Glyn Coy)

spread of Christianity and literate monks employed by kings to document their conquests.

Assuming Penda was in his early 20s when he first fought in 628, it would not be unreasonable, therefore, to suggest his grandfather, Creoda, may have been born in the late 540s or the 550s. However, the exact order of descent among Wessex kings throughout the entire sixth century and early-seventh century is open to considerable debate. This is evidenced by how Cynegils who ruled from 614 is recorded as both the son and grandson of Cuthwine, the son of Ceol and the son of a Ceolwulf. This begs the question whether Creoda was the father of Cynric or his brother – as Alfred the Great's biographer, Asser, mentions both are the sons of Cerdic. Asser also describes Cynric as a son of Creoda in a separate genealogy.

Cynric, whose death is notably not stated in the chronicle, supposedly reigned for twenty-six winters but is only recorded fighting in two battles as a king without Cerdic.[39]

The civil warfare that erupted in Wessex in the late-sixth century revolved around warring factions related to the Cynric–Ceol and Creoda–Ceawlin line. This also coincided with a massive expansion of territory, which was almost certainly divided between the Gewisse princes and kings, resulting in the internal conflicts that culminated at Adam's Grave.

The safest conclusion would be that all the named Wessex kings, including Creoda, were ultimately descended from Cerdic, which was imperative for all subsequent rulers up until the age of Alfred the Great.

At some point between 560 and 592, when Ceawlin reigned according to the chronicle, which clearly contradicts the seven or seventeen years given in the regnal list, it appears Wessex had another ruler in the shape of the shadowy Creoda who must have led the capture of the former Catuvellauni and Dobunni civitas, which became central to Mercia in 571 and 577 respectively.

Territory around Adam's Grave close to East Wansdyke was contested in a bitter and protracted struggle for power between Wessex and Mercia over the next two centuries. The reasons are obvious. Tan Hill, where the dyke can still be viewed in all its glory, has huge strategic advantages as the third highest point between modern Bristol and London. The adjacent Milk Hill, which remarkably is exactly 26cm taller at its highest point, is second.[40]

Ecgberht's triumph in this vicinity had finally swung the balance in favour of Wessex and revenged the chastening loss of the prized former Dobunni civitas.

In a wider context, this supports Professor Dumville's conclusion that Cerdic began to reign later and the highly unlikely account of his landing in 495 when his recorded son Creoda died around 100 years later.

As for why Cerdic's timeline was pushed back by nearly forty years, Professor Dumville concludes 'a need may have been felt in the late ninth century to close the gap between the dates for the Kentish and South Saxon settlements and the dates in the 530s'.

Rival English-speaking kingdoms, such as Kent and Sussex, had been founded before Wessex and so could be seen to have more prestige. Kent's origins for example date to the mid-fifth century, more than eighty years before Cerdic supposedly landed in 532. By the late-ninth century, Kent and Sussex were now part of a greatly expanded Wessex, but the fact they had been in existence much longer may have been a sore point.

Crucially the study, with the addition of Cerdic's erased son Creoda, has produced more logical reigns. This also places Cerdic's kingship in a turbulent era in British history. One of famine and plague that devastated large portions of the island. Far from being an all-conquering invader, the biggest struggle for Cerdic and his peoples may have just been surviving this decade of extreme hardship.

Chapter 5

The Volcanic Winter and Justinian Plague

Darkness Descends Around the World

His fidelity is an encircling shield. You need not fear the terror by night, or the arrow that flies by day, the plague that stalks in the darkness, or the scourge that ravages at moon.

A sign dated to the sixth century on
a church in Petra, Jordan[1]

Comets were seen as the 'terrors of kings' in medieval times[2] and a prophecy of future disasters for superstitious people, who feared they were an act of God to punish mankind for their sins and to offer a last chance for redemption. Such unexplained events were seen as a manifestation of God's will for change and repeatedly linked to the deaths of rulers, plagues and warfare. Halley's Comet, which reoccurs every seventy-five to seventy-six years, filled the nobility with gloom of impending upheaval every time it was sighted.

Bede wrote how in 729 two comets appeared 'seeming to portent disaster' before the Muslim Saracens army 'ravaged Gaul with cruel bloodshed', while the chronicle associated the death of King Edgar in 975 with a comet in which the 'vengeance of the Ruler manifested widely through the people, a famine over the earth'.[3] Major comets can be seen on average once every five years. In his influential *On the Nature of Things*, Bede wrote: 'Comets are stars with flames like hair. They are born suddenly, portending a change of royal power or plague or wars or winds or heat.' The Bayeux Tapestry famously depicted Halley's Comet before the Norman Conquest, which William the Conqueror took as an omen of victory and the English greeted with anguish.

Roman senator Cassiodorus writing to his deputy Ambrosius in 537/538, then an aide to the Ostrogoth kingdom in Italy but believed to be writing from Constantinople, provided a startling first-hand account of a climate disaster. It reveals in detail the widespread consequences of a sudden change in the earth's atmosphere during the sixth century, an event which would become known as the 'year without summer'. At a loss to explain the disastrous cosmic events, Cassiodorus is clearly fearful of their implications. Here is the incredible account in full[4]:

> '*Since the world is not governed by chance, but by a Divine Ruler who does not change, His purposes at random, men are alarmed, and naturally alarmed, at the extraordinary signs in the heavens, and ask with anxious hearts what events these may portend. The Sun, first of stars, seems to have lost his wonted light, and appears of a bluish colour.*
>
> '*We marvel to see no shadows of our bodies at noon, to feel the mighty vigour of his heat wasted into feebleness, and the phenomena which accompany a transitory eclipse prolonged through a whole year. The Moon too, even when her orb is full, is empty of her natural splendour. Strange has been the course of the year thus far. We have had a winter without storms, a spring without mildness, and a summer without heat.*
>
> '*Whence can we look for harvest, since the months which should have been maturing the corn have been chilled by Boreas? How can the blade open if rain, the mother of all fertility, is denied to it? These two influences, prolonged frost and unseasonable drought, must be averse to all things that grow. The seasons seem to be all jumbled up together, and the fruits, which were wont to be formed by gentle showers, cannot be looked for from the parched earth. But as last year was one that boasted of an exceptionally abundant harvest, you are to collect all of its fruits that you can and store them up for the coming months of scarcity, for which it is well able to provide. And that you may not be too much distressed by the signs in the heavens of which I have spoken, return to the consideration of Nature, and apprehend the reason of that which makes the vulgar gape with wonder.*

> *'The middle air is thickened by the rigour of snow and rarefied by the beams of the Sun. This is the great Inane, roaming between the heavens and the earth. When it happens to be pure and lighted up by the rays of the sun it opens out its true aspect; but when alien elements are blended with it, it is stretched like a hide across the sky, and suffers neither the true colours of the heavenly bodies to appear nor their proper warmth to penetrate. This often happens in cloudy weather for a time; it is only its extraordinary prolongation which has produced these disastrous effects, causing the reaper to fear a new frost in harvest, making the apples to harden when they should grow ripe, souring the old age of the grape-cluster.*
>
> *'All this, however, though it would be wrong to construe it as an omen of Divine wrath, cannot but have an injurious effect on the fruits of the earth. Let it be your care to see that the scarcity of this one year does not bring ruin on us all.*
>
> *'Even thus was it ordained by the first occupant of our present dignity, that the preceding plenty should avail to mitigate the present penury.'*

Something truly terrifying with far reaching consequences happened in the sky around the year 536, which one historian Michael McCormick described as possibly 'the worst year to be alive'.[5] Medieval chroniclers around the world all recorded similar stories of destructive weather that severely reduced daylight and led to famine. They describe days with only a few hours of sunlight, of being unable to see your own shadow before midday and of snow falling during the summer in China.

Europe, the Middle East and parts of Asia were plunged into near day-long darkness for as long as eighteen months, while summer temperatures plummeted from 1.5 to 2.5°C, which caused crops to fail and millions to starve.[6] The Byzantine historian Procopius recorded:

> *'And it came about during this year that a most dread portent took place. For the sun gave forth its light without brightness, like the moon, during this whole year, and it seemed exceedingly like the sun in eclipse, for the beams it shed were not clear nor such as it is accustomed to shed.'*

Zacharias Rhetor, a Syrian bishop and historian, documented a darkening of the sun and moon along with a severely cold winter between March 536 and June the following year in Turkey.[7]

> '*The sun began to be darkened by day and the moon by night, while the ocean was tumultuous with spray from the 24th of March in this year till the 24th of June in the following year. And, as the winter was a severe one, so much so that from the large and unwonted quantity of snow the birds perished, there was distress among men from the evil things.*'

According to Marcellinus Comes' *Constantinopolitan*, there was a massive migration of 15,000 people from Iran to Syria because of 'excessive drought' in pastureland.[8]

Such reports of darkness and famine in 537 were not just recorded in the northern hemisphere but also in various provinces of China according to an eighteenth-century encyclopedia called *Gujin Tushu Jicheng*. In China and Japan, the author of the *Nan Shi* (*The History of the Southern Dynasties*), documented how late in 535 'yellow dust rained down like snow'.[9] The population of one kingdom north of the Yellow River is said to have declined by up to 80 per cent, while harvest failures were reported in Korea.

In *Constantinople*, the writer John Lydus said in 535–36, for nearly a whole year in Europe, moisture 'gathered into clouds dimming the light of the sun, so that it did not come into our sight or pierce this dense substance.'[10]

The chronicle of Michael the Great, Patriarch of the Syrians, states how the 'sun darkened and stayed covered with darkness a year and a half, that is eighteen months. Although rays were visible around it for two to three hours (a day) they were as if diseased with the fruits that did not reach full ripeness. All the wines had the same taste of reject grapes.'

In his 2018 book, environmental historian Dr Timothy Newfield of Georgetown University explained that two years of a failed harvest would have been devastating.

> '*Back-to-back years of extremely poor growing conditions were certain to take a toll. Sharp cooling of 1.5 to 4°C in consecutive years should be expected to have generated significant subsistence crises – true famines, in other words.*'

Extreme weather was also recorded in Britain in the tenth-century chronicle, the *Annales Cambriae*, which reported a 'mortality in Britain and Ireland' in 537 whilst the Irish annals of Ulster and Innisfallen documented a 'failure of bread' and claimed it lasted for three years and impacted 90 per cent of islanders.[11] Notably, in the same year, the *Annales Cambriae* recorded the Battle of Camlann in which 'Arthur and Medruat died' and which led to the Mordred character. Although this battle may have occurred slightly later in the early 540s or the 520s based on different theories it is notable how the death of Arthur was associated with the famine. Even the Arthurian legend seemingly refers to the devastation when they talk of a wasteland in the quest for the Holy Grail, where trees have fallen, crops have been destroyed and all inhabitants are dead.

One of my most enlightening realizations in researching Cerdic has been how he seems to have entered the picture just after this extreme weather event. As his reign is believed to have begun around 537/538 and lasted until 554, it became apparent Cerdic may have ruled during one of the toughest decades in the past 2,000 years, when unexplained climate disasters created the environment for a bubonic plague.

More extreme weather in 540 leading to a similar global blackout for most daylight hours prolonged the suffering and famine for millions of people.

A year later, the world was gripped by the first recorded plague pandemic just as the Eastern Roman Empire looked set to reclaim its power in the west. In 541, the Justinian Plague, named after the serving eastern Roman emperor, was first documented at the Byzantine trading port of Pelusium in Egypt and spread around the globe killing millions of people. An excellent chapter in the 2019 book, *The Fate of Rome* by Professor Kyle Harper (no relation), documented many references that describe the unfolding terror across the Eastern Roman Empire and what remained in the west.

John of Ephesus witnessed villages whose 'inhabitants perished altogether' as he is believed to have travelled from Alexandria in Egypt to Palestine then Mesopotamia (modern-day Iraq, Kuwait, Syria and Turkey), before onto Asia Minor, which encompasses largely Turkey.[12] Near Egypt's borders an entire city was killed with just 'seven men and only a little boy remaining', while as he made his way through Syria, he described in his Ecclesiastical History passing 'houses and waystations occupied only by the dead, corpses lying in the fields and along the roadside, and cattle wandering untended in the hills.'

Even at sea people were not safe as John of Ephesus recalled 'ships in the midst of the sea whose sailors were suddenly attacked by God's wrath, and these ships became tombs for their captains and they continued adrift on the waves carrying the corpses of their owners.'

In a startling account of its impact on Constantinople, Roman historian Procopius remarked 'there was a pestilence, by which the whole human race came near to being annihilated'.[13]

Victims developed a fever followed by a bubonic swelling within days, below the abdomen and sometimes in the armpit and on the ear, and then often a 'deep coma' and 'violent delirium (and) distorted imagination'. Procopius added 'in those cases where neither coma nor delirium came on, the bubonic swelling became mortified and the sufferer, no longer able to endure the pain, died.'[14] Many sufferers were said to have nightmares of a supernatural being in headless form touching them and passing on the disease. Most people died within days, but some managed to survive when the swelling grew unusually large and discharged pus, but those who did 'lived on either lisping or speaking incoherently and with difficulty'.

Describing how the disease seemed almost planned, Procopius remarked it was slow at first, before eventually reaching every person in every corner of the land.

> *'For it seemed to move as if by prearranged plan, it would linger for a set time in each place, just enough to make sure that no person could brush it off as a slight matter and from there it would disperse in different locations as far as the end of the inhabited world, almost as if it feared any hidden corner of the earth might escape it. It overlooked no island or cave or mountain peak where people happened to live.'*

The deadly disease was transmitted to humans far and wide largely from rats on grain ships heading to and from the Byzantine capital Constantinople (Istanbul). According to a paper by Professor Peter Sarris of the University of Cambridge, the plague 'Probably travelled with traders and armies, with food supplies and the flea-bearing rodents that accompanied them, in a series of steps drawn out over the course of several centuries, evolving as it passed through different climates and hosts.'[15]

Carriers of bubonic plague have typically been fleas borne by rodents such as the black rat found in east and south-eastern Africa from southern

Zambia to Zanzibar as well as the former Roman Mediterranean. Once rats infected with the disease had died, some were seen with 'swollen tumours', their fleas started to feed on humans, which sparked the bubonic plague. Black rats were widespread across the Roman Empire, with hundreds living on grain ships. The females could produce five litters a year and newborns could be reproductive after three to five months.[16] One theory suggests the extreme cold drove the rodents into homes and close contact with malnourished and weakened humans created the perfect breeding ground for a plague to spread.

The academic essay by Professor Sarris theorized that climate conditions had forced plague-bearing rodents in east and south-eastern Africa to 'forage ever further afield for food', transmitting the disease via fleas to local black rat populations and then via the fleas (and disease) to humans.[17] This could have spread through trade ships to Pelusium and then the Mediterranean via Constantinople, however, the paper cautions the earliest bubonic plague has also been linked to Central Asia.

It spread rapidly around the world and became the first known pandemic as it was carried across Asia, North Africa, Arabia and Europe. The worst period of transmission lasted for about eight years, but it is believed to have remained in the Mediterranean for up to thirty years and around the world for two centuries with plagues reported in Britain in 664 and 684. At its height, up to 16,000 people a day were said to be dying from the plague in Constantinople, which had a population of almost half a million people.[18]

Even Emperor Justinian was infected with a reported swelling on his groin but recovered. In measures to support the 'banking sector' of the imperial economy between 542 and 545, Justinian described how the 'impending presence of death' had 'spread to every region'.[19] In 544, the emperor attempted to impose price and wage controls, as labourers, artisans and agricultural workers took advantage of labour shortages from deaths to the plague to obtain higher wages or extract higher prices for goods or services.

Describing the scene in the capital of the Eastern Roman Empire, Procopius said: 'It seemed no easy thing to see any man in the streets of Byzantium, but all who had the good fortune to be in health were sitting in their houses, either attending the sick or mourning the dead.' The city ran out of space to bury the dead and some corpses were thrown into the sea as the initial plague lasted for four months but returned to Constantinople sixteen years later.[20] In the first outbreak, Procopius said:

> *'And when it came about that all the tombs which had existed previously were filled with the dead, then they dug up all the places about the city one after the other, laid the dead there, each one as he could, and departed; but later on those who were making these trenches, no longer able to keep up with the number of the dying, mounted the towers of the fortifications in Sycae [Galata], and tearing off the roofs threw the bodies there in complete disorder.'*

Agathias, a principal historian of Emperor Justinian, wrote how the Eastern Roman Empire's military force had been decimated, falling from 645,000 to 150,000 men following the plague.

By the year 547, Procopius claimed just 500 people were remaining in Rome.[21] Although disputed, this highlights the dramatic decline of the former 'capital of the world' where between one and two million lived in the first and second centuries.

After Justinian's death in 566, the Germanic Lombards captured large parts of Italy, while the Persians, in the shape of the Sassanid Empire, overran Syria and the Eastern Roman Empire was severely weakened. Just as the chroniclers feared, the climate disasters and plague led to a massive change in the balance of power and the ancient order, but it seems in the darkest hours, religion was a source of salvation and experienced a resurgence. As apocalyptic fears spread among religious leaders, there was a call for repentance and conversion, before the final judgement, even Justinian claimed it demonstrated 'God's love for mankind', by giving humanity one last chance. Great community rituals were held to ward off the plague, including by the Bishop of Clermont in France in 544, who led his congregation to a remote shrine during Lent.[22] Meanwhile, church building continued across the globe despite the ravages of the plague.

Some 800 years later, another devastating pandemic emerged, which was linked to the same strain of bacteria called *Yersinia pestis* that had caused the Justinian plague. The Black Death killed 50 million Europeans between 1347 and 1351 alone.

Part of a study of twenty-one archaeological sites in western Europe, including Britain, involved analyzing 171 teeth from 122 individuals from France, Germany and Spain to search for traces of the strain, confirmed the Justinian Plague and fourteenth-century Black Death were 'from the same lineage'.[23] It was also behind the third plague pandemic in nineteenth-century China.

Genetic data has pinpointed the Qinghai-Tibet Plateau in China as the original origin of *Yersinia pestis* and it has been in a maintenance phase for most of its existence.[24] The disease can infect any mammal, but its main 'reservoir' is said to be among rodents such as gerbils, which are more conducive to flea-bearing transmission. *Yersinia pestis* is said to block the digestive system of flies causing them to search for blood and spread the bacteria.

While people living during the Justinian Plague may have believed the darkness had biblical implications, it is only in the recent decade that scientists have also begun to understand what was behind the extreme weather. Since the early 1990s, tree-ring studies have suggested the summers around both 536 and 540 were exceptionally cold because there was a lack of growth. Trees in the British Isles and Germany have displayed extreme lows in 536 and 540–41, which could only be explained by a significant drop in temperatures.[25] In 2015, the clues emerged from ice cores in Greenland and Antarctica, which contained volcanic ash and debris. When a volcano erupts, it spews sulphur, bismuth and other substances into the atmosphere, creating a dust veil, which reflects the sun's light back to space and cools the planet.

Researchers led by Michael Sigl, now of the University of Bern, discovered evidence of a massive volcanic eruption in early 536, which was followed by another one in 540 leading to a prolonged spell of darkness and cold.[26] They worked this out by matching the ice record of the chemical volcanic traces with the tree-ring records of climate. According to the data, nearly all extreme summer cooling events in the northern hemisphere in the past 2,500 years can be traced to volcanoes.

Michael McCormick and glaciologist Paul Mayewski at the Climate Change Institute of the University of Maine (UM) reported the volcanic eruption had originated in Iceland and spewed ash into the atmosphere in 536 and then again in 540 and 547.[27] The scientists studied ice in the Swiss Alps and were able to go back 2,000 years by drilling down and extracting slivers of ice.

Researcher Laura Hartman found two microscopic particles of volcanic glass from the spring of 536, which they discovered by bombarding the shard with X-rays to establish its chemical footprint. These particles matched other particles in lakes and peak bogs in Europe and Greenland, which in turn were linked to samples of volcanic rock from Iceland. This chance discovery by the University of Maine team explained one of the most destructive weather events in modern times, one which sparked widespread famine around the world. McCormick, a historian and archaeologist, said: 'It was the beginning of one of the worst periods to be alive, if not the worst year.'

Dr Newfield explained how eight volcanic events in European sources between 750 and 950 can be linked to harvest failures.[28] In his paper, 'The Climate Downturn', he wrote how he believes the volcanic eruptions in 536 and 540 sparked 'widespread and ruinous harvest failures. A cluster of very large volcanic eruptions triggered exceptional cooling and possibly drought across several parts of the globe.' The world suffered 'a decade and a half of marked cold', Newman adds, with lows in the summer of 536, 540–41, and 545–46. It has been suggested the second volcanic eruption was even bigger and a tropical event recorded at both poles. For the second time in four years, massive clouds of sulphates were blasted into the sky blocking out the energy of the sun.

The volcanic eruption could possibly have originated in Mexico. Scientists from Utrecht University in the Netherlands discovered the El Chichón volcano in southern Mexico erupted in 540, which sparked the decline of the Mayan civilization. Ash layers in the Maya lowlands matched with ice core records, according to the research team.[29] The same volcano erupted in 1982 killing 2,000 people after it spewed vast quantities of sulphur dioxide and other particulates into the atmosphere, but the Utrecht researchers believed the eruption in 540 would have been much bigger. The location of the 540 volcano is still subject to debate, and some scientists have also identified Lake Ilopango, a volcano in El Salvador, Central America, as the one which erupted.

Dr Matthew Toohey, a climate modeller at the GEOMAR Helmholtz Centre for Ocean Research in Kiel Germany, who led research into the impact of the two volcanic eruptions, described them as the 'most powerful volcanic event affecting the northern hemisphere climate over at least the past 1500 years'.[30] He claimed the devastating impact lowered temperatures by 2 degrees Celsius (35.6 degrees Fahrenheit) during what is probably the coldest decade in the last two millennia.

The subsequent plague reached the shores of Britain, but the dearth of contemporary records make it difficult to assess. This was until an incredible discovery a few years ago.

Chapter 6

The Volcanic Winter and Justinian Plague

Plague Hits Britain, Raiders Cherished and Rewarded

In 2018, a Cambridge University study of DNA preserved in remains found in an early 'Anglo-Saxon' burial site known as Edix Hill in Cambridgeshire revealed many died – including an adult woman and a child aged around 10 or 11 buried together – carrying the disease.[31]

The site is near a Roman road that ran between London and Lincoln. Further analysis revealed the strain of *Yersinia pestis* in 40 per cent of the bodies examined. It was the earliest identified lineage of the bacterium involved in the sixth-century pandemic, which meant it hit Britain before other discovered sites such as in Bavaria. Dr Craig Cessford, from the University of Cambridge, said:[32]

> *'There are no documentary sources that definitely record that the Justinian Plague of the 540s reached Anglo-Saxon England, so its identification at Edix Hill represents a major discovery. It is unlikely that this site is unusual in being affected by the plague; more probably most, if not all, of Anglo-Saxon England was ravaged by it.'*

Plague is invisible on skeletons because it kills within days and leaves no trace explained Dr Cessford.[33] The discovery of Black Death sites was found through documents and mass graves. New techniques mean researchers can now examine DNA from the teeth of ancient skeletons, which can show traces of disease including the plague. As the first use of this type of DNA testing at Edix Hill revealed plague victims, Dr Cessford believes it must have been 'widespread' across England.

The disease also reached Wales. It claimed the life of the notorious Maelgwn, the post-Roman Brittonic ruler of Gwynedd, who as mentioned is recorded as dying from a 'great mortality' in 547.

A few years later a St Teilo escaped the country as the pestilence took hold, which suggests Britain was hit by at least two outbreaks, most likely more, in the early 540s and again around 549.

Several monasteries in western Britain, Ireland and south-western Scotland contained pottery imported from Egypt and southern Gaul (France), which is part of the reason of how the plague is believed to have spread to Britain.[34]

Gildas described how Britons were unable to visit the shrine of martyrs because of the 'unhappy partition' with the Saxons and did not venture into eastern territories controlled by English-speaking peoples, which implies they may have not passed on the infection.

Grave goods indicated the imports of English-speaking peoples were the ornaments and weapons of northern and north-eastern Gaul and of the Franks of the Lower Rhine, areas which did not suffer as badly from the plague according to Gallo-Roman historian Gregory of Tours. Writing from modern-day Marseille, Gregory revealed the arrival of a slave ship from Spain led to the instant death of eight people, and after a brief lull, the disease spread rapidly, adding, 'Like a wheat-field set alight, the whole town was ablaze with pestilence.'[35]

It is theorized Anglo-Saxon communities relied more heavily on an insular trade network and subsistence farming, producing enough crops for themselves, which meant they were less exposed to the disease as it spread rapidly through Europe.

Tintagel, a spectacular rocky settlement on the cliffs of north Cornwall and now a hugely popular English Heritage site, must have been impacted by the plague. During the post-Roman period, Tintagel was almost certainly a royal site with trading links reaching from the Celtic Sea to the eastern Mediterranean. It was most likely the seat of the rulers of Dumnonia, encompassing modern-day Devon, Cornwall and parts of Somerset, whose kings would have stayed there seasonally. The site's headland was connected to the mainland only by a narrow neck of land which made it almost impenetrable, while offering extensive and spectacular views across the channel.

The coastal fortress, linked to the King Arthur legend, had flourished after the Roman troops departed, with a remarkable complex of around

Tintagel was mysteriously abandoned between the sixth and seventh centuries, which could be linked to the Justinian Plague (Paul Harper/ English Heritage)

100 stone buildings, featuring slate floors, stone steps and walls three feet thick arranged in a grid system on the cliff.

A thriving settlement idyllically placed, which now seems remote but was then incredibly well networked. Charles Thomas, an archaeologist and the foremost scholar on Tintagel, said the quality of its imported goods was 'dramatically greater' than any other site in Britain and Ireland in the 150 years after Roman troops departed. He believed Tintagel was a site where ships docked to deposit their cargo from southern Europe and these ships could be packed with between 600 to 700 all-purpose ceramic vessels known as amphorae, which contained luxury items.[36]

Merchant captains would sail their ships around the Mediterranean collecting what they knew would sell in Britain, and they traded the luxury items in exchange for Cornish tin, which was shipped out of Britain in the form of ingots.[37]

Lavish goods found at Tintagel included glassware from Spain, wine amphorae from Byzantium, and oil jars and fine tableware from the north African coast. Elites who controlled Tintagel and revelled in 'Cornwall's first golden age' feasted on pork, fish and oysters. Archaeologists found evidence of the butchering and burning of sheep, goat and cattle, with other finds such as a cod cranial bone pointing to the first signs of deep-sea fishing.

The pandemic could have had a huge impact on this booming trading site in the south-west because it was spreading rapidly along trade routes from the Mediterranean. Within the next century, the site appears to have been largely abandoned. Tintagel is one of several post-Romano-British settlements in either reoccupied hill forts or in former Roman towns that were abandoned in the sixth century, such as Cadbury Congresbury Fort, Wroxeter, Silchester and Birdoswald. The plague may have been the catalyst for these abandonments because centres of civilian population would have been an obvious breeding ground for the disease. Professor Sarris in another paper explained urban environments 'provided opportune conditions for the contagion' and would be more 'structurally vulnerable to the shock of the plague and reoccurrences' because of the loss of a tax-paying population.[38]

Cadbury Congresbury Fort in North Somerset, which maintained similar trading links as Tintagel, was reoccupied and fortified in the fifth century with ready-made enclosures for the livestock of new settlers, who most likely included refugees from surrounding communities along with villa owners and their peasants. In the post-Roman period, a watchtower and around 200 structures of mostly Iron Age style round houses were built, along with a timber hall for feasts and celebrations, in which they ate beef from the large number of cattle they controlled, dined on Roman tableware

Tintagel was a thriving settlement in post-Roman Britain thanks to lucrative trade with the Mediterranean (Paul Harper/English Heritage)

The ruins at Tintagel, which was once thought to be the home of rulers from the kingdom of Dumnonia (Paul Harper/English Heritage)

and drank Greek wine.[39] There was evidence of a flourishing settlement for around 150 years run by a local lord. This lasted until some point in the sixth century, most likely through the trade of tin with foreign merchants, which was a rarity in Europe and a precious ingredient for producing bronze, popular for tools and weapons.

Inhabitants at the similarly named South Cadbury in South Somerset, which featured a spectacular 66ft-timber hall in the post-Roman period, also left without a trace in the sixth century.[40]

Much further north, the old Roman fort of Birdoswald, next to Hadrian's Wall, thrived following the end of Roman rule, where remnants of the Roman legion stationed there may have continued to guard the site and offer protection to local people in return for supplies.

Inhabitants remodelled the stone-built Roman granaries with hypocaust heating, a space under the ground in which hot air was pumped into and fit to store a year's supply of dry goods.[41] The north granary was turned into a timber domestic building, evidenced by fireplace hearths built above the stone floor, and the space continued to be used for storage below.

Birdoswald featured a massive wooden hall near its main gate but grinds to a halt in the sixth-century period, along with Wroxeter, which is another post-Roman survivor. Once a booming Roman town with a basilica (public building), which fell into ruin, a new settlement built using a Roman system of measurement and layout with several timber buildings, including one massive timber hall that has been identified as another possible Camelot, sprung up in the ruins of the empire during the fifth century.[42] The basilica may have been the home of a seasonal market where local farmers traded, but Wroxeter was most likely quietly abandoned in the mid-sixth century, although a small village grew in another corner of the town.

Signs suggest a post-Roman settlement in the former thriving town of Silchester, where an Ogham stone with an inscription hinted at the presence of Irish-speaking people, but abandonment occurs at Silchester at some point in the fifth or sixth centuries.[43]

Undeniably, there seems to be a pattern with these thriving self-sustaining communities that emerged from the ashes of Roman Britain and enjoyed extensive trade links and a degree of wealth fading away or being evacuated in the sixth century, which must be linked to the plague.

Various research has connected dramatic upheaval in Sweden during the sixth century with the volcanic winter and subsequent plague.[44] Academic Daniel Löwenborg argued that the archaeological evidence from southern Sweden, which included abandoned settlements and the termination of burial grounds, pointed to a crisis sparked by the volcanic winter and that elites used the opportunity to seize land and construct large burial mounds to reinforce their claims.[45] It was estimated the number of occupied sites fell by 75 per cent during the sixth century in the Uppland region of Sweden. Swedish archaeologist Professor Bo Gräslund, who has extensively studied the impact of the volcanic winter and plague on Scandinavia, said:[46]

> *'A significant depopulation caused by the climatic catastrophe in 536–545 contributed to a large number of farms and perhaps whole hamlets being abandoned, land that remaining protoaristocratic families took over with reference to relationships or by force. In this manner, the environmental disaster might also have contributed to the general economic concentration of power to a land-owning upper class that characterises the end of the Iron Age and the Early Middle Ages.'*

Professor Gräslund said the 'use of the sun symbol in Scandinavia came to an end' during the sixth century after 2,000 years of continued use, which could be attributed to the blackout.

It is possible to imagine several sudden deaths would have terrified most people into fleeing to a more isolated setting with their families. In some medieval accounts, there seems to be an understanding that the plague spread through the air, but the extent to which this was shared by the wider population was unclear. It is also suggested plaques with inscriptions of the words of Apollo during the second-century Antonine Plague, believed to have been smallpox, were designed to ward off the disease and stated the god prohibited kissing, which implies a basic understanding of transmission.[47]

While the post-Roman British settlements were being evacuated, Cerdic's kingdom was expanding as he put down a rebellion and recaptured the Isle of Wight in the last significant event before his death.

Cerdic's stronghold is less apparent. Traces of post-Roman occupation in Winchester, which was the heart of the Belgae civitas, are thin, but as discussed in Chapter 1, there are signs of occupation based on what is described as a 'remarkable cluster' of burials just outside its walls, indicating it remained in use as a tax-paying administration. Famine and plague would have led to a marked increase in raiding. Cattle raids on rival clans were common during the early medieval period in particularly hard winters, and some of Cerdic's conflict could have been a consequence of such raiding.[48] Medieval sources in Wales repeatedly refer to a *teulu*, which now means 'family' in Welsh but at the time meant 'retinue' and 'warband', loyal followers of a lord or chieftain drawn from his kingdom, who would raid neighbouring settlements and be rewarded with a slice of the plunder.[49]

One theory on the origin of King Arthur suggests he was a leader of such a warband in North Wales during the sixth century, and his evident success and reputation spawned the later legend. Nennius, who attributed the famous twelve battles to Arthur, was recorded as a 'disciple of Elvodugus', a bishop of Gwynedd who died in the early-ninth century.[50]

Cerdic led a similar warband, almost certainly including Germanic warriors such as Bieda and Stuf. Rather than the pitched affairs involving thousands of men in three entries in the *Anglo-Saxon Chronicle* – involving Cerdicesora, Cerdicesleaga and Portchester – Cerdic's forces confronted roaming warbands from neighbouring kingdoms or launched their own raids and expanded the realm after victories. The concentration of battles in the former Belgae civitas around its boundaries more than hint at such a scenario.

Intriguingly an apparent contemporary reference to such raids comes from Gildas, who refers to how the tyrant kings are 'engaged in plunder and rapine, but always preying on the innocent' and how 'robbers', the definition being taking possessions by force, are favoured by the tyrannical rulers: 'Those who sit at table with them are robbers, and they not only cherish but reward them; they give alms plentifully, but in contrast to this is a whole pile of crimes which they have committed.'

Raiding armies would have been led by kings or successful warriors with other famed local fighting men, and as they made a living from war, they would have been armed with shields, spears and only basic leather as protection. High-born warriors may have worn chain mail and wielded swords. On small farms, they would have faced peasants armed with spears and shields, while confrontation resulted in often fatal close combat.

Forces would have ranged in size from between 100 and 300 strong and despite the small scale of combatants, the conflicts were brutal. Hundreds of men fought at close quarters, crashing together in shield walls on both sides, until one broke and they were effectively doomed. Fleeing men would have been savagely cut down and pursued by cavalry.

Raiders would have travelled by horseback along the extensive network of Roman roads and ancient trackways to position themselves deep in enemy territory without being spotted before launching an attack.[51] Notably, the Old English word *rad* can mean 'go riding on a horse' and 'to go raiding'. Targets of raids could have been largely cattle, other food supplies and in some cases slaves, while kings and warriors who led successful raids would have increased their power, but the consequence was most likely a cycle of retaliatory attacks.

Local people would have readily looked to Cerdic and his forces for protection as the raiding increased and he took advantage of the uncertainty to cement his authority and proclaim himself king, having previously been the equivalent of a ninth-century 'ealdorman', as stated in the *Anglo-Saxon Chronicle.* His forces may have supplied grain through large stores accumulated from tribute to those in desperate need as the Old English word for Lord (*hlaford*) means 'bread giver' or 'loaf guardian'.

The communities of the reoccupied forts and former Roman towns survived the plague but in smaller and new settlements. Several most likely formed smaller regional and local estates, which from the seventh century began to fall under the overlordship of English-speaking rulers. The presence of some of these places is found with a Latin word *saete,* which in Old English is believed to mean a 'place or seat of residence'.

This is found in several smaller regional groups such as the *Sumorsaete* in Somerset, the *Magonsaete* in Herefordshire, the *Cilternsaete* in Oxfordshire and Cambridgeshire, and the *Grantasaete* who controlled the Cam valley.[52]

Further north, there was the *Pecsaetan* occupying the Peak District, along with the *Elmetsaete* based on the former Brittonic kingdom of West Yorkshire, including modern-day Leeds, while a small tribe called the *Arosaete* was thought to be close to modern-day Droitwich in the Midlands. In a similar region, Wrotexter evolved into the *Wrocensaete*, a large territory which according to the Tribal Hidage document had a value of 7,000 hides; the same as Essex and Sussex and the *Magonsaete* of the time.

Another example was the *Dornsaete*, based on the former Roman civitas of the Durotriges in modern-day Dorset, where South Cadbury emerged as a fortress in the post-Roman period. Both the *Dornsaete* and the *Sumorsaete* began to appear in names after Wessex took over the regions in the later-seventh century. From the mid-sixth century, new buildings emerged at a site that later became a great hall complex at Cowdery's Down, just 7 miles from Silchester. Many of these regions in central and southern England were fought over by Wessex and its great rival Mercia over the next 200 years.

The extreme weather and plague dramatically altered the political landscape. English historian John Maddicott believes 'the seeming origin of many Anglo-Saxon kingdoms in the years after c.550 – Bernicia, Deira, Essex and Kent, for instance – could indicate a new start after a demographic and political hiatus'.[53] The Anglo-Saxon age truly began at this point.

When the dust settled towards the end of the sixth century, major new kingdoms took centre stage in East Anglia, Deira, Bernicia, Kent and Essex led by English-speaking elites descended from migrants who had arrived in the past 150 years and grew eventually to encompass dozens of smaller tribal territories from which they demanded tribute.

The volcanic winter and plague had served to accelerate the rise of Anglo-Saxon kingdoms as Rome's power, trade and influence faded in western Europe. Deserted settlements in Sweden, empty villages in Syria and the drastically reduced population in Rome show how the effects were far reaching. Power shifted and a new landowning class seized the abandoned territories. Climate catastrophes led to dramatic political and social upheaval just as the chroniclers feared. As Cerdic's kingdom emerged in this vacuum, its fate rested on a confrontation that would shape the future of Britain.

Chapter 7

The Solent and the New Forest

Cerdic's Landing and Natanleod

Remembered kinsmen press through his mind; he singeth out gladly, scanneth eagerly men from the same hearth. They swim away, Sailors' ghosts bring not many known songs there. Care grows fresh in him who shall send forth too often over locked waves his weary spirit. Therefore I may not think, throughout this world, why cloud cometh not on my mind when I think over the life of earls, how at a stroke they have given up hall, mood-proud thanes. So this middle earth each of all days ageth and falleth.

The Wanderer, Exeter Book, late-tenth century[1]

The Lookout is a perfectly placed cafe in front of Lepe Country Park with views extending towards the Isle of Wight across the Solent. Elevated two and a half metres above the sand on pillars, to combat the high tide level, it boasts hut-style wooden decor and large open framed windows for diners who can admire the many passing sailing boats.

The coastline between Calshot and Lepe on the Solent has long been favoured as the region of Cerdic's landing at Cerdicesora.[2] The word *ora* in both Latin and Old English describes a 'bank, shore or the edge of land', and Ower near Calshot stems from *ora*. Stansore Point near Lepe also contains the same element and is just a half mile north along the beach from The Lookout.

An old Roman Road, which the Legio II Augusta used to conquer the Isle of Wight, is believed to have run from Lepe in a north-westerly direction towards Southampton Water.[3] There is evidence to suggest the existing Lepe Road heading towards Totton follows the course of the old Roman Road.

The Lookout cafe is next to an old Roman Road and close to where Cerdic and his warriors landed

Lepe Road is believed to follow an old Roman Road towards Southampton Water, which Cerdic's forces would have used

At points along Lepe Road, traces of the Roman Road can be seen in maps and on the landscape, including near Stone Farm.[4] While, according to Bede's narrative, there may have been a ferry running to the Isle of Wight in the seventh century from near Stansore Point, which originated in Roman times. One early-twentieth century academic, Osbert Crawford, who extensively researched Cerdic's battles, believed it would have been an 'excellent haven for ships' and linked mysterious earthworks near Stone Farm to a small ferry port.[5] A marshy nature reserve, fenced off with barbed wire, now divides the farm site from the shoreline of Stansore Point.

Disturbed ground with nettles around Stone Farm hints at former occupation along with a concentration of Roman finds, including a second- or third-century ring in moulded glass with an intaglio design, where an image is incised into the design and the sunken surface holds the ink.[6] Other discoveries include badly corroded and burned Roman coins,[7] featuring the second-century emperor Aelius Caesar[8] and a Roman bronze phallic amulet, which were often good luck charms, featuring a rude hand gesture and male genitalia.[9]

When Alfred the Great's chroniclers recorded Wessex's history, they began with Cerdic's fated landing at Cerdicesora. This was the moment

The sand and pebble beaches of Lepe are just a few miles across the Solent from the Isle of Wight

when the Gewisse ruler sailed over from the Isle of Wight with a menacing fleet of armed warriors. This warband was intent on conquering the rest of the former Belgae civitas for their leaders Cerdic and Cynric. And for the fame and the glory.

The origin of the English nation almost certainly begins near The Lookout cafe. With a history as a ferry port, a well-established trackway inland and one of the nearest mainland spots to the Isle of Wight, the beaches at Stansore Point and Lepe would have been chosen for Cerdic's landing. This stretch of coastline also played a key role in another seismic moment in British history as 6,000 men departed from Lepe for the D-Day invasion in 1944.

Despite the short distance and lowered risk of detection, this journey was not without hazards because Lepe is notorious for its strong currents. The public are advised against swimming, with large red signs near Stansore Point warning of the dangerous offshore currents. This trip would have been carefully timed to avoid such dangers.

After reaching land, Cerdic and his powerful warband would have followed the Roman Road all the way to Applemore Hill in Dibden, then towards Marchwood and Totton before stopping near Winsor, which is just

Cerdic's warriors most likely landed at Stansore Point, where thousands of troops also departed for Normandy in 1944

2 miles from Cadnam. This 15-mile hike would have taken five to six hours interrupted.

Situated at the junction of no less than three Roman roads, Cadnam seems like a 'classic situation for the later battle of Natanleaga', according to archaeologist Arthur Clarke.[10] However, it seems more plausible Cerdic and his forces marched inland after landing and fought the Britons at a place such as Cadnam, where the opponents were 'put to flight'. As the 'cad' element derives from the Old Welsh word *cat*, meaning battle, this current and historic site of crossroads between Southampton and towns in Dorset, seems a primed place for warfare.

It is notable that Lepe is close to a 'Cadland', retained in Cadland Estate a mile up from the coast, and in all probability, there had been skirmishes before the main battle near Cadnam within a day or two of the landing. The region, between Cadnam and Lepe, is likely to have been sparsely populated as it remains today, with the bus route ending a mile from Lepe beach out of season.

With Cerdic already ruling on the western side of Southampton Water, the Gewisse ruler surely would have wanted to avoid wanton destruction and pillaging to keep the civilians on side. Instead, his forces would have sought a decisive victory.

When confronted, Cerdic's warriors would have launched a volley of arrows, javelins and possibly throwing axes at their opponents. They most likely formed a *scield weall*, 'shield wall', a closely packed wedge formation learned from the Romans, and slowly advanced on the enemy.[11] The army boasted a royal bodyguard, a local militia drawn from the former Belgae civitas along with the Jutish foederati, who were given land in return for military assistance.

Generals such as Cerdic, Cynric and Stuf were equipped with swords, which were an expensive commodity, and clad in a mail shirt made up of hundreds of interlocking metal rings sewn onto a leather lining, which could provide protection against bladed weapons. Swords were around 30 inches long and their hilts and scabbards were often highly decorated.[12] The cavalry wore iron helmets fashioned with gilding or with silver ornaments, and they would have been armed with javelins and a small oval shield to block blows. Meanwhile, the militia and the Jutes would have been equipped with thrusting spears of about seven feet in length and made up the heavy infantry in the centre. Spears were made of ash wood with a leaf- or lozenge-shaped iron head. These men may have also brought up to three or four javelins and carried a small single-edged knife or dagger, known as a *seax*, which gives the Saxons their name.

Those in the shield wall would have stood shoulder to shoulder with shields protecting their body in multiple lines, with the men at the back

Cerdic's fearsome warband would have worn similar military attire to this depiction of Anglian, Mercian and Anglo-Saxon warriors from the early-seventh century (Illustration from *Arthur and the Anglo-Saxon Wars* (MAA 154) © Osprey Publishing)

jabbing their spears over the top at the enemy. The cavalry would have been kept at the back and occasionally rushed forward to launch javelins, before retreating to avoid retaliation. The key moment of the battle was when the commander deployed his cavalry reserve to pick off the fleeing opponents once their shield wall was broken. Casualties would have been extremely high, but loyal followers who survived would be rewarded with spoils and land captured in the campaign.

The story of Cerdic's conquest has become considerably muddled with the passage of time.

> **Original *Anglo-Saxon Chronicle* (*ASC*) dated 495**: 'In this year came two ealdormen to Britain, Cerdic and Cynric his son, with five ships, at the place which is called Cerdicesora; and on the same day fought against the Welsh.'
>
> ***ASC* 514**: 'In this year came the West Saxons to Britain, with three ships, at the place that is called Cerdicesora, and Stuf and Wihtgar fought against the Britons and put them to flight.'
>
> **Revised *ASC* early 530s**: 'In this year, ealdorman Cerdic, his son Cynric and Stuf landed in eight ships at the place which is called Cerdicesora [Stansore Point, Lepe] and fought against the Britons and put them to flight.'[13]

Annals documenting the aftermath of Roman Britain were written centuries later, often drawn from folk tradition with a mix of Latin, Brittonic and Old English names and titles. The academic Gordon Copley explained that such tales 'legendary or historical, would be modified and diversified by generations of oral transmission in scattered and isolated communities'.[14]

As outlined in Chapter 4, evidence suggests the account of Cerdic's reign was the same tradition told twice and backdated thirty-eight years from its original date. Landings at Cerdicesora in 594/595 and 514 and entries featuring Cerdicesford in 508 and 519 appear to be duplications, which would resolve many confusing aspects. Despite having a British name, Cerdic must have landed after he sailed the short distance from the Isle of Wight across the Solent with his militia and a Jutish warband. He commanded five ships along with Cynric, together with three led by

Stuf packed with around forty to fifty armed warriors each, which would tally with the two versions of the landing.

Another puzzling aspect is how Cerdic and Cynric are given an official title of 'ealdormen' despite being apparent invaders. Gildas speaks of how after Badon all kings, public magistrates, priests and clergymen 'lived orderly by their profession by their vocation', which suggests a return to the established Roman political system of civitas. According to Gildas, there were *rectores* who were equivalent to officials working for powerful kings and he shows familiarity with Roman terms for taxes, which supports a military force in the case of *annona*, *hospites* and *epimenia*.[15] Notably, Gildas appears to have legal training suggesting a form of Roman law existed in the administrations modelled on Rome's former civitas. This strongly implies Cerdic was labelled an 'ealdorman', equivalent to the chief magistrate of a shire in later Anglo-Saxon times, because that was his role before he took over the whole kingdom and ruled without paying heed to any authority.

Moreover, the reference to Stuf as a 'West Saxon', when according to Alfred the Great's biographer Asser he had Jutish and Gothic heritage, can also be easily explained. 'Saxons' became a catch-all term for all Germanic people in Britain in the same way as the 'Danes' and 'Northmen' (and in modern times 'Vikings') referred to all raiders from Scandinavia, even though they came from separate regions now made up of Norway, Sweden and Denmark. Tribes who settled in post-Roman Britain included Saxons, Jutes, Franks, Angles and Frisians, which is confirmed by Bede. Given the kingdom only became known as Wessex from the late-seventh century, the duplicated entry for 514 would have derived from a later translation when the 'West Saxons' moniker had come into force.

Many scholars suggest the first clash broke out on a low-lying headland between Calshot and Lepe at the mouth of Southampton Water and abutting the Solent, which had been a thriving centre of trade throughout Roman and Anglo-Saxon times. This is a place where merchants could safely dock along the navigable Test and Itchen rivers from Southampton Water to unload supplies.

The Roman settlement of Clausentum in the Bitterne Manor area of Southampton on the River Itchen and nearby Hamwic during the Anglo-Saxon period were booming trading ports with the continent. The *wic* element, an old English word meaning 'village', was also found in coastal and river trading settlements from the seventh century, most notably including Lundenwic (now Aldwych in London) and Ipswich.

Excavations have revealed dozens of post-Roman burials at Clausentum indicating continued occupation.[16] At least 138 burials, 96 of which were aligned east to west suggesting a Christian burial, have been found in a cemetery within the area enclosed by the inner ditch of the Roman settlement of Clausentum, which dates between the fifth and eighth centuries. One nineteenth-century antiquarian and astronomer, Sir Henry Englefield, described how the dead were buried in coffins with iron nails and speculated they had been soldiers killed in a battle.[17]

> *'It is remarkable that all the teeth in every one of the jaws were quite perfect, a circumstance which seems to indicate that the bodies were young men, probably soldiers, slain in some engagement; evidently, however, by the mode of sepulture (burial), at a period later than the Roman inhabitancy of the spot.'*

Investigations found Clausentum was built at a similar time to Portchester Fort, which is around 13 miles away, and it seems likely they were controlled by the authority headed by Cerdic and his ancestors after Roman troops departed. Clausentum was connected to Winchester via a Roman road.

Hamwic emerged in the seventh century on the opposite side of the River Itchen in the heart of the city, which includes the modern-day St Mary's Stadium of Southampton FC, where forty graves from the seventh century were discovered.[18]

The Durotriges realm may have extended as far as Southampton Water and included the New Forest based on hordes of coins minted by the tribe that were found in this region before the Belgae arrived in the mid-first century BC.[19] It seems post-Roman rulers in the former Durotriges civitas reclaimed this territory.

Faced with a rival warlord on the south-eastern side of Southampton Water, Cerdic landed with his warriors to seize a section of the former Belgae civitas not under his control and secure the coast around the Solent. Four man-made earthworks, ditches and banks, with some extending in parts for 1,600 feet, formed a complete ring in part of the land captured on the south-eastern side of Southampton Water, which extended to the Solent.[20] Afterwards, his followers may well have been stationed within the earthworks and reinforced existing dykes to defend from reprisals.

Further westwards around the coast, near the end of Beaulieu River, there is an earthwork that is thought to be known as Cerdic's Bridgehead on Hatchet Moor, Beaulieu Heath, which could also be linked to Cerdic's forces.[21]

The next decisive confrontation saw Cerdic pitted against Natanleod, who may have been licking his wounds from defeat and gathered a huge warband to gain revenge. The story of this conflict again became garbled when it was recorded more than once hundreds of years afterwards.

> ***ASC* 508**: 'In this year Cerdic and Cynric slew a British king, whose name was Natanleod, and five thousand men with him; after that the land was named Natan leaga as far as Cerdicesford.'
>
> ***ASC* 519:** 'In this year Cerdic and Cynric assumed the kingdom; and in the same year they fought against the Britons, where it is now named Cerdicesford.'
>
> **Revised *ASC* late 530s:** 'In this year Cerdic and Cynric assumed the kingdom after they slew a British king whose name was Natanleod and five thousand men with him at Cerdicesford [North Charford] and afterwards all the land was named Natan leaga [New Forest] up to Cerdicesford.'

Confusion arose from separate sources describing a battle at Cerdicesford and victory over Natanleod, and it is notable how no actual location is provided for the latter unlike every other entry related to Cerdic.

A separate West Saxon Genealogical List of King Alfred, which serves as a preface to Manuscript A of the *Anglo-Saxon Chronicle*, supports the theory of duplication. It states how Cerdic and Cynric 'conquered the West Saxons kingdom' six years after they landed, but in the *Anglo-Saxon Chronicle*, it would be thirteen or twenty-four years from 495 to 508 and to 519.

The tenth-century chronicler Aethelweard, a descendant of Alfred, also believed the West Saxons assumed the kingdom six years after landing. The entries that speak of extending territory or assuming the kingdom are both 508 and 519, which both happen to include Cerdicesford, and the later entry explicitly states this as the location. This suggests there was a gap of six years between the landing at Lepe and another decisive confrontation at Cerdicesford.

If Cerdic as suspected had begun to reign in 532–33 this would mean his rebellion and capture of the entire civitas happened before the Justinian

Plague outbreak after 541. The first mention related to Cerdicesford can be traced to around 120 years after his death.

Cenwalh was the first of the Gewisse-Wessex kings to be recorded issuing charters, which are legal documents normally involving the grant of land and have proved a rich resource of Anglo-Saxon history. In one charter, Cenwalh gave 100 hides to the Church of St Peter and Paul, the Old Minister in Winchester, which was space for 100 farming families and later made up Downton Hundred.[22] While the date is not stated, two other grants from Cenwalh were issued in 670/671, so it must be of a similar time frame before his death in 672.

Within Cenwalh's charter, there is the place name Fegerhilde Forde, which includes the Old English terms *feger* (fair) and *hilde* (battle). The charter was drawn up a little over a century after Cerdic's death when the triumph would have been fresh in the memory. Fegerhilde Forde's exact setting has remained a mystery, but there are clues from the original text and the extensive research by Crawford.

In 1910, the charter was also interpreted by Arthur Du Boulay Hill, a former vicar of Downton, which has proved crucial in pinpointing the exact spot.[23] Hill, who had a passion for Anglo-Saxon history, established the charter had begun near a nature reserve known as Great Yews around 6 miles east of Salisbury. It then covered a vast stretch of land and woodland as far as Bramshaw Woods, around 8 miles from Totton, near Southampton, and returned across a ridge to its original starting point.

The charter, which made up the area of Downton Hundred, was split into two sections and one of these parts included the hamlet of North Charford. This area has been traditionally associated with Cerdicesford because Charford was called Cerdeford in the Doomsday Book, when it featured a settlement of twenty-eight families. Before and after the reference to Fegerhilde Forde, the boundary description states: '*Anlang herepathes to Fobban Wylle. anlang herpathes to thas hagan ende to Fegerhilde Forde, on thone hagan, on Ceorles Hlawe, on Cradan Crundul.*' This roughly translates, based largely on Crawford's interpretation, as: 'Along the highway to Fobba's Spring; along the highway to the end of the enclosure at the Fair Battle Ford; along beside the enclosure to the Churl's Hill (or barrow) to Crada's Crundle (or, reading Crawan, to the Crow's Crundle).'

The key to identifying the charter's course lies with an ancient trackway known as the Cloven Way, which must be the 'highway' referenced.[24] Medieval armies used ridgeways and highways and battles occurred along such routes, which were known in Old English as *here paths*, with the 'here' thought to be a term for 'army'. Raiders most likely used such ancient trackways to position themselves deep in enemy territory before launching an attack, and the Cloven Way led from Totton all the way to Old Sarum in Wiltshire. As it happens, this ancient trackway passes through North Charford, where it crosses the Avon and takes its name from the Cloven Hill Plantation a few miles away. In the charter there's reference to a 'Brember Wudu', which related to the existing Bramshaw Woods, just beyond the plantation.

According to Wiltshire Historic Environment Records, the Cloven Way can be identified by undated trackways – at Landford Common, Risbury Plantation and Pimlico Bottom – captured in aerial photography and traced as one visible earthwork running in a northwest-southeast direction and parallel to the modern-day Forest Road (B3080).[25] Based on Hill's description, the route takes a sharp turn in the direction of the River Avon. A trackway, the 'highway' in question, is still in existence and crosses the Avon Valley Path and runs between small copse woods – Hookers and Lodge – towards North Charford, where the 'Fobba's Spring' must be located. This would tie in with the charter, which references *haga*, an Old English word for 'hedged enclosure' often associated with enclosed deer parks and woodland.

It is interesting to note the seventeenth-century map by John Speed refers to a 'Searchfield deer park' near the ford.[26] What appear to be several springs in the woodland can be found near the trackway based on Ordnance Survey (OS) maps. As described, the trackway ends at the river crossing, where a ford is highlighted on OS maps near a property known as Searchfield Farm. There has been a cluster of flints discovered in this very spot, and just across the river, which are often associated with arrows and spearheads.[27]

Charford sits next to the existing modern-day division with Wiltshire and this boundary could date all the way back to Cerdic's victory. It is striking how the charter appears to follow its exact course, with the distance between the trackway and modern boundary just 500 metres around North Charford Drove.

I visited the potential battle site on a planned day off, which unfortunately landed on possibly one of the worst days for exploring. Heavy rainfall had left the fields between Breamore Road and Moot Lane resembling a mini swamp, with the River Avon running through the land and several small tributaries.

You can follow an old track running from Breamore Road, which includes a series of tiny old wooden bridges over the streams towards Moot Lane, where a large bridge is sited just before St Mary's Church in Hale. Further up the lane, between the fields and woodland, the charter's boundary becomes evident.

Across from Searchfield Farm is where the ford – marked on OS maps – can be found connecting to the River Avon. It was hard to detect on my visit when, with permission from a resident, I'd scaled a rickety old fence and followed a path down to where the ford was located. There was certainly a stream running from the Avon and the point where two rivers diverged, but both were filled to the brim.

This was otherwise a very typical agricultural field with troughs and a barbed-wire fence on collapsing wooden posts, but there was clearly enough open field around the river where large armies of thousands of men could have gathered.

It was common for battles to be fought at fortifications and at fords near the edge of kingdoms with an aggressor seeking to enter and conquer territory.[28] Given Natanleod's forces were almost certainly from further west in modern Dorset and parts of Wiltshire, it would seem Cerdic was

The site of Cerdic's greatest victory at Fegerhilde Forde near the River Avon at North Charford

A muddy field between the River Avon (behind hedges) and Moot Lane was where Cerdic and Natanleod locked horns

defending his realm, having enforced his authority and conquered the New Forest since landing at Lepe.

What was telling was how a trackway that runs alongside the farm, which became apparent when strolling a few hundred metres up towards Woodfalls, matches the 'hedged enclosure' from the description and does lead to a ford as stated. There can be no other place for the Fegerhilde Forde. Even after 1,500 years, it is remarkable how the same route can be pinpointed in this largely rural landscape. The landmarks have remained remarkably similar, just as one study of the countryside noted that 'trackways often seem to act as a constant in the landscape especially with dispersed settlements'.[29]

It did make me consider whether this must have clearly been an arranged battle at a key point in the Cloven Way. Perhaps there had been negotiations that collapsed after one side failed to surrender, and the armies engaged in a standoff across the river, with both sides cursing their enemies.

After Fegerhilde Forde, the boundary heads towards Wick Down following the North Charford Drove, which must be the old Cloven Way. Such droves were used to drive sheep to new pastures and markets, and were often found on well-established highways. An old property called

Muddy public path running alongside Searchlight Farm must be the 'haga' from the charter before the ford where Cerdic and Natanleod clashed

Lions Lodge, with four small statues of the beasts on either entrance, is situated on this route at the start of the drove.

North Charford Drove boasts a steep incline where with the dramatic change in terrain to one of large rolling hills shows why this landscape became dotted with large, fortified hill forts. In a two-mile radius, there was a concentration of old Iron Age forts, such as Whitsbury, Clearbury Rings and Odstock Copse, along with a dozen burial mounds and cemeteries, including several spectacularly long barrows, some more than 100ft in length, often bearing the name 'giant' as they appeared big enough for one.

This had been a sacred and contested place for thousands of years, long before Cerdic arrived on the scene. Logically, it would seem this area divided Iron and Bronze Age tribes, who buried their dead on the edge of their kingdoms and built huge earthworks to act as barriers.

Whitsbury Fort, which was served by a well during Roman times, may have been aligned to a Romano-British authority further west during the wars of Cerdic.[30] Situated in a formidable position on the summit of Whitsbury Down, which rises to 400 feet above sea level, the fort featured three banks and ditches covering 18 acres. For any aspiring warlord, there would have been few better strongholds.

Horses feeding next to North Charford Drove, which was formerly part of the ancient Cloven Way

The start of North Charford Drove, where the charter's boundary headed after the ford

Just before Wick Down, around a mile up, is Gallows Hill next to a Grim's Ditch earthwork, which were defensive structures or marked boundaries, and a nearby tumuli, recorded as a bowl barrow originally measuring 60ft in diameter.[31] Hill believed Gallows Hill is actually 'a phonetic modification of *Ceorles low*, or hill (the C having a hard sound)'.

The trackway reduces to a narrow winding path alongside Breamore Wood, where the rush to grab my camera and photograph two deer led to an embarrassing slip in the mud. Thankfully, no one was nearby, apart from the deer, which were long gone when I rose to my feet.

Just beyond the woods, I ran into the summit of Wick Down where what appeared to be banks of the Grim's Ditch in front of another small woodland. This part of the ditch runs for around a mile between Whitsbury and Wick Down. There are 14 miles of a linked Grim's Ditch around the borders of Hampshire, Dorset and Wiltshire, but there is uncertainty over whether it is one monument or separate sections.

The final landmark in the charter, the 'Cradan Crundul', may also relate to another barrow, given the 'Crundul' element is associated with such mounds, or refer to a long barrow situated on the Wiltshire–Hampshire border near the Great Yews documented for a staggering 600 yards.[32]

Dramatic changes in the landscape to one of steep rolling hills are evident further along North Charford Drove

Alternatively, a group of six barrows were documented on the outskirts of the nature reserve in the late-nineteenth century but had been destroyed by the 1950s, as had a nearby cluster of five small barrows.[33]

Though Cerdic and Natanleod locked horns 'on the Avon', just as Aethelweard described, the chronicle claims the 'British king' boasted a massive force of 5,000 men, which implies the conflict was spread out over a large swathe of countryside having begun at the ford.

The potential burial site of Natanleod hints at such a scenario. Natanleod has long been suspected to be a product of folk etymology to explain *Natan leaga,* because in Old English it could possibly derive from *naet*, meaning 'wet', and *leaga* that translates as 'wood', which would be an accurate description of Netley Marsh.

An early form of Netley Marsh dating from the thirteenth century was 'Natele'.[34] Evidence linking Natanleod to Downton around 9 miles away,

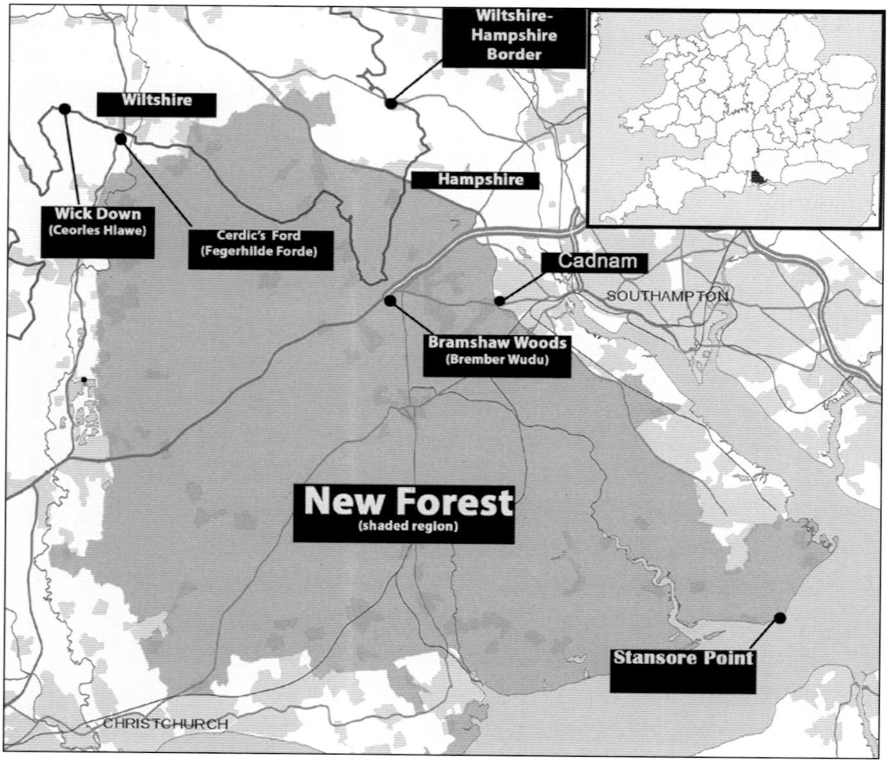

The location of Cerdic's Ford, the New Forest and modern Hampshire-Wiltshire borders (Howeard/Wikishire/CC BY-SA 4.0)

however, would make it seem unlikely the name applies to Netley Marsh, and there's an explanation in the name itself.

The *leod* is the Old English word for 'chief, leader, prince' and the *Natan* element shares obvious parallels with the British *Neithon-Nectan* and the Pictish *Naiton-Nechtan*.[35] Dun Nechtain was the setting for a famous Pictish victory over Northumberland forces in the late-seventh century, which ended any further Anglian encroachment. The name would equate to 'chief or prince Natan'.

The word 'leaga' is an alternative form of 'leah' which has been associated with woods, clearings and meadows. The New Forest landscape is covered in mires, bogs, ponds and rivers, making it one of the most intact networks of wetland habitat in western Europe. It boasts ninety of the remaining 120 valley mires, areas of waterlogged deep peat, in north-west Europe.[36]

It seems logical the name 'Natanleaga', meaning 'Natan's woodland', applied to this unique environment in the same way as the Wash on the East Coast, rather than one of the dozens of small woodlands that included Netley Marsh. With another Netley situated on the outskirts of Southampton, the name Netley is translated as 'nettle leah' and denotes features of the landscape.[37]

Nearly all of Cerdic's warfare fell within or just outside the New Forest. Honouring the region with the name Natanleaga clearly demonstrates the significance of the mysterious ruler.

Cerdic's rebellion caused alarm among Romano Britons of modern Dorset and parts of Wiltshire, who formed a massive coalition judging by the size of the force. Mustering a warband would have been an easy task for the Natanleod as they had a vested interest in stopping Cerdic's army breaking out over the chalk downlands of Cranborne Chase with its fertile plains for farming. This confrontation would shape the future of the south-west.

Chapter 8

The Solent and the New Forest

The Battle for the South-West

As I looked to uncover the truth behind Cerdic's battles, the picturesque village of Downton, where 'The Bull' pub greets visitors, was the next stop. Rows of thatched cottages, including a striking property in a mustard colour, line the main road and feature names such as 'Cymbeline' and the 'Yew Tree'. Downton has retained its rural nature with the cottages surrounded by open fields and a leisurely path running through the heart of the village along the River Avon. One cottage across from 'The Goat' pub in the middle of the village even bears the plaque: 'On this site, Sep 5 1782, nothing happened.'

Nothing of note did happen on 5 September 1782 other than an inconclusive naval battle between British and French naval forces during the American War of Independence, long after Britain's crushing defeat at Yorktown as well, but during the early Anglo-Saxon period something seismic did unfold in Downton, and it is crucial to solving the mystery of Wessex's foundation.

I headed to a site next to a former corn mill and across from an old tannery where a row of cottages can be found tucked away next to the fast-flowing River Avon. I had been aware of this street for some time but seeing the sign bearing the name was memorable. This street is known as 'Natanbury' after Cerdic's mysterious opponent who according to legend had been buried in this vicinity, while the road leading to this very spot is called 'Lode Hill'.

What is particularly significant is how Natanbury backs directly onto the stunning Downton Moot, an area rich in history as a former twelfth-century motte-and-bailey Norman castle. Henri of Blois, the Bishop of Winchester, brother to King Stephen and grandson of William the Conqueror, built the castle in 1138 during a civil war.

Natanbury street directly outside Downton Moot and next to the River Avon

Walking through the entrance, the outer ditches of the castle were visible along with the distinct sunken gardens, and the main path heads through a small wooden section over a bridge to the central feature of Downton Moot.[38] This is a remarkable amphitheatre built in the eighteenth century from the earthworks of the castle, which once staged Shakespeare plays and hugely popular fairs attracting thousands of people. As part of the landscaped gardens, the amphitheatre features six grass curving terraces on a steep bank above a former central stage.[39] A small lake in the shape of a three-leaf clover, traditionally a symbol of good luck, lies just behind. Backing onto the lake was an Italian loggia (lodge), a covered outdoor area in the same vein as a porch, of which the wall remains. At the top of the steep row of terraces. there was once a small Greek-style hexagonal Temple of Mercury, overlooking the stunning landscape. The view remained as impressive as ever during my visit in late January, when a father and son were fishing in the lake.

The name 'Downton Moot' hints at a history stretching back long before the Norman conquest. It was once a meeting place for Saxon chiefs and takes its name from the 'folkmoot', where Germanic tribes traditionally thrashed out issues.

Striking former amphitheatre overlooking a lake at Downton Moot near to where Natanleod was possibly buried

Downton Moot was a meeting place for Saxon councils and the site of a Norman motte-and-bailey castle

Traces of a ringed enclosure dated to the Anglo-Saxon period have been found during excavations of Downton Moot. It is tempting to consider Cerdic and his chieftains may have convened the 'folkmoot' at the very place where Natanleod had supposedly met his demise. Surely few venues would have offered as much prestige.

The Wiltshire Historic Environment Record did not show evidence of a former barrow, but a previous owner of Downton Moot estate until the early-twentieth century – Euas Squarey – stated in a private paper there had indeed once been a tumuli in the grounds but it had been destroyed.[40]

The actual name 'Natanbury' implies a fortress of Natanleod because 'bury', which is found across Britain, is derived from the Old English word *burh*, meaning 'castle, stronghold or fort'.

Another discovery provided further signs of Downton being a thriving settlement in the Roman age. Just east of Moot Lane in Downton, a resident was digging up his garden to create a washing line when he stumbled upon a Roman villa featuring a spectacular mosaic.[41] This plush villa, which was excavated in the 1950s, had included a dry corn furnace, bathhouse and seven rooms, as well as, most notably, a mosaic floor in the main room, featuring a central cup bearing dolphin-shaped handles; it remains on display in Salisbury Museum. Archaeological finds associated with the villa around the River Avon suggest the estate covered roughly eight acres and dated to the late-third and early-fourth centuries.

Another substantial Roman villa in Fordingbridge known as Rockbourne was discovered around 2 miles west from Downton.[42] Here, excavations uncovered a hypocaust (underfloor) heated bath house, mosaic floors and gardens, a hoard of 1,700 coins and oyster shells, which were a rich delicacy in Roman times.

Based on the extensive historical discoveries in Downton, including the Moot, Natanbury and Fegerhilde Forde, we can begin to see a chain of events unfolding.[43] Thousands of men engaged in a brutal confrontation on the fields around North Charford and the River Avon, and as the pendulum swung in Cerdic's favour, it appears Natanleod held a last stand a mile away at the current Downton Moot.

The use of horses in early Anglo-Saxon warfare is open to debate, but the discovery in 2018 of a 6ft powerfully built chieftain buried in Marlow in Buckinghamshire, who was dated to the later-sixth century, revealed he had been a mounted warrior.[44] His grave goods included a 35-inch double bladed sword still in a well-preserved scabbard made of wood and leather

Mosaic in the dining room at Rockbourne Roman villa from the late-third century, displaying an intricate swastika decoration (Mike Faherty /Rockbourne, Roman mosaic/CC BY-SA 2.0)

with decorative bronze fittings. A deadly mounted royal guard, possibly including Cerdic himself, armed with swords may have cornered the rival warlord and delivered the killer blow, reminiscent of how William the Conqueror is said to have personally joined a hit squad and hunted down Harold at Hastings.

The rest of Natanleod's retreating forces were pursued back towards Wick Down, where individual and small groups of barrows could have been hastily created to bury some of the dead. Fields would have been a gruesome sight in the days and weeks afterwards, filled with corpses that were stripped of their armour and weaponry. Bodies were left to the mercy of scavenging wolves, ravens and eagles, which became synonymous with battlefields.[45] Their presence beforehand was a sign of impending death and bloodshed as referenced in the epic Old English poem *Beowulf*: 'The raven, eager for the fated to die, shares many conversations with the eagle about how he succeeded at the feast when he plundered the corpses against the wolf.'

Natanleod's fall was a decisive moment for Cerdic, who was now firmly in control of the former Belgae civitas, including the Solent, with an elite retinue of warriors known as the Gewisse at his disposal. With this new hegemony over defeated rivals, Cerdic was proclaimed a king, having previously been a magistrate. This was the dawn of Wessex.

Warfare had been confined to a specific area of Hampshire, but it had huge ramifications because the spread of Anglo-Saxon culture and settlements across the south-west over the next 250 years is tied to Wessex's expansion.

Land from the Solent encompassing the New Forest up to Charford and to the Dorset border, which is marked by the Bokerley Dyke, was incorporated into the realm.

Cerdic appears to have offered land to Jutish followers near the contested borders after the victory based on a remarkable discovery, which gained national attention, at Breamore, less than 3 miles from Downton, in 1999. Metal detectorist Steve Bolger discovered a stunning copper alloy Byzantine bucket in the village at a site called Shallows Farm next to the river.

The body of the bucket was made from a single sheet of metal, hammered and then hand-decorated by stamping and incising with punches and a chisel.[46] Three naked warriors armed with spears, shields, swords and a discus are depicted fighting a leopard and a mythical beast or bear. An inscription in ancient Greek on top of the bucket reads: 'Use this in good health, lady, for many happy years.' Possibly part of a late Roman soldier wash kit, it was described as 'exceptionally rare' and a 'significant piece of Byzantine art', which is only found in graves of people who appeared to have considerable wealth.

Only two similar buckets have been found in England, at Chessell Down on the Isle of Wight and Bromsewell in Suffolk, a mile from Sutton Hoo. Only eighteen such decorated examples, produced in copper alloy, glass or silver, are known worldwide. They were crafted at a workshop in the Eastern Roman Empire in Antioch on the Syrian-Turkey border in the sixth century and hint at the wealth of the occupants. One theory suggests the Breamore bucket may have arrived via someone connected to the burial site who had visited the Byzantine court and brought it back as a gift.

Time Team launched a three-day investigation at Breamore two years later and uncovered burials with a high number of weapons alongside, before a four-year excavation, which was documented in a report by David Hinton from Southampton University and Sally Worrell from the Institute

Rare copper alloy bucket from Byzantium uncovered in a burial site at Breamore linked to Cerdic's reign (Hampshire Cultural Trust)

of Archaeology at University College London.[47] The excavation of the cemetery, situated close to the River Avon and within a prehistoric burial mound, examined eleven skeletons, which included signs of two double burials and one triple burial, with the suggestion up to thirty people may have been laid to rest. Nine spear heads, nine shields, seven possible knives and two confirmed adult male weapons burials and the fact everyone over

17 had been buried with such goods was 'exceptional for Anglo-Saxon England in relation to the small number of excavated burials'. The report concluded:

'Its location, its artefacts and its multiple burials all suggest that The Shallows cemetery was not an ordinary one. The number of weapons from it might favour the view that it was a warrior graveyard associated with the honoured dead slain in a particular battle. Weapon injuries were not noted on any of the bones, though the poor survival conditions of those could mean that battle damage would not be identifiable.'

The dead were from a 'warrior retainer community' or linked to a 'household royal guard', according to one report, which compared Breamore with a similar seventh-century site in Rendlesham.

Among other finds was a bowl made of pale-green glass with faint white trails below the rim, which significantly matched a bowl found at a burial site at Carisbrooke Castle on the Isle of Wight (to be discussed at length in Chapter 10) unearthed in the grave of a possible prince or king. A Visigothic coin found in the body's mouth was dated to the period 520–25 and deposited within twenty-five years of being produced, but it is thought the deposits at Breamore could be placed from 550, which would fit the later reign proposed for Cerdic between 538 and 554. Taken together, the discovery, along with the bucket and a square-headed miniature silver brooch, connected the site to the Isle of Wight, which was crucial in terms of Cerdic's kingdom.

After Natanleod's defeat, this would appear to be a band of Cerdic's Jutish followers, who must have settled here and had a strong military tradition evidenced by the high number of weapon burials. This 'frontier community', which included children and women, wanted to express themselves in an 'ostentatious way', by being buried with goods from overseas and for feasting.

The River Avon would have been navigable by single boats and there may have been trade and exchange, evidenced by the weights unearthed at Breamore, which were used for judging the value of goods.

Despite the victory over Natanleod, the war was far from over. After securing the Solent, New Forest and region up to Downton, the focus seems to shift to land further west and south, including Salisbury Plain, where Stonehenge could date as far back as 3000 BC.

Control of the chalk downlands of Cranborne Chase (now an Area of Outstanding Natural Beauty), a huge 380m^2 area of countryside straddling the modern Hampshire, Dorset and Wiltshire borders, was the prize for the Gewisse kings, who continued to wage war against remaining Romano-British resistance. The site of 'Cerdicesleaga' demonstrates the conflict.

> ***ASC* 527 (revised mid-to-late 540s)**: 'In this year Cerdic and Cynric fought against the Britons at the place which is called Cerdicesleaga [Odstcock Copse].'

In the Cenwalh charter, there's a reference to 'Fyrdinges Lea', in the vicinity of Odstock Copse, which is another former Iron Age hill fort.[48] This is very close to the start of the charter and suggests the boundaries directly relate to the land captured during Cerdic's reign. The word *fyrding* is an Old English word meaning an 'army on a war footing', while the *lea* is the Old English word for 'woods', which would imply that part of Cerdic's warband had been stationed at Odstock Copse, around 4 miles from Downton, following the confrontation. Alternatively, an enemy force may have gathered here in preparation for a raid on Cerdic's new settlements around Breamore and Charford. Either way, this must have been the setting for the memorable battle of Cerdicesleaga, which carried through the ages in folk tradition.

The word Odstock, named as 'Odestoche' in the Doomsday Book, is thought to mean 'Odo's stockade'.[49] Odstock Copse was naturally my next destination, and it was a slightly unnerving experience during a tour of Cerdic's battle sites because as I trudged up the very steep Whitsbury Road leading to the woods, a couple warned me that a 'man with a shotgun' had just entered the woodland and was presumably hunting deer.

Having reached the top of the lane, I nervously waited on the outskirts of the woods where traces of a southern rampart and the outer ditch of the old fort together with a section of parallel earthworks have been documented, but the northern earthworks had been erased by cultivation. I peered along a central trackway and spotted a pair of deer sprinting through the woods. With sunset approaching in less than an hour, I avoided venturing any further and decided to return another day as this began to feel like the start of a horror movie. What was clear from first visiting Odstock Copse is that this would seem a perfect place to station an army as described.

Massive Iron Age hill fort discovered in Odstock Copse – the setting for the battle of Cerdicesleaga

An ancient charter from King Cenwalh described an 'army on a war footing' near Odstock Copse

To the east, the site directly faces Clearbury Rings, which is just under 2 miles away and offers extensive views from the top of a valley towards Salisbury, where the cathedral's spire could be made out.

Walking up the steep hill along the narrow lane reminded me of the setting of Solsbury Hill, on the outskirts of Bath, which has been theorized as the site of Badon Hill for good reason. The flat top hill, a former Iron Age fort that sits more than 600ft above sea level, also lies at the top of a very steep and narrow lane and overlooks the famed former Roman city.

Much like the West Country setting, I could imagine the early stages of a battle, with forces charging up the slope from the direction of Salisbury towards the enemy positioned on the higher ground in front of the woods.

Incredible view from Solsbury Hill overlooking the city of Bath, where many believe the battle of Badon took place

The chronicle notably remains silent on the victor, which suggests the Gewisse held their territory and withstood the assault but not in the conclusive manner of previous battles.

The site of Ceardiceleaga has also been linked to Chearsley in Buckinghamshire because it was recorded as 'Cerdeslai', which could translate as 'Cerdic's Clearing' or 'Cerdic's Meadow', in the Domesday Book.

However, this could be explained by the village of Cuddington, just 2 miles away, which is believed to be named after Cuthwine, a seventh-century Wessex prince and son of Cerdic's recorded grandson Ceawlin. It is possible Cuthwine, whose name is also linked to Cuddesdon some 12 miles away, gave this name to the meadow in Chearsley, the site of an ancient spring, to honour his ancestor.[50]

The use of 'Cerdicesora', 'Cerdicesford' and 'Cerdicesleaga' has often cast doubt on the chronicle, but academic Frank Stenton argued doubts involving the use of Cerdic's name 'involves the improbable assumption that three separate placenames, each containing the same anomalous personal name, existed before these traditions were written down, in the small area to which they relate'.[51]

Evidence has helped pinpoint the real locations such as 'Cerdicesora' (Stansore Point), 'Cerdeford' 'Fergerhilde Ford' (Charford) and 'Fyrdinges Lea' (Odstock Copse), while more prominent ones such as Portsmouth Harbour and the Isle of Wight were referred to by their commonly known names.

The presence of culturally Anglo-Saxon settlements in large parts of modern Wiltshire and Dorset remained sparse until the seventh century. South of Salisbury Plain, the existence of such communities has not been recorded beyond Teffont in the Nadder Valley and Warminster on the River Wyle before this date in Wiltshire.[52] Cynric's capture of Old Sarum in 552 is seen as the starting point of an English advance into Wiltshire, but this has been confused by other archaeological finds.

It would, however, fit more logically with Cerdic reigning between 538 and 554 rather than 495 to 534 as the distance between Old Sarum and Odstock is less than 4 miles, which are the scenes of warfare in 527 and 552 respectively. Surely Cerdic's warband would not have waited twenty-five years between 527 and 552 as the chronicle claims to clash with what appears to be considerable opposition from a neighbouring warband situated a few miles away.

Old Sarum appears to have been held by a rival warband during Cerdic's reign

At Harnham Hill, 3 miles north of Salisbury, burials with Jutish grave goods from the early-sixth century have been discovered, while other similarly dated Germanic-style finds include a strap end with an animal ornament unearthed near burials in East Harnham, a saucer brooch with five spirals found at Britford and distributive spearheads (C1 and C2 types from the twenty-one types of Anglo-Saxon spearheads identified by the historian Michael Swanton) dug up at Odstock Down and Winton. Such discoveries point to the significant 'early presence of Germanic farming communities, living in small, probably kin-based, groups' around Salisbury Plain, according to one academic paper.[53]

There are indications of a Germanic foederati guarding the Portway Roman road – an ancient route between Silchester and Old Sarum – with a 'Frankish' axe dated to the mid-fifth century found at Winterbourne, along with a zoomorphic penannular brooch at Salterton Down in a rich male burial suggestive of a foederati. Decapitated burials, suggesting warfare or executions, were found at another possible cemetery at Winterslow around 6 miles north of Salisbury.

At one Anglo-Saxon site in Market Lavington, around 20 miles west of Salisbury, which was in continued use from the fifth to seventh century, a new settlement was situated on a ridge overlooking the clay lowlands where wheat, barley and rye were grown.[54] Half of the bones found at the site were from cattle and 37 per cent were sheep or goats. The notably larger size of the animals, with sheep kept for wool, was indicative of knowledge of Roman husbandry practice, and there was no sign of an overtly military theme among the Anglo-Saxon grave goods.

Romano-British warlords in modern-day Dorset and Wiltshire may have welcomed small Germanic farming groups, along with foederati in the early-fifth century, or some communities may have begun adopting an Anglo-Saxon inspired culture as in Hampshire.

Warlords around the present Hampshire borders with Dorset and Wiltshire became locked in a battle for control of territory based on ancient divisions, rather than focused solely on ethnic groups, and they may have launched devastating raids on each other, particularly during the extreme hardship of the volcanic winter and the aftermath of the plague.

Over time, however, the expansion of Wessex would eventually coincide with the widespread adoption of Anglo-Saxon material culture in the areas further west that it conquered. Cerdic's defeat of Natanleod proved pivotal in the birth of a new Anglo-Saxon nation. Had Cerdic's army been defeated, and the emerging kingdom stopped in its tracks then the Anglicization of the south-west may have been delayed for several hundred years or permanently. By the middle of the ninth century, when the Moot was convening at Downton, the kingdom of Wessex now included the whole of south-western England. In the same region, a legendary warrior had been remembered in a famous elegy dating all the way back to the sixth century. Many believe the ruler had fallen at the hands of Cerdic's forces.

Chapter 9

Elegy for Geraint

In Llongborth I saw spurs and men who did not flinch from the dread of the spears. Who drank their wine from the bright glass. In Llongborth I saw the weapons, of men, and blood fast dropping. After the war cry, a fearful return.

Elegy for Geraint, attributed to Llywarch Hen, sixth century

While based around London for the past decade, I have always relished the train journey back home to Devon on the seaside railway line. Heading south, the first sight of water after Exeter is the Exe Estuary, which begins a calming 11-minute stretch next to rivers, beaches and the internationally protected Dawlish Warren Nature Reserve with its meadows and marshes. Spectacular red cliffs, formed from windblown sand in a desert climate millions of years ago, appear from the point of the tiny Elephant Rock Cafe just past Dawlish Warren. A remarkable section of railway gets underway as the train hugs the waterfront, offering sweeping sea views, which are interrupted only briefly as the line heads through a series of tunnels built into the rock.

The English Channel is a captivating spectacle on a sunny day next to compact beaches packed with families, couples and their dogs, who can be seen bounding excitedly across the sand. Small trawlers, thatched cottages and the Georgian architecture of the idyllic fishing village of Shaldon can also be witnessed as the train continues alongside the River Teign, before the water disappears just before Newton Abbot. Further along, before Totnes, there are closely spaced dramatic hills resembling a field of giant barrows on your left near Wrigwell Hill, and the whole brief section of railway provides a snapshot of the coastal and landscape delights of Devon awaiting visitors.

Devon was once central to the post-Roman kingdom of Dumnonia based on an Iron Age tribe of the same name, whose region also included modern-day Cornwall, west Somerset and possibly parts of Dorset. The name 'Dumnonia' is believed to mean 'deep valley dwellers' in Welsh.[1]

I've been fascinated with how the fall of a legendary warrior supposedly from the south-west has been closely connected to Cerdic's reign. This stems from a poem, which could be more than 1,500 years old, commemorating a hero known as Geraint, who is said to have originated from Dumnonia. The tragic tale is known through the words of a bard, who were a fixture of the medieval world.

Bards sang of heroic victories and warriors at the courts of kings as halls full of jovial civilians drinking mead and feasting would fall silent when they recalled tales of heroism and bravery. Powerful warlords who caused them offence could end up the subject of a cruel satire and they were best advised to bask in the glory instead. One bard, Taliesin, who gained notoriety through singing for three kings in the sixth century, including Urien of Rheged, became known for mocking his enemy, Maelgwn from Gwynedd, who Gildas singled out as the most powerful British king of his age, but it seems not everyone was in awe.

In the late Iron Age, the bards were considered by Julius Caesar and the Greek geographer Strabo to be one of three intellectual classes of the continental Celts, alongside poets and musicians. Originally, the word 'bard' is derived from the Indo-European root word *bardos*, which means 'singer of praise', but unlike the druids, they survived Roman occupation and the rise of Christianity.[2]

Works they composed have often provided the only known contemporary records of battles in the post-Roman period, including *Y Gododdin* by the northern British poet Aneirin, concerning the disastrous raid by warriors on Anglian forces at Catraeth in the late-sixth century. If you visit Edinburgh Castle, then you will see a reference to *Y Gododdin* at the top because it is believed this is where the men from various parts of northern Britain stayed in the months before the raid. Aneirin was possibly one of just three or four from a 300-strong warband to survive, and his famous work includes a reference to Arthur because when praising a warrior Gwawrddur for slaying enemies on the ramparts he remarks: 'He fed black ravens on the rampart of a fortress. Though he was no Arthur.'

Another famous elegy written before *Y Gododdin* is known as the *Elegy for Geraint*. It also mentions Arthur and celebrates a warrior from the late-fifth or early-sixth century. It has been attributed to the sixth-century bard Llywarch Hen from the kingdom of Rheged. Vivid details, such as the 'silver-tinged mane' of grey horses and how men 'drunk their wine from the bright glass', suggest the possible author Llywarch Hen witnessed the carnage of the battle and fought alongside Geraint or perhaps learned second-hand from descendants of survivors.

According to the dramatic elegy, Geraint charged bravely on the battlefield and 'committed slaughter', as his men were left 'blood stained', and before being overpowered, they 'did not flinch from the dread of spears', which speaks of cavalry charging at the shield wall. The 'gates of Heaven' would be open for the fallen Geraint, the 'enemy of tyranny', who was clearly a leader of considerable standing in post-Roman Britain. The elegy reads:

'Before Geraint, the enemy's scourge,
I saw white horses, tensed, red,
After the war cry, bitter the grave
Before Geraint, the unflinching foe,
I saw horses jaded and gory from battle,
After the war cry, a great driving force
Before Geraint, the enemy of tyranny,
I saw horses white with foam,
After the war cry, a terrible torrent.
In Llongborth I saw the rage of slaughter,
And biers beyond all number,
And red-stained men from the assault of Geraint.
In Llongborth, I saw the clash of swords,
Men in terror, bloody heads,
Before Geraint the Great, his father's son.
In Llongborth I saw spurs,
And men who did not flinch from the dread of the spears,
Who drank their wine from the bright glass.
In Llongborth I saw the weapons,
Of men, and blood fast dropping,
After the war cry, a fearful return.
In Llongborth I saw Arthur's
Heroes who cut with steel.
The Emperor, ruler of our labour.
In Llongborth Geraint was slain,
A brave man from the region of Dyvnaint,
And before they were overpowered, they committed slaughter.
Under the thigh of Geraint swift chargers,

Long their legs, wheat their fodder,
Ruddy ones, swooping like spotted eagles.
Under the thigh of Geraint swift chargers,
Long their legs, grain was given them,
Ruddy ones, swooping like black eagles.
Under the thigh of Geraint swift chargers,
Long their legs, restless over their grain,
Ruddy ones, swooping like red eagles.
Under the thigh of Geraint swift chargers,
Long their legs, grain-scattering,
Ruddy ones, swooping like white eagles.
Under the thigh of Geraint swift chargers,
Long their legs, with the pace of the stag,
With a nose like that of the consuming fire on a wild mountain.
Under the thigh of Geraint swift chargers,
Long their legs, satiated with grain,
Grey ones, with their manes tipped with silver.
Under the thigh of Geraint swift chargers,
Long their legs, well deserving of grain,
Ruddy ones, swooping like grey eagles.
Under the thigh of Geraint swift chargers,
Long their legs, having corn for food,
With the assault of brown eagles.
When Geraint was born, open were the gates of heaven,
Christ granted what was asked,
Beautiful the appearance of Glorious Prydain.'

What makes this memorable elegy so intriguing is the association with Cerdic through one of the entries in the chronicle referring to Portchester Fort. As this warrior possibly originated from the West Country kingdom, the location was puzzling and the reason for why Geraint was engaged in a conflict so far away seemed questionable, as romantic as it was to link these iconic battles.

Portchester Castle is one of the most visually striking of the more than 400 historic sites maintained by English Heritage. It developed within the huge Roman fort, which dates to the late-third century, at the northern edge of Portsmouth Harbour.[3] This is another incredible feat of Roman engineering which has stood the test of time. It once featured twenty

Portchester Castle was built within a massive Roman fort, which dates to the late third century (Paul Harper/English Heritage)

(sixteen remain) projecting D-shaped towers, which were a common feature of Roman military architecture, and presumably used as watching points and defensive positions during raids. Its 20ft high walls still stand to their original height today and much like the still flawless stone structure of Hadrian's Wall evoke admiration for Roman ingenuity. This fortress, which has an inside area of about nine acres, was most likely enclosed on all sides

Thick Roman walls at Portchester have stood the test of time and sixteen of its twenty original watchtowers remain (Paul Harper/English Heritage)

by a double ditch. As you walk around the boundaries of this remarkable fort, it remains as intimidating as hundreds of years ago, with the thickness of the huge Roman walls and protruding towers awe-inspiring.

Portchester may have been part of the Saxon Shore Forts, which were a series of forts along the eastern seaboard of Britain listed in the fifth century. *The Notitia Dignitatum* documented the administrative organization of the western and eastern Roman empires, and Portchester is thought to have been logged as 'Portus Adurni' alongside eight other forts. The term Saxon Shore Forts is believed to signify either the forts were built to defend against pirates of Saxon origin or guarded by Saxon foederati.

Given the accounts of post-Roman Britain describing the Saxon pirates as arriving in small groups of three to five ships, questions remain why such raiders would have posed any threat to well-armed defenders behind towering walls or taking aim from the multiple towers.

Instead, these forts may have served primarily as a centre of trade, a theory advocated by the academic John Cotterill, who believed fortresses such as Portchester had an economic function for military and commercial shipping.[4]

Troops may have stayed there on transit to places such as Gaul. Cotterill argued they were intended as bases for where goods could be stored and then shipped inland to garrisons.[5] Such a theory is supported by how the forts were all located near navigable waterways and in the case of Caistor and Reculver were constructed long before references to piracy in the England Channel, when according to historian Andrew Pearson, it would have at best been an ‘intermittent and nagging problem’. Winchester, which became a military centre in the late-fourth century, would have been served by Portchester’s fort.

Portchester may have held agricultural and mineral commodities from the region, which were in turn dispatched to Rome’s troops over in Gaul, such as in AD 359 when Julianus demanded the resumption of grain shipping to supply his army on the Rhine frontier, and it is thought some 600 ships were required for the monumental task.

When Roman currency collapsed, the fort may have served as a collection point for taxed goods from the local population, which would be sent to troops in places such as Gaul or the Rhine.

Just outside Portchester Castle, the locality of ‘Wicor’, with a local school bearing the name, hints at an ancient marketplace.[6] As discussed in the previous chapter, the ‘or’ and ‘wic’ elements could mean it translates as ‘trading place on the shore’.

Post-Roman trade around the Solent during the sixth century is unclear, and the association of ‘wic’ with trading or marketplaces is not entirely certain according to place name expert Dr Jillian Hawkins, who stressed it had a ‘variety of significances’ as the English language developed.[7] Moreover, Lundenwic (London) and Ipswich are assigned to the seventh century.

With several of the chronicle entries placed around the Solent, it is clear Cerdic fought against powerful Romano-British forces from the south-west for control of the region.

Documentary sources, however, remain sparse and the first time the fort is officially recorded was in AD 904 when King Edward, Alfred the Great’s eldest son, received ‘Porceastra’ from the Bishop of Winchester.

The *Anglo-Saxon Chronicle* entry related to the elegy was undoubtedly a crucial factor in the foundation of Wessex. It reads:

> ***501***: ‘In this year came Port to Britain, and his two sons, Bieda and Mægla, with two ships, at the place which is called Portesmutha, and there slew a very noble young British man.’

This confrontation was so memorable historians believe it was documented by both Welsh and English chroniclers in the *Elegy for Geraint*, which can also be found in the *Black Book of Carmarthen*, the fifteenth-century *Red Book of Hergest* and in part in the fourteenth-century *White Book of Rhydderch*. They believe the 'Llongborth' of the poem, which is believed to mean 'ship's harbour', was a fitting description for the huge Roman port at Portchester on the south-east coast.

The poem, based on the reference to Dyfnaint, which was the Welsh name for Devon, has been associated with two documented kings of Dumnonia who were named Geraint, according to genealogies from the late fifth to sixth centuries and the late seventh to eighth centuries.

So, who are the Geraints? What we know of the late-seventh century one comes from a row over the religious date for Easter. A letter from Aldhelm, Bishop of Sherborne and possible Wessex royal, was sent to a 'King Gerent' in the late-seventh century to request the Britons of Dumnonia follow the Roman Catholic date for Easter.

In the letter, which implies peace and cooperation between Wessex and Dumnonia, Gerent is referred to as the 'most glorious lord of the westerly kingdom' but also describes him ruling over a province, suggesting he was a sub-king of Wessex.[8] Gerent agreed with the request from Aldhelm, which one scholar, Duncan Probert, dates to around 695–97 based on Bede's references to Aldhelm.

The chronicle then mentions a battle in 710 between Wessex's King Ine and Northelm of Sussex against King Gerent, and the twelfth-century monk and chronicler John of Worcester believes Gerent died in the battle. No more is heard of him in written records.

One theory states that 'Llongborth' could be Langport in Somerset, a region then fiercely contested between Dumnonian and Wessex kings.

According to the Annales Cambriae, there were further battles between Wessex and Dumnonia forces in 722, while Aethelburg, the wife of King Ine, destroyed a fort at Taunton in the same year.

The identification with the later Geraint is less favoured due to the reference to 'Arthur', which implies this detail was added hundreds of years later or Geraint was fighting for the famous ruler.

Author John Morris is forthright[9] on the *Elegy for Geraint*, which he writes has a 'sense of personal loss' comparable to near contemporary bardic poems, such as *Y Gododdin*, and must have been the same event as the entry in the *Anglo-Saxon Chronicle*: 'It would be absurd to suppose that the poet learnt English, read, interpreted, and elaborated the pedestrian language of the chronicler or that the chronicler learnt Welsh and condensed a poem. The common source of the two accounts is an event, differently remembered.'

I turned to the excavations at Porchester Castle by Sir Barry Cunliffe, an emeritus professor at the University of Oxford, to find out what archaeology had shown.[10] Excavations discovered traces of eighteen buildings dated between the fifth and eighth centuries, including six *grubenhäuser* style sunken-featured buildings (SFBs).

The study found one of the sub-rectangular pits, which measured 5ft by 7ft and 1ft 3in deep, included mixed domestic rubbish including charcoal, oyster shells, flints and redeposited brick earth. One of the SFBs, which was approximately 16m (52ft) long, boasted a 6ft-wide entrance leading down to the Roman road cobbling outside the fort. Shards of early Anglo-Saxon period pottery, such as bowls, jars and dishes all finished in a sandy ware, indicate these were domestic dwellings.

Professor Cunliffe believed the occupation of Portchester was probably continuous based on his excavations, which revealed a 'gradual Germanization of the shore fort community'.[11] He believed that by the mid-fifth century, the 'mixed population was now using a Saxon-inspired culture rather than a Romano-British one'.

A large urn was unearthed that was out of place as they would be more common in a cremation site, but unfortunately a large burial site associated with Portchester, which would shed more light on its inhabitants, has not yet been discovered.

The base of an early Anglo-Saxon bowl was characteristic of a type that can be traced from the North German coastlands to the lower Elbe to the Weser and to the Ems into Frissia and then eventually England.

The first excavation included the examination of twenty-two graves dated between the fifth and eleventh centuries. Some of the graves included brooches that were most likely modelled on a Vermand brooch, which was popular for more than 100 years in the early Anglo-Saxon period. It normally featured a Star of David formed from interlocking triangles and was associated with items such as a large, decorated pin, a sub rectangular buckle and an undecorated pottery cup.

A five-pointed brooch from Long Wittenham, the site of the seventh-century Upper Thames elite settlement, was found in one grave, alongside a saucer brooch with a compressed form of a heart-shaped motif in each quadrant. Another grave included a similar brooch to the Long Wittenham

Portchester was an important part of Cerdic's kingdom and the scene of a famous victory (Paul Harper/English Heritage)

one and, with the presence of a pair of bronze tweezers and beads, suggests a date of the early-sixth century.

Professor Cunliffe concluded the collection of ceramic debris indicates the site was occupied in the sixth century around the time of the battle at Portchester:

> *'It thus only possible to say they provide evidence for some degree of occupation during the 6th century, for this is the sort of ceramic debris that one would expect from hut fills of that period. The whole collection who thus indicate there was some degree of Anglo Saxon occupation within this part of the Roman enciente at Portchester from quite early in the 5th century, when the place may have still been controlled by some sub-Roman regime until the middle or late part of the 6th century.'*

This 'sub-Roman regime' must have been based on the former Belgae civitas and headed by Cerdic, and the occupants, using an Anglo-Saxon inspired culture, were his forces.

The chronicle depicts a simple war between Britons and invading Saxons, but the name of Port's sons, Bieda and Maegla, are thought by most scholars to be English and British names respectively. It seems strange that these names would be invented by the chronicle writers because, as with Cerdic, why choose a British name if supposedly describing an English hero who arrived and conquered lands from the natives? This makes me believe the entry in the chronicle relates to a real event.

Bieda as one of the leaders is particularly significant because it could feasibly relate to Cuthwulf's victory over Britons at Biedcanford, some thirty to forty years later, and the capture of four towns: Limbury, Aylesbury, Bensington and Eynsham. This area is believed to be the Chilternsetna, which comprised 4,000 hides in the Tribal Hidage document, compared to Essex's 7,000 hides for example.

Originally known as Bedanford, the name of Bedford was based on Aethelward's use of this form in his tenth-century Latin translation of the *Anglo-Saxon Chronicle*. Bedford could conceivably translate as 'Bieda's river crossing'.[12] Meanwhile, the name Bieda is also found in a small village called Biddenham adjacent to Bedford.[13]

Perhaps the name implies Bieda was a significant ruler among the early Gewisse leaders and the town was named to honour him. Interestingly, just across the harbour from Portchester Fort lies Bedenham in Gosport, which was possibly translated as 'hamlet of Bieda's people'. It was once part of the Manor of Alverstoke and owned by the Old Minister church in Winchester, which was closely linked to Wessex's rulers.

John Morris believes the local British and English-speaking warriors were allies who beat off a 'British army' but dates the battle to 480, nearly sixty years before Cerdic began his reign.

Neither does a late-fifth century date correspond with the contemporary source available for a Geraint of Dumnonia, where records for the post-Roman kingdom before the sixth century are confusing.

One point of reference appears in an ancient near contemporary book about the life of a famous sixth-century British monk and bishop called St Teilo, who founded various monasteries and churches. According to the 'Life of St Teilo' in *The Book of Llandaff*, angels told him to escape the Yellow Plague sweeping through the island in 549 by fleeing to Armorica (Brittany).

On route, St Teilo stopped in Cornwall and was received by a Gerennius (a Latinized version of Geraint), the king of the region. At the request of the king, Teilo received his confession and promised the king 'would not see death until he had received the Body of the Lord which he [Teilo] himself would have consecrated.'

Teilo then headed to Armorica to escape the Justinian Plague, which had ravaged large parts of Europe and Asia. When he learned Geraint was sick and on the verge of death, he returned to Britain seven years and seven months after leaving and arrived at Din Gerein harbour, believed to be the modern-day Gerrans[14] in Cornwall[15] on the east coast and around 9 miles from Truro. King Geraint received the sacrament and 'joyfully departed to the Lord'. His body was buried in what was described as a vast sarcophagus, which had been miraculously transported across the sea from Armorica.

This means the Geraint who met St Teilo died in 556–57 and is a near contemporary to Cerdic in his revised reign, but the vivid poem clearly recalls the famed warrior being 'slain'; it is the whole point of the elegy. The account of St Teilo written a few decades later does not imply death on a battlefield or from injuries.

Moreover, a clash between a contemporary Geraint and Cerdic's forces, based on his revised reign between 538 and 554, would have presumably occurred in the 550s, but the chronicle clearly states it was at the start of his reign and it appears unlikely they altered the order of battles so significantly.

The conflict of Port and his sons would have happened thirty-seven or thirty-eight years later than documented between 538 and 540, following the extreme weather event after a battle with neighbouring Romano-British warbands.

A force, based at Portchester and led by Bieda, were forced to repel an attack, with the absence of Cerdic being explained by this being an unexpected attack on his coastal stronghold when he was based elsewhere. This attack could have resulted from either Cerdic's forces rebelling and refusing to pay tribute to a leading Romano-British ruler – the 'young noble man' – sparking a conflict or have been an opportunistic raid on the occupied fort of Portchester, following the extreme weather, with the added prize of controlling the vital Solent.

Capturing Portchester must have been an unenviable task, as defenders armed with spears could conceivably have been positioned in the twenty towers. References to crossbows are non-existent between the fifth and tenth century, and spears were the favoured weapon of choice among the rank-and-file troops. Massive outer walls of the fort were 20ft high, 10ft thick, 630ft long and constructed of coursed flint with bonded limestone slabs.[16] Surrounding the port would have been a double ditch, which would have proved another obstacle for attacking forces. Part of the ditch is still visible around Portchester Castle today.

Excavations by Professor Cunliffe would not support the link between Portchester and the *Elegy for Geraint* because no mass burial was found at the site or nearby, which given the brutality of the apparent conflict would be suspected. The carnage is reflected in the use of 'biers beyond all numbers' in the elegy, with 'biers' a wooden frame on which a corpse is laid before burial.

In the Portchester battle, Cerdic's military muscle defended his kingdom, and the victory was remembered for centuries, but it was construed as an invasion by Port and his sons.

During extreme hardship, clashes would have been localized skirmishes and raids for livestock and supplies, which makes it unlikely a king such as Geraint in Cornwall would have been engaged more than 300 miles away.

There is also a logical alternative explanation for the identity of the 'young noble man' if it wasn't in fact the Geraint from folklore. The name Maegla derives from the British word 'Maglos' which is thought to mean 'prince' and was most probably confused with the young nobleman. A similar prefix features in the name of the infamous sixth-century king, Maelgwn from Gwynedd. Maegla would have hailed from a Brittonic enclave in the southwest or Armorica.

Another later sixth-century ruler called Mailcun reigned in Armorica, which was settled by British migrants, and has a similar prefix. Mailcun led repeated incursions into Frankish territory, but he was killed in a separate battle according to Geoffrey of Tours.[17] No less than twenty saints, princes and kings including 'Mael' can be found in Welsh medieval history.[18]

It is interesting how there is no reference to a battle or 'Britons', which suggests a raid by a young prince eager to make a name for himself by attacking the fort of a chief nemesis but was then met with fierce resistance.

It seems chroniclers knew of three associated names through folklore or an ancient list but not their exact role in the form of Bieda (Cerdic's fort commander), Maegla (the nobleman) and Portesmutha (the location). This then became Port and his two sons Bieda and Maegla to fit with an established pattern of semi-legendary or mythological founding pairs of brothers or father and son. Notably, this would also support a theory

Stunning view from the top of Portchester Castle towards nearby Portsmouth Harbour (Paul Harper/English Heritage)

Cerdic's force was led by English-speaking warriors such as Bieda and in conflict with neighbouring British kingdoms.

> ***ASC* 501:** 'In this year came Port to Britain, and his two sons, Bieda and Mægla, with two ships, at the place which is called Portesmutha [Portchester], and there slew a very noble young British man.'
>
> ***ASC* revised late 530s**:'In this year Bieda slew Maegla, a very noble young British man at a place which is called Portesmutha [Portchester].'

So, what was the *Elegy for Geraint* related to? A battle between Cerdic and the Geraint based on the contemporary reference to St Teilo would have meant far too much manipulation in the *Anglo-Saxon Chronicle*.

Ultimately, one Geraint was killed in something akin to a slaughter and the other died peacefully in a Cornish coastal village so the two didn't add up and neither did the timeline.

Focusing on an alternative for the *Elegy for Geraint*, favoured by Welsh historians, helped make sense of this mystery, as this theory places the battle near Cardigan Bay and is supported by significant Welsh place-name evidence. A historic farmhouse right next to the coast in Dyfed, Wales, is known as Llanborth and, intriguingly, a local site 10 miles inland is called Beddgeraint (the grave of Geraint).

Based on Dyfed Archaeological Trust records, there are at least three sites in a very small area near Penbryn beach that feature 'Llanborth', including the medieval farmstead and an ancient corn mill. A site nearby was reported to be called Maesglas ('the field of killings'), which was also known as Maes Galanas ('field of the massacre'), while just a few miles away is a village called Glynarthen[19] ('Glen of Arthur').[20] The link is undeniable and, in addition, the nearest Penbryn beach, 300m from the farmhouse, is a wide shallow bay in which Geraint could have easily berthed his ships in low tide and his men departed to the shore.

According to the Dyfed Archaeological Trust, a potential burial spot for Geraint and his men was scanned in a geophysical survey in 2004 in a field in Beddgeraint, near Newcastle Emlyn.[21] The trust stated 'no buried metal coffin was found within the mound but several shallow targets were located on and off the mound confirming the area was used as a location to deposit artefacts or debris'. The record adds that the origin of the objects is unknown and remains a mystery as the field has not been 'disturbed by farming practices'. It is interesting to note that a later castle at Newcastle was seized by the famous Welsh prince Llywelyn the Great in the thirteenth century, before later being recaptured by the English.

Wales was subject to raids by Irish tribes in post-Roman Britain, many of whom settled and marked their presence through Ogham memorial stones across the west coast of Britain.

Notably Vortipor, a ruler of Dyfed then known as Demetae, which may have had a joint British and Irish ruling elite, was condemned by Gildas as one of the five tyrant kings of Britain and accused of incest with his daughter. As Vortipor lived between 470 and 540, based on Demetae pedigree and Gildas' description that he was nearing death, he could have been the opponent of Geraint with a battle sometime between 500 and 530.

A carved stone found near a church in Castelldwyran in Carmarthenshire,[22] which has the inscription of 'in memory of Vortipor the Protector' includes both Latin and Irish writing, indicating there were important people living in the kingdom who were Irish speakers.[23]

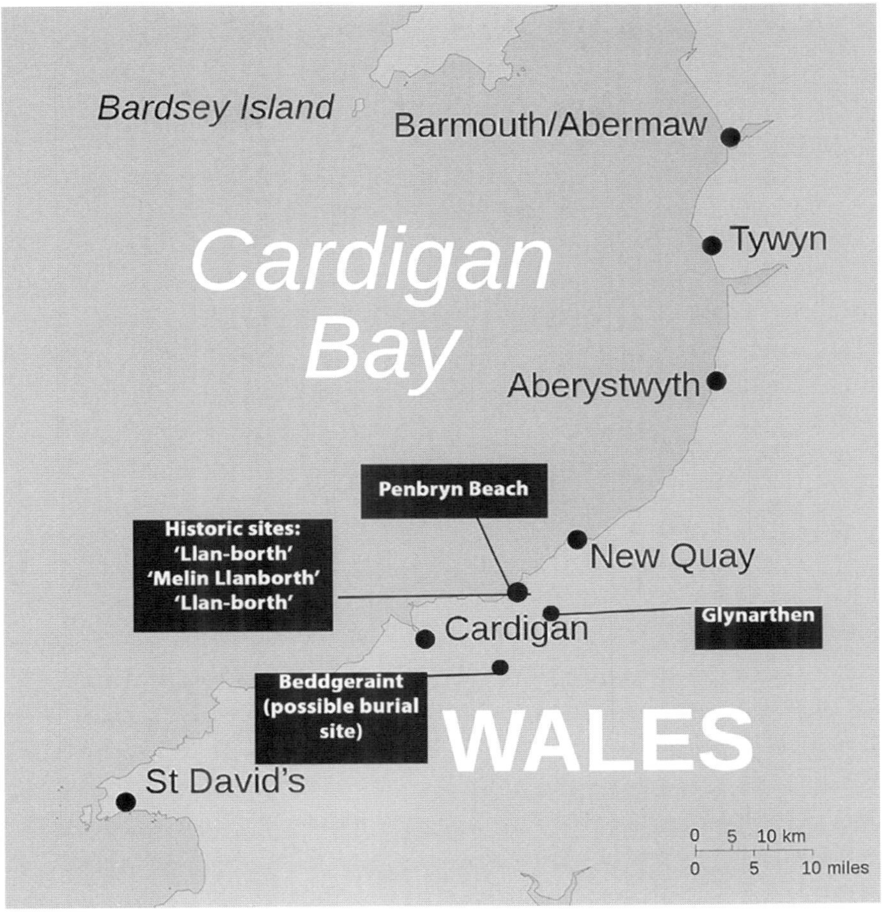

The location for the battle of the *Elegy for Geraint* in Wales (Wereon/Wiki Commons)

A confrontation pitting Geraint against the tyrannical Vortipor and Irish warriors would seem appropriate for the 'enemy of tyranny' against a king later derided as a ruling tyrant.

Geographically, a battle involving Geraint in western Wales could make more sense because Tintagel, further along the western shores, was a thriving post-Roman trading settlement and possible seat of Dumnonian royalty.

This would mean another Geraint from Dumnonia beside the two referenced contemporarily, but Welsh Triads describe the Geraint Erbin as a cousin of Arthur, and he is also referred to as one of the 'three seafarers of Yns Prydien (Island of Britain, although originally thought to be Island of Wales).'[24]

The possibility of the Geraint who welcomed St Teilo sharing the name of a heroic warrior from the same kingdom, or a famous Briton a few decades later when his deeds were fresh in the memory, would mirror the occurrence of the name Arthur in noble British families during the later-sixth century.

The issue is whether this Geraint was based in Dumnonia or as the strong local tradition suggests in Cardiganshire Bay, where up until the eleventh century it is claimed the site of Old Cardigan Castle was known as 'Din Geraint' (the fortress of Geraint).

Several different locations in Wales are named 'Dyfient', however, its later association with Devon and the ties with the powerful post-Roman kingdom of Dumnonia and the Arthurian legend, including Tintagel where Arthur was purportedly conceived, mean an identification placing Geraint in the west country is plausible but not as convincing as west Wales.

Either way, it is almost certain the *Elegy for Geraint* relates to a massacre of Britons in this part of Wales, which led me to conclude Cerdic or his forces did not cross swords with the much heralded warrior.

The battles involving Port and remembered in the *Elegy for Geraint* were real events, which lived long in the memory, but they were not connected, despite repeated associations by historians and writers. Geraint may have passed through the gates of Heaven, but his heroic death was never forgotten.

Chapter 10

Isle of Wight

Night thickened, and from north snowflakes, hail fell on the frost bound earth, coldest of grains. There come thoughts now, knocking my heart, of the high waves, clashing salt-crests, I am to cross again. Mind-lust maddens, move as I breathe, soul to set out, seek out the way, to a far folk-land flood-beyond.

The Seafarer, The Exeter Book, late-tenth century[1]

Carisbrooke Castle is a mile or so from the island's capital of Newport and its remarkable keep on top of a huge conical mound in the north-east corner is unmissable. Even as you reach the perimeter, the surviving medieval landscape becomes instantly apparent with a path on a steep bank alongside the huge ramparts that surround this fortress.

Structures of the former Norman castle, now a popular English Heritage site, have stood the test of time, including the commanding gatehouse entrance and the curtain wall with its projecting towers built on top of the massive earth banks, which can be followed around the site.

Carisbrooke's most famous resident was Charles I, who was kept as a prisoner for ten months from November 1647 after losing the English Civil War before being transferred back to the mainland and executed a few months later in London in January 1649. During his imprisonment, Charles I attempted to escape by lowering himself 10ft down a silk cord into the unguarded courtyard, but he became wedged between an iron bar and the window frame. Carisbrooke Castle museum has an account of Henry Firebrace, one of his household grooms, who recalled: 'His Majesty put himself forward, but then too late found himself mistaken; he sticking fast between his breast and shoulders... I heard him groane, but could not come to help him.'

The actual bedroom Charles I stayed in for the first five months, before he was relocated after a failed uprising by his followers in Newport, can

Stunning gatehouse entrance to Carisbrooke Castle on the Isle of the Wight, which is visited by thousands of people each year (Paul Harper/English Heritage)

still be viewed at the castle, but I was more intrigued by a much older resident. More than 1,000 years before Charles I's botched escape, a prince or king had been buried in the castle grounds with a rich array of grave goods. It remains perhaps the most significant archaeological discovery related to the reign of Cerdic.

The small island across the Solent has been a key location throughout British history. Vikings docked there regularly, and it was the setting for a pivotal moment in the Spanish Armada battle.[2] English ships with better cannons harried and forced the seemingly invincible fleet from Spain into treacherous shallow waters far out from the shore, caused by sand banks, around the northeast side of the Isle of Wight.

Faced with destruction, the Spanish abandoned their mission amid cheers from the large crowd that had gathered on the stunning cliffs of the Isle of Wight. Describing the engagement, Sir George Carey, the captain of the Isle of Wight, wrote: 'This morning began a great fight betwixt [between] both fleets south of the island which continued from five of the clock until ten.'[3] What could have been a disastrous invasion that changed the course of British history was averted by the island's hidden hazards.

At some point in the mysterious aftermath of Roman Britain, the island became a destination for new arrivals from the North Sea. Written records and archaeological studies reveal it was settled by Jutish tribes, originating from Jutland, which is a peninsula made up of Denmark and north Germany. In Bede's account of their arrival, he said:

> *'Those who came over were of three of the more powerful peoples of Germany: the Saxons, the Angles, and the Jutes. From the Jutes are descended the Cantaurri (men of Kent), the Victuarri, that is to say the people who inhabit the Isle of Wight, and that people who are today called the Jutes and are located in the kingdom of the West Saxons, opposite the Isle of Wight.'*

The *Anglo-Saxon Chronicle* describes how the two warriors Stuf and Wihtgar arrived in 514 and fought the Britons. Cerdic and Cynric captured the island in 530 after killing men at Carisbrooke (referred to as Wihtgara burh) and then handed the Isle of Wight back to Stuf and Wihtgar, who are described as their nephews after Cerdic's death in 534. There are several

Carisbrooke Castle has a fascinating history as a former motte-and-bailey Norman castle and an Anglo-Saxon stronghold (Paul Harper/English Heritage)

The inner bailey and courtyard of Carisbrooke Castle, where Charles I stayed as a prisoner (Paul Harper/English Heritage)

issues with this traditional account not least as established in Chapters 7 and 8 that the arrival of Stuf and Wihtgar is almost certainly a duplication of an earlier battle and that all events are likely to have taken place nineteen years later to fit with an established pattern of dating. Throwing further doubt on the chronicle version is how pagan cemeteries with Jutish origins date to the late-fifth and early-sixth century on Bowcombe and Chessell Down, before the reported landings of Stuf and Wihtgar, while metal detector finds have indicated a further six cemeteries of similar date.[4]

As suspected with the suspicious Port of 501, the name Wihtgar is another product of folk etymology derived from the island's existing Latin name Vectis, pronounced 'wechtis' or 'wekhtis'. The different forms of Wihtgar's stronghold in the Parker manuscript of the *Anglo-Saxon Chronicle* with one stating '*Wihtwara burh*' (the stronghold of the men of Wiht) and '*Wihtgara burh*' (the stronghold of Wihtgar) demonstrates the confusion.[5]

Following the death of Wihtgar in 544, nothing more is heard of the Isle of Wight for more than a century, until the Mercian King Wulfhere captured and handed the island to King Aethelwealh of Sussex, around 680 according to Bede. Months before, Wulfhere had seized the Upper Thames as well as

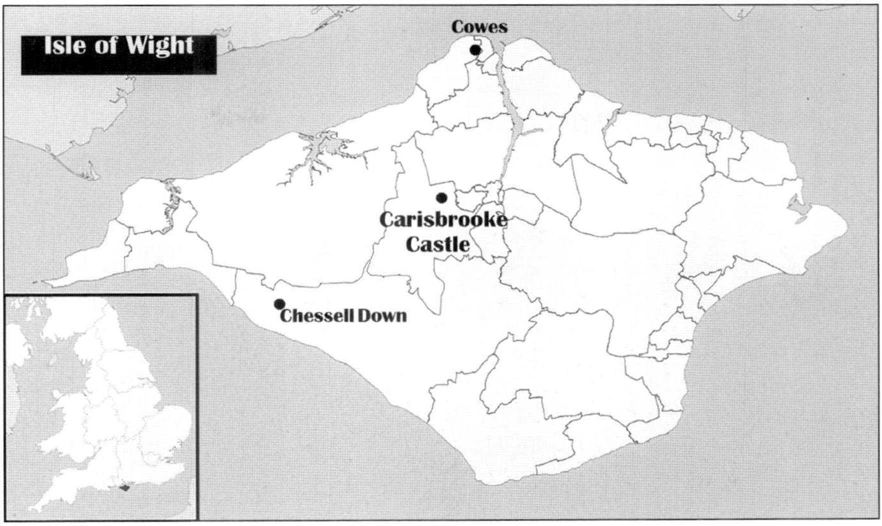

Key sites on the Isle of Wight during Cerdic's reign (Nilfanion, created using Ordnance Survey data/CC BY-SA 3.0)

the Isle of Wight from his bitter rivals the Gewisse-Wessex, which led to its prince, Caedwalla, invading Sussex and killing Aethelwealh, before being driven out by the slain ruler's elders, Berthun and Andthun. Later, Caedwalla recaptured Sussex, killed Berthun and then conquered the Isle of Wight. According to Bede, the king by 'cruel slaughter endeavoured to destroy all the inhabitants' and replace them with 'people from his own province'.

Around 1,200 families lived there under the rule of Adwald, the last pagan king of Anglo-Saxon England, who must have been subordinate to Wessex and then Sussex for a brief period. Two young brothers of Adwald fled the island but were betrayed and handed over to Caedwalla at Stoneham near Southampton. Before being killed, they were baptized by a local bishop, Cynibert.

The Isle of Wight became the last province to embrace the Christian faith in Britain but remained under 'foreign leadership' and was situated across the Solent opposite the division between Sussex and the Gewisse.

According to Bede, Caedwalla's victory proved fatal, and he died in Rome, having been baptized on 20 April 688, around the age of 30 after suffering 'wounds fighting on the Isle of Wight'.

Up until this point, it is claimed by some scholars that the island and parts of neighbouring Hampshire around the Meon Valley were independent

Jutish regions, possibly with Kentish overlordship. A connection is certainly evident in the royal houses of Kent and the Isle of Wight, with the inclusion of Uecta as a son of Woden in the genealogy of the kings of Kent. Meanwhile, Uictgisl and Uitta are described as the father and grandfather of Hengest, and Bede calls the Isle of Wight inhabitants '*Uictuarii*' (with 'u' and 'v' interchangeable in the medieval period other translations may read Vecta, Victgisl, Vitta or Victuarri), which links to Kentish royal ancestry.

Professor Barbara Yorke, one of the leading scholars on Wessex's early history, believes chronicle writers were aware of a 'common origin of the two peoples and close links between the rulers of the two provinces'.[6] She said that the flourishing kingdoms of Kent and the Isle of Wight shared a passion for the same brooches influenced by southern Scandinavia, while cemeteries in both regions contain imported prestige objects, which are rare in England, such as bronze Byzantine pails and bird brooches from Francia. Rare runic inscriptions have also been found dating from before 650 in the Isle of Wight, Kent and the Upper Thames.

It seems unlikely the Isle of Wight possessed Kentish overlords, which is 100-plus miles further along the coast instead of across the water. As soon as Wulfhere captured the Upper Thames, then the heartland of Wessex, his next step was to secure the island, which is implied because records state both the Upper Thames and the Isle of Wight were part of the same kingdom.

More than 130 graves were found at Chessell Down cemetery dating from the late-fifth and sixth century, with many of the rich and exotic grave goods now stored in the British Museum. Excavations at Chessell uncovered more than 200 items largely traced to Kent and Francia with Frisian pottery, and almost nothing distinctly Saxon in origin.[7] Grave goods included mediocre quality imitations of Kentish keystone garnet disc brooches.

There were several warrior burials of men with weapons. One chieftain, seemingly of high rank, had been buried with a sword, spearhead, shield-boss, bow and arrows, a hanging bowl with three bird-shaped escutcheons, an imported pail (possibly from Byzantine) and a bucket.[8]

As the place name Chessell may derive from the Old English word *ciest* meaning 'chest or coffin' combined with *hyll* ('hill'), it implies locals were aware of its history as a final resting place for island dwellers.[9]

Chessell Down is located within an Area of Outstanding Natural Beauty on the southwest corner of the island in an almost mythical landscape, sparsely settled barring the occasional stone-built isolated property, such

The dramatic Church of St Mary the Virgin Brook perched on a hill around half a mile from Chessell Down

as the plush Shalcombe Manor, once a monastic grange, and the Church of St Mary the Virgin Brook perched on top of a dramatic mound with the graves on a steep bank.

Ordnance Survey directed me into a wood known as Brighstone Forest, which at first seemed unusual when searching for Chessell Down, but the actual spot is now a Forestry Commission plantation.[10] It is striking how the ridge includes an abrupt and dangerous vertical spot in the middle of the woods, where the graves were sited, along with possible cremations. Standing on the edge of the woods, you can begin to see why it was chosen.

Mottistone Downs, further up from the Chessell burial site and the other side of the forest, is better known because it features four barrows, between six to nine feet high, that can be found on a chalk ridge with spectacular views out over the English Channel and west across the island's trademark white chalky cliffs.[11]

Inhabitants using the Chessell site decided to bury their dead on a slope facing in the other direction, which speaks of how they were paying heed to local ancestors but stamping their own identity. Situated at the bottom of a slope of chalk downlands on a ridge 114m above sea level, the site offers

Sweeping views towards the Solent in front of Chessell Down, where a large Anglo-Saxon burial site was unearthed

stunning views westwards over the hill towards the Solent and landing places in Hampshire.[12]

Presumably the idea was the deceased would continue to watch over their realm in the afterlife, which is in keeping with burial practices. Archaeologists believe Chessell Down could be one of a dozen cemeteries located on the main central chalk ridge, while the opposite Shalcombe Down features a barrow cemetery, cremation and burials dating to the post-Roman period.

Francia, which was initially based in modern-day France but grew to include the areas of Belgium and Germany before it was divided in three in the ninth century, was formed from the former Roman province of Gaul. It is named after its rulers, the Franks, who had evolved into a powerful Romanized Germanic tribe and could have even ruled Kent itself during the late-sixth century. Aethelbert, king of Kent, had a Frankish royal wife, Bertha, the Christian daughter of Frankish king, Charibert I. She was influential in inviting the missionary Augustine at the end of the sixth century, which led to the spread of Christianity among Anglo-Saxon people.

Among the fascinating graves at Chessell Down, one young woman buried in the second half of the sixth century wore three large Kentish square-headed brooches on her breast in addition to another brooch, which was a Frankish import. She was also buried with an elaborate necklace of beads, a headband of gold braid in Frankish fashion, a crystal ball and perforated spoon positioned between her legs, a bronze pail from Byzantium and two silver-rimmed cups. Her stunning Frankish-style gold braid dress fittings have led to a theory she may have been born in Francia and arrived via Kent. Professor Yorke concluded that the elaborate grave goods matching rich female burials in Kent suggest she may have been a princess who married into an island family.[13]

Nine women were found buried at Chessell Down with Frankish-type brooches popular in Kent, leading to the suggestion they were the female relatives, or possibly slaves of an elite woman who brought them along as one big community, perhaps when she embarked on a religious life. Brooches were an essential item for holding clothes together before the advent of buttons, and they were popular throughout nearly the entire Anglo-Saxon period.

One grave at Chessell Down featured a stunning silver-gilt, square-headed brooch decorated in the Style 1 format, which was popular in the late-fifth and sixth centuries in northern Europe. This art was decorated with

Looking over the Anglo-Saxon burial site discovered at Chessell Down, which is now a plantation

scrolls and animals and based on Scandinavian styles. Closer inspection reveals the remarkably intricate design includes at least twenty-four different animals with a mixture of birds' heads, animals, serpents, human faces and masks.[14]

These images can, however, be interpreted in different ways, which is central to the ambiguity of Style 1 animal art, and four heads appear on

Remarkable silver-gilt square-headed brooch uncovered in the grave of a woman at Chessell Down (©The Trustees of the British Museum)

the rectangular head of the brooch when it is turned upside down. At the foot of the brooch, a bearded face with a helmet underneath two birds may represent the Germanic God Woden with his two companion ravens, which offered symbolic protection to the wearer. With a zoomorphic style and various animal shapes, an Anglo-Saxon cruciform brooch in Bloodstone Copse on the Isle of Wight was dated 450–500 and then popular in Anglian settlements in Britain.

The brooch at Chessell Down was from a primary or reused barrow burial because a possible nearby cemetery included thirteen primary or reused barrows. It was unearthed just 100m from an existing Newchurch/Brading parish boundary, which evolved from a Roman villa estate one.[15]

Just under half of the early cemeteries from the Anglo-Saxon period are located near parish boundaries, which could preserve ancient land divisions predating the Romans. Early Jutish settlers must have lived and farmed within visual contact of the barrow cemeteries, and there appears to be continued occupation among island residents and new arrivals.

Significantly, Bede stated the name for the Isle of Wight dwellers was '*Wihtwara*'. The *wara* is a plural of the Old English noun *waru*, which translates 'to watch, guard, protect or defend'. *Wihtwara* could then mean the 'guards of Wiht', implying some of the Jutish inhabitants were defending its primary stronghold, which must have been Carisbrooke Castle, where a powerful fortress seems to have been located for more than 1,000 years.

The famous Isle of Wight cliffs from Mottistone Down just further up from the Chessell Down burial site

The existing name of Carisbrooke would describe a 'watercress brook', which relates to the nearby 'Lukely Brook'. However, a fourteenth-century document listing beacons refers to '*Wyghtberg*' when mentioning the castle site.[16] It is believed the site of Carisbrooke Castle was once an Iron Age hill fort. During excavations, a Roman wall was discovered at Carisbrooke Castle, which suggested it formed part of the Saxon Shore Forts, along with nearby Portchester. No solid evidence has been found of Roman occupation, but three Roman villas have been found within the local area.[17]

Another Jutish tribe, which became known as the Meonwara, emerged across the Solent in the Meon Valley that also features the *wara* element, while 'Meon' is derived from a Celtic word meaning 'swift one'.[18] The River Meon runs for 21 miles from East Meon, 4 miles west of Petersfield, to the Solent.

Bede refers to a Jutish enclave in southern Hampshire, which he describes as a 'province of the dwellers of the Meon', while the place name Ytedene in east Meon translates as the 'valley of the Jutes'. A very similar place name Ytene (of the Jutes) was also attached to describe the New Forest up until the eleventh century.

One site was uncovered at Shavards Farm at Meonstoke in the Meon valley, which featured twenty-one burials, including five children and sixteen adults, and revealed a sunken feature timber building cut into the remains of a Roman villa.[19] Among the grave goods was a K1 Swanton series spearhead, which mirrors a British design with leaf-shaped blades and a stepped section, dated to the late-fifth and mid-sixth centuries and is also found at sites in Andover, Worthy Park and the Upper Thames.

A belt mount of the Quoit brooch style was found east of the villa. This was a popular design in the Anglo-Saxon period, featuring geometric motifs of animals and human face masks based on late-Roman military belt buckles from northern Gaul and Britain but most likely replicated in British metalworks. The belt buckle and spearhead have been associated with mercenaries, but the people at Shavards Farm appear to have led a peaceful farming existence.

An examination of burials at the site noted:

> *'The degree of trauma and stress injuries was high, as is often the case in rural populations whose main occupation is farming. Overall, the group appears to have been relatively healthy and physically robust, all skeletons showing large muscle markings and little evidence of disease beyond the stresses and strains of daily life.'*

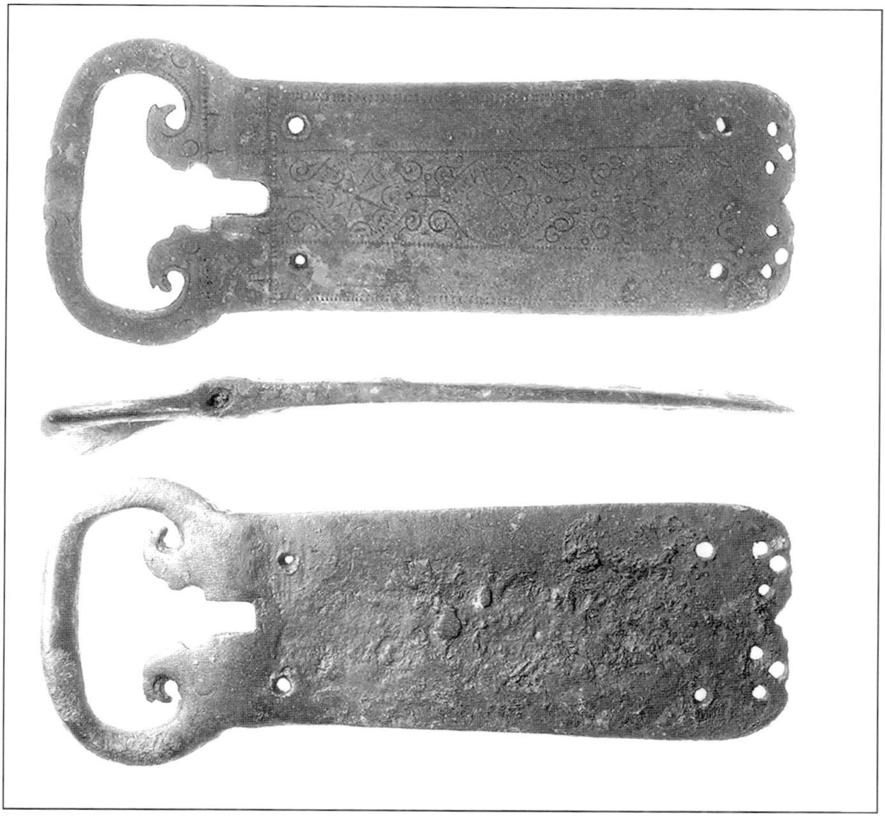

Incomplete cast copper alloy buckle dated 425–75 found in the Isle of Wight decorated in Quoit Brooch style (The Portable Antiquities Scheme (IOW-0CB093)/The Trustees of the British Museum/CC BY-SA 2.0)

According to academic Jillian Hawkins, the lack of Anglo-Saxon settlements around the Solent, besides Portchester and the Isle of Wight, and prevalence of 'Ora' place names, as discussed in Chapter 7, which are derived from a Latin word for 'edge of land, shore', suggests a British authority was in control and allowed Germanic migrants to travel up the Meon to find new land for farming:[20]

> *'The cemetery near Shavards Farm demonstrates that people with Germanic tastes settled, worked, lived and died here. Again, instead of the incomers taking territory after fierce battles, killing the natives and destroying their way of life, in fact something else was going on. The new people did not have all the power, or gain overall control, they had to negotiate with the residents.'*

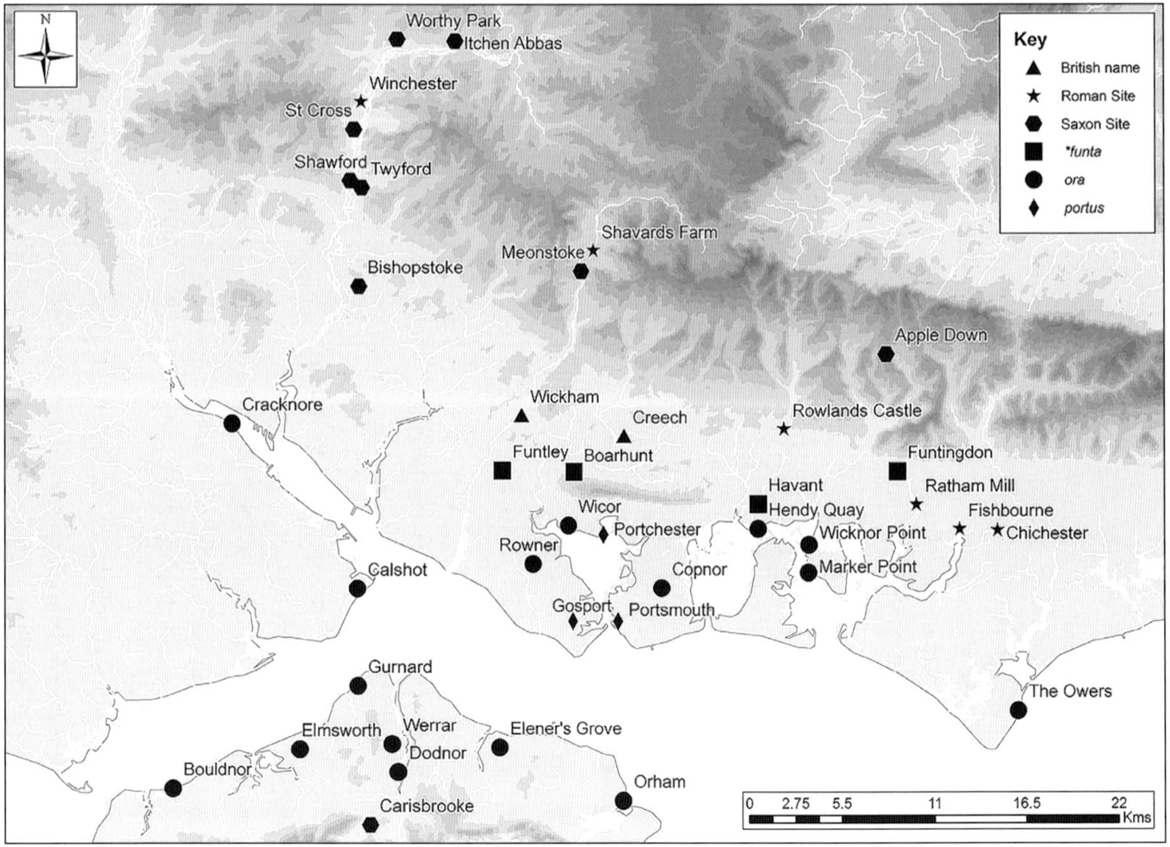

The distribution of *funta, ora* and *portus* place-name elements against select archaeological sites dated to the Roman and Saxon periods. As outlined in Chapter 2, these place names appear to be derived from Latin loan words and suggest Romano-British settlements (Jillian Hawkins/ CC BY-SA 4.0)

Part of this agreement may have included defending the region as Shavards Farm was situated close to a fording point of the Meon, which is suggested by a burial site a few miles away in Droxford near the river.

Excavations revealed eight of the forty-one graves contained spearheads, roughly one in five. As there were forty spearheads recovered from the site, there may have been at least 200 people buried at Droxford over 150 years from the late-fifth century, which is equivalent to a small medieval village.

The location of the Anglo-Saxon settlement in Droxford remains a mystery. Later charters also made references to a 'heathen burial place' in Droxford, which has caused further confusion. Such descriptions also feature in ten Hampshire charters, and it is believed they may have been reference to an executed criminal buried outside of a church burial ground and placed near the boundaries of a division such as a Hundred.

Droxford lies around 10 miles west of the border with Hampshire and Sussex. Among the forty-one graves, were twelve males, twenty-one women and six juveniles, while the remaining people cannot be identified. Nearly half of the people died between the age of 20 and 30 and the majority before the age of 25. More than 200 beads, made of glass, amber or shale, were uncovered which were most likely part of a woman's necklace. The number of spearheads and six iron swords recovered, along with six burials featuring one or more weapons, hint at the militarized nature of the site, as swords were a sign of wealth or high rank in a society. A burial report noted: 'The lack of decorated scabbard mounts on the Droxford swords, however, suggests that none of them were buried with a warrior of exceptionally high status.'[21]

Droxford inhabitants appear to have guarded the Meon in return for land, perhaps to prevent further North Sea settlers from rowing up the river and carving out a new territory.

Jutes on the Isle of Wight and the Meon arrived following the foederati influx described by Gildas in the mid-to-late fifth century, which is supported by the close links with the Jutes of Kent. According to Nennius, they were continually increasing their numbers, implying they were inviting friends and family from their homeland. In the rebellion which followed, the post-Roman authority in the former Belgae civitas retained an allegiance with the new Jutish inhabitants.

Surely the post-Roman authority led by Cerdic and his ancestors would have wanted to ensure the island a few miles off the mainland was not left to the mercy of barbarian tribes who were capturing vast swathes of the western Roman empire. The foederati became vital to Cerdic's kingdom as they protected the island and provided military muscle in the campaign against Natanleod. However, there appears to have been a rebellion because Cerdic and Cynric are described as capturing the island.

> ***ASC* 530 (late 540s, early 550s):** 'In this year Cerdic and Cynric took Wihte ealond [the Isle of Wight] and slew a few men at Wihtgarabyrg [Carisbrooke Castle].'

The severity of this confrontation involving Cerdic on the island is unclear as two manuscripts of the chronicle have used both 'slew a few men at Wihtgarbyrg' and 'slew many men at Wihtgarbyrg'. It appears Cerdic's forces seized the island or reinforced their authority after a rebellion or dispute. Who was rebelling remains unclear, but it could have been a faction of the Jutish guards or a barbarian group trying to muscle in and take over the island. Both scenarios are possible, but by the time of Cerdic's death, he had secured the island and handed it over to his nephew, Stuf.

The sequence of events would imply a rogue element among the existing group and, possibly with newcomers, they had holed up at Carisbrooke, which historically appears to have been a fortress long before the Norman castle. As discussed, this is evidenced by how Stuf and the fictional character of Wihtgar – named after the island itself – are described in the *Anglo-Saxon Chronicle* as landing some sixteen years before Cerdic captured the Isle of Wight, and how the presence of Jutish inhabitants is attested to the late-fifth century, up to fifty years beforehand. Given the natural defences of Carisbrooke, it could be theorized Cerdic had landed with a considerable force on the Isle of Wight and met up with Stuf's contingent before swamping the fortress in sheer numbers and removing the enemy.

Nothing more is heard of the Isle of Wight in the chronicle until the wars of Caedwalla around 150 years later. After the rebellion was squashed, it seems the Jutes were quickly back in favour and rewarded with land around the New Forest, which became known as *Ytene* (of the Jutes) up until the eleventh century.

Carisbrooke was central to the arrangement as the stronghold of the Jutish foederati and it was the site of a spectacular discovery, which could be dated to Cerdic's reign.[22] This was covered in a fascinating report by archaeologists Tania Dickinson and Elaine Morris.

In the 1960s, excavations at the castle[23] revealed a richly furnished burial, alongside two other graves, which featured stunning finds comparable with other princely burials from the late-sixth and seventh centuries at Taplow Barrow, Sutton Hoo and Prittlewell. Traces of a Saxon fort have been found at Carisbrooke, and its Norman inner bailey occupied the same area.

The burials were found at the bottom of the inner bailey lawn, which survived despite the construction of a nearby 48m-deep well for the motte and keep.[24] One burial was of a female aged between 17 and 19 years old, who displayed signs of spina bifida, which occurs when the backbone does not fully develop during pregnancy. Along with the princely burial, there were signs of arrested growth, based on dental examinations, between the age of 2 and 3 because of dietary deficiencies, which can lead to shortened arms and legs. Likewise, there was no sign of a coffin, but both graves had been packed with greensand blocks taken from nearby Roman sites. Grave goods included an iron knife with a horn handle possibly made from leather and an iron bar believed to be part of a barrel key, which hung from a belt, and has been found in another burial at Alton in Hampshire.

While the sex of the third grave was undetermined, based on the objects placed alongside, such as a squat glass bowl and derivatives of Roman belt buckles typically found in female graves, it is thought to have been a woman buried in the late-fifth or early-sixth century.

Described as of 'exceptional importance', the princely occupant was laid to rest alongside 'four different prestige items', including two drinking vessels, a drinking horn and a glass bowl. Tiny ivory counter pieces from a medieval board game were found next to the princely burial in Carisbrooke Castle, which were extremely rare and only matched at the famous Sutton Hoo site. Excavations found fifty-one ivory counter circular pieces for a medieval board game known as 'tafl' based on a Roman military tactics one called *Ludus latrunculorum* in which the aim was to capture the king. This was a popular ancient board game in which the blue-coloured glass counter pieces represented the king, while the ivory ones would have distinguishing marks or colourings.

Ivory pieces were found at Sutton Hoo in the richly furnished main burial thought to be King Raedwald and dated to around 625. Such counters were more commonly made of bone or more rarely copper, pottery and copper-alloy, while non-glass pieces, fifteen in total, have only been found elsewhere in Oxton, Nottinghamshire. Using ivory was so unique it suggested the burial occupant possessed access to extensive trade networks and could have been a prince or king. The burial report stated: 'The playing pieces from Carisbrooke are then exceptional for their time and place and represent a grave good of the highest calibre.'[25]

By the seventh century, a large settlement had developed at Carisbrooke that, judging from coins finds, also possessed extensive trade links, which had been seemingly established 100 year earlier.[26] The male occupant was believed to have been aged between 20 and 25 and lived in the sixth century, most likely in the second quarter.

More than one prestige item found in a grave was rare, let alone four, but the grave did not include a wooden chamber, such as at the princely burial at Prittlewell (dated 575 to 605), which suggests a date closer to the mid-sixth century.

Green discolouration in the man's mouth was most likely because a coin had been placed in it, while the grave also included an iron knife believed to date from the fifth to seventh centuries.

A stunning glass bowl, complete with light yellow brown soda glass, placed next to his left knee was uncommon in Britain but has been found at contemporary sites such as Lavoye in France and Nennig in Germany, while bowls with similarly decorated moulding have been unearthed in the Rhineland.

Drinking horns, rather than wooden cups and bottles, are rare in early medieval graves, and the Isle of Wight is the only one to have a particular type of zoomorphic Style 1 mount asides from one discovered in Taplow.

Clearly the occupant was someone with considerable standing in Cerdic's burgeoning kingdom based on the former Belgae civitas.

Visigothic tremisses (gold coins) minted between 509 and 520 and found in one grave mean a burial at least after the second decade of the sixth century. It is thought such gold coinage did not arrive from Europe until at least the 530s–40s.[27] The coins are particularly noteworthy as Asser, Alfred the Great's biographer, records the king's grandfather was descended from the Goths and Jutes via Stuf and Wihtgar, a detail not included in the chronicle, but suggested by the Visigothic coins.

Another Visigothic tremissis of 509 to 520 at the cemetery at Bowcombe Down, along with embossed rim copper alloy bowls from the Rhineland and a Frankish helmet from a weapon grave, highlight how island dwellers clearly had access to an extensive foreign trade network and the resources to purchase luxury goods.[28]

Early-medieval Visigothic gold tremissis, dating to the sixth century before 580 – similar to the coin found in Carisbrooke Castle burial (The Portable Antiquities Scheme (IOW-715794)/ CC BY-SA 2.0)

Asser's reference to the ancestry reads:

> *'Moreover, his mother, the daughter of Oslac, was called Osburgh. And this Oslac was of the Gothic race, for he descended from the Goths and Jutes, namely from the stock of Stuf and Wihtgar, brothers and companions in arms who received the Isle of Wight from their uncle, King Cerdic, and from his son who was their cousin.'*

What is particularly fascinating about the original Latin text is how Asser uses the term *Con Sobrino*, implying Stuf and Wihtgar were blood relations of Cerdic's wife, who must have had Jutish and Goth ancestry.[29]

The use of *Con Sobrino*, which includes 'Con-With', is generally associated with the cousin of the child of a mother's sister and it is said to be composed of the Latin word *con* derived from 'cum- with', while *sobrinus* equals 'cousin', from 'soror-sister'.[30] This is hugely significant as the first recorded hint of a mixed heritage kingship emerging, something suggested by scholars such as Myres and common throughout the early Anglo-Saxon period. It is a very specific detail and surely one Asser would not have included without foundation.

Cerdic's union with a Jutish bride may have secured the support of the Isle of Wight rulers who gained a stake in the royal dynasty and kingship reflective of the mixed population. This intriguing detail may have marked the start of the anglicization of the Wessex kingship; however, it is possible Cerdic himself and his predecessor had Jutish-Goth ancestry given the Isle of Wight dwellers arrived in the late-fifth century.

What this reference implies, is the ninth-century chroniclers, such as Asser, were better informed than is often believed and privy to genealogies that never surfaced. Before Seaxburh, the wife of Cenwalh who ruled for two years after the death of her husband in 672, there are few details about the wives and mothers of Wessex kings. It should be noted that in a later passage Asser seems to imply Cerdic is a grandfather of Stuf and Wihtgar, however, this seems unlikely given they are part of the same timeframe in the chronicle.[31] The same passage clearly uses *avunculo* to refer to Cerdic, which in classical Latin means 'maternal uncle'.

The princely male grave occupant on the Isle of Wight had suffered from attested growth between the age of 2 and 3 years. Whether this relates to a famine around the year 536 after a volcanic blast caused atmospheric dust veils is unclear but given the hardships of life compared to modern standards when most people did not live long beyond 30 years, it is perhaps not as unusual as it might seem.

As Chapter 4 explained, it does appear the landings at Cerdices Ora in 495 and 514 were duplications and confused from two separate sources. Stuf, Cynric and Cerdic landed near Stansore Point in a powerful warband of several hundred men in the early 530s.

As one of the few non-princes or kings in early Wessex history, Stuf must have been a key part of the campaign and commanded Cerdic's forces. He could have been described as a 'leader of battles'. Stuf appears crucial in the entries related to the Isle of Wight. Given the confusion with the chronicle entries written hundreds of years afterwards, it does appear a title associated with Stuf or his force with a reference to Wiht (Isle of Wight) led to the invention of the Wihtgar name. The word *gar* in Old English means 'spear', possibly relating to the favoured weapon, or it could stem from the Proto-Germanic word *garu*, i.e. 'ready, prepared' which may refer to Stuf's forces arriving primed for battle.

The death of 'Wihtgar' at Carisbrooke in 544 would have been at the height of the Justinian Plague if correctly dated.

> **ASC 544:** 'In this year Wihtgar died, and they buried him at Wihtgarabyrg [Carisbrooke Castle].'

Up until the past decade, with advances in DNA, it has been impossible to detect the plague in skeletons because it kills so quickly and leaves no trace. The story has clearly become confused as the chronicle has 'Wihtgar' landing in 514 and dying thirty years later, which is longer than the lifespan of the prince or king buried in the castle grounds. Given the man's relatively young age, this must have been a son or younger brother of Stuf who died during the plague in 544 or later in the early 560s around ten years after Cerdic's death. The lavish burial presumably reflected the outpouring of grief at his untimely death.

The exact identity of the man buried in the princely burial will remain a mystery. Its existence and dating to the second quarter of the sixth century, however, once again highlights how the chronicle's entries are drawn from actual conflicts and events. Characters such as Stuf were real life warriors whose impact was profound.

Just as the Isle of Wight played a crucial role in saving England from the might of the Spanish Armada, it was pivotal in the birth of the kingdom that grew into the English nation.

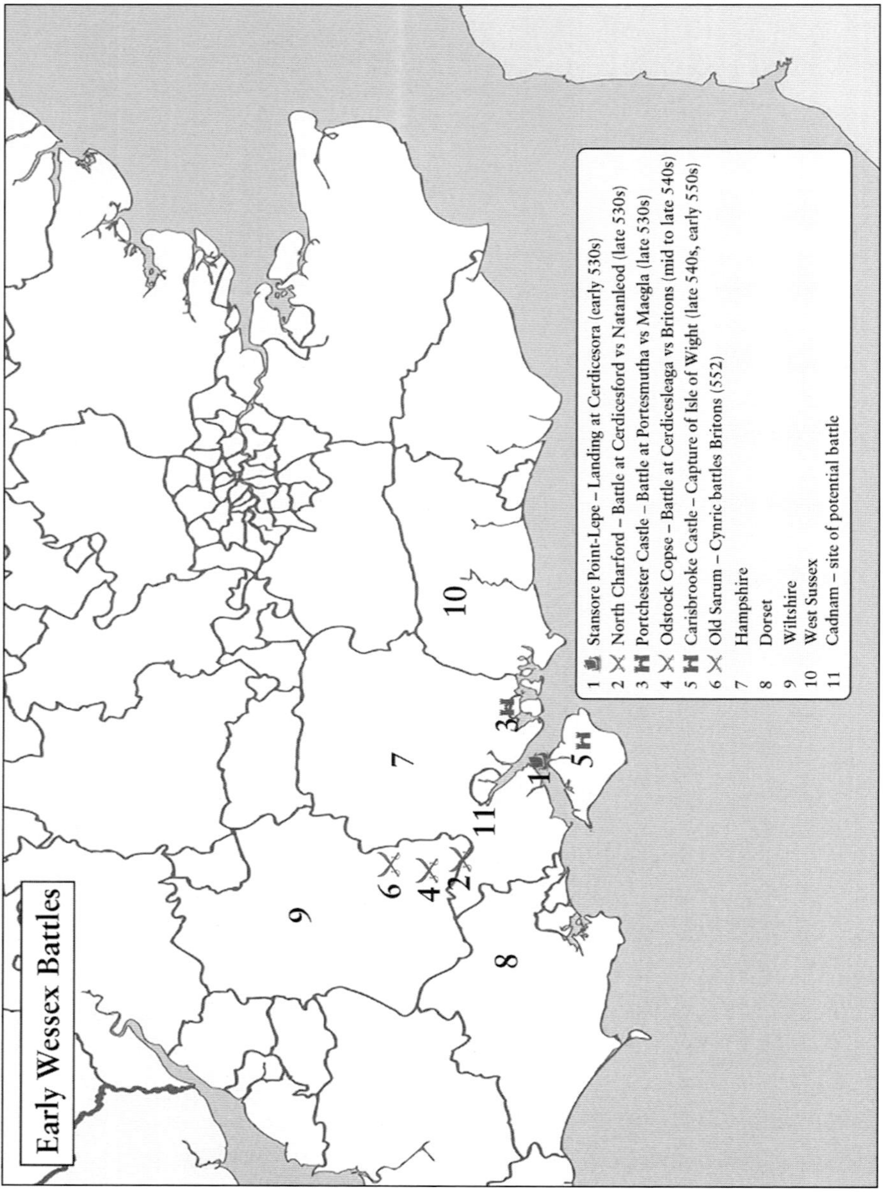

Early Wessex battles

Chapter 11

Gewisse and the Upper Thames

The fortunes of war favoured Hrothgar. Friends and kinsmen flocked to his ranks, young followers, a force that grew to be a mighty army. So his mind turned to hall-building: he handed down orders for men to work on a great mead-hall meant to be a wonder of the world forever; it would be his throne-room and there he would dispense his God-given goods to young and old but not the common land or people's lives. Far and wide through the world, I have heard, orders for work to adorn that wallstead were sent to many peoples. And soon it stood there, finished and ready, in full view, the hall of halls. Heorot was the name he had settled on it, whose utterance was law.

Beowulf, author unknown, seventh century

The legendary Old English poem *Beowulf* conjures up images of kinsmen crammed on long narrow benches drinking mead as bards serenade the masses with tales of great victories. Characters epitomized the male culture of being loyal, brave and strong, with Beowulf described as having the 'strength of 30 men'. Warriors would feast in the mead hall of Danish king, Hrothgar, known as the Heorot, before falling prey repeatedly to the monster Grendel at night. Eventually, the Geatish hero Beowulf confronts and slays the beast in an epic battle and pays a debt to the ruler Hrothgar. Afterwards, Grendel's severed arm remained hanging in the rafters as another raucous celebration in the hall was staged to honour Beowulf's triumph.

The tale is widely believed to include real characters who appear in Scandinavian sources, such as Hrothgar, Healfdene, Eadgils and Ohthere, along with the clans of Scyldings and Scylfings. Kings and clans from Anglo-Saxon England are also mentioned, such as Hengest, the founder of Kent, and the Wulfings, who are thought to have created the East Anglian dynasty. *Beowulf* may even have been composed in East Anglia during the seventh century.

Reconstruction of a Viking house, resembling the Beowulf mead hall, from the Fyrkat ring castle near Hobro, Denmark (Malene Thyssen/CC BY-SA 2.5)

The poem shines a light into the tribal and warrior societies of the North Sea in which a mead hall was pivotal. Mead halls were the heartbeat of warrior communities, where they gathered to socialize, rejoice and remember the fallen and often became a statement of wealth and power, with rulers bidding to make their hall bigger and more spectacular than rivals.

Based on the *Beowulf* text, these mighty buildings were made of timber, featured gold decorations, such as glittering wall tapestries, had wide gables, contained many mead benches, boasted mosaic flooring, had a reinforced external door and a separate internal one and were approached via a stone path which accentuated its grandeur.[1]

Such sites were not just an Anglo-Saxon phenomenon and were common across northern Europe, particularly in Scandinavia as more than eighty sites have been identified around the North and Baltic seas.[2] One study has suggested as many as 195 such royal halls in Anglo-Saxon England but less than twenty have been discovered and only a handful excavated.[3] Archaeologists have uncovered great halls in the Upper Thames, which became the focal points of seventh-century elite settlements in Wessex and linked with a shadowy group known as the Gewisse, described as a powerful Anglo-Saxon tribe based in Dorchester. Matching the Heorot, their obvious prestige led to a radical new outlook, which places Wessex's foundations in the Upper Thames and not Hampshire and the high concentration of Germanic grave finds has served to strengthen this argument.

Many scholars now believe the kings of the Upper Thames later conquered Hampshire and hijacked the local tradition of rulers named Cerdic and Cynric as their own to explain how the kingdom was founded. This seemed unlikely but not impossible given how the *Anglo-Saxon Chronicle*'s early entries have been manipulated to a degree.

Wessex had originally been known as the Gewissae (Gewisse) according to Bede, who labelled its late-seventh century king, Caedwalla, as a 'daring young man of the royal house of Gewissae'. Cerdic's pedigree, which is a literary invention beyond his grandfather, includes a Gewis as his great-grandfather, and the Gewisse is possibly derived from the Old English word for 'reliable' or 'sure' that is commonly associated with confederates.

One of the most puzzling aspects of Cerdic's mysterious reign is the connection with the kingdom in Hampshire and the later Upper Thames settlements. The Upper Thames was historically a barrier between the Iron Age Atrebates and Catuvellauni tribes before the Romans arrived. The large Atrebatic tribal region had been divided into a Roman province, with three districts encompassing the Belgae centred in Winchester, the Atrebates in Silchester and the Regni in Chichester, which became Sussex (South Saxons).

In the final years of Roman Britain, it appears Germanic foederati may have been employed to guard the Upper Thames.[4] Such a positioning would make sense because the Upper Thames may have also marked the northern boundary of the former Britannia Prima province, an administrative region during Roman rule that was created in the early-fourth century and covered the southern part of modern-day England. There is some suggestion that the political structure remained in place for several decades after Roman troops departed.

Several burials in Dorchester displayed a fascinating mix of Roman military-style items and Germanic dress and 'it served as a centre of authority in the final decades of Roman rule and beyond', according to a large study called the 'Origins of Wessex', led by the University of Oxford's School of Archaeology.

In 1874, a male burial containing an early-fifth century military-style Roman belt set was found in Iron Age linear earthworks known as the Dyke Hills near Dorchester, while a nearby female burial was found with an intriguing mixture of Romano-British and Germanic dress items.[5] *The Origins of Wessex* study stated:

> *'There is nothing inherently Germanic about burial with weapons, but the female burial does suggest the presence of mercenaries and their families, some of whom, at least, came from north-west Germany. Indeed, the Upper Thames region as a whole has long been recognised as containing an exceptional concentration of early fifth century finds of this kind.'*

Among the graves in the northern end of Dorchester were applied brooches decorated with a design identical to ones found in North Friesland, the northernmost district of modern Germany, which may relate to a force transferred from Bavaria to Britain for garrison duty.[6]

In 2010, more late-Roman burials were uncovered from Dyke Hills, with the bones found close to late-Roman metalwork, including a buckle and plate of another very fine military-type belt, which was most likely manufactured in early-fifth century northern Gaul.[7]

A further three burials with late-Roman belt buckles of the Hawkes and Dunning Type 1b (from the classification of Roman zoomorphic buckles

Dyke Hills in Dorchester where late military Roman burials were uncovered (Philip Halling/CC BY-SA 2.0)

into four types with sub-types by Christopher Hawkes and Gerald Dunning) have been excavated in the southern part of the town, along with one from a female Dyke Hill burial. These eye-catching zoomorphic buckles, which dated to between 350 and 450, were D-shaped, with the front of the design featuring a fish or dolphin with large bulbous eyes. The objects 'demonstrate the existence at the very end of Roman Britain and beyond of a dominant, arguably military, group at Dorchester which buried at least some of its dead in an ostentatious way in the Iron-Age earthworks'.[8]

However, in a report on the late-Roman burials at Lankhill near Winchester, which featured 451 graves from the third to fifth centuries and included burials with four Hawkes and Dunning buckles, Giles Clarke said they were 'wrongly' thought to have solely Germanic affinities.[9] The buckles had been produced locally based on continental designs, and the population was 'as capable as adopting Germanic fashions as they were of imitating Romans'. Clarke explained they were distributed only in Britain so it would be 'absurd' they were only worn by foreigners. He linked the buckles to a native force, which had been raised after 350 under the command of a 'Vicarius' who was a military commander.

The Great Barbarian Conspiracy in 367, which was a series of devastating raids by Saxon, Frank, Picts and Scotti tribes, explains why such a force was raised and stationed in places such as Dorchester and Winchester.

A study by Dr Heinrich Härke argued the late-Roman weapons burials in Winchester, Dorchester and in West Heslerton in North Yorkshire were

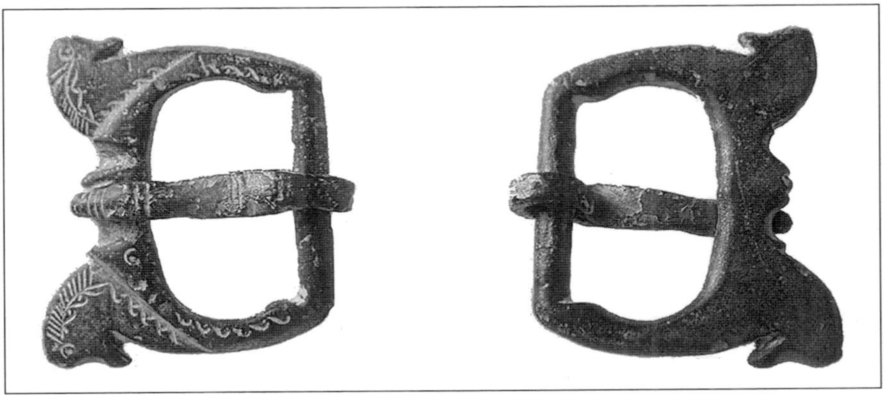

Late Roman copper alloy zoomorphic buckle frame of Hawkes and Dunning type 1B found in Hampshire and matching a similar find in the Upper Thames (The Portable Antiquities Scheme/Trustees of the British Museum/CC BY-SA 2.0)

suggestive of a foederati with Germanic roots in late Roman times.[10] At the latter, West Heslerton, Dr Härke claims 17 per cent of burials in the first cemetery had originated from Scandinavia or eastern continental Europe, while fourth-century 'exotic' burials in Lankhill in Winchester reveal a dispersed pattern of origin from the continent. Dr Härke believes this pointed to a foederati in the latter stages of the Roman empire who were from central and southern Europe. An examination of forty-seven Anglo-Saxon burial sites found 47 per cent of male adults had been buried with weapons, which Dr Härke claimed was a symbolic and social marker of families of immigrant descent, and those males without weapons must have been native.[11]

At the cemetery of Berinsfield near Dorchester, which was in use from the late-fifth to the early-seventh centuries, twenty-five of 105 inhumation burials included weapons and the proportion of male adults (64 per cent) was above average for the Upper Thames (35 per cent).[12] Male adult burials with and without weapons occur across three burial plots, but it has been discovered the men with weapons have different genetic traits in their teeth than those without weapons.

Germanic immigrants and their descendants lived together with native Britons in the same settlements but did not intermarry, which Dr Härke argued could imply a different social status and possibly even prohibition of mixed marriage. The first immigrants formed kin groups and communities, which grew with further immigration in years to come, Dr Härke added. This kin group could well have evolved into the warrior tribe known as the Gewisse, which many scholars are convinced gained power in Dorchester and began exacting tributes from neighbours before later conquering Hampshire.

Professor Barbara Yorke, in her 1995 book *Wessex in the Early Middle Ages*, speculates the Gewisse only began calling themselves West Saxons in the late-seventh century, when they had taken over new territory, and its rulers were based in the Upper Thames, which 'produced the earliest and most intensive evidence for Germanic settlement within Wessex'. In the book, Professor Yorke said, 'it is not surprising that it was also at the heart of what seems to have been the most powerful of the region's kingdoms'.

Archaeologist Jim Gunter also believes the kingdom emerged from the territory of the Gewisse in Dorchester and the story of Cerdic 'subduing locals' was a '9th century rewrite of history to justify how come Wessex had emerged as the leading Anglo-Saxon realm' and to project it into the 'same mould as the other early Germanic kingdoms of Kent and Sussex'.[13]

Dr John-Henry Clay, from Durham University, found the term '*Rex Gewissorum*' appears in just one charter as a late donation of King Cuthred dating from 745, and the first so-called Gewissian kings, Centwine (who reigned between 676 and 685) and Caedwalla (685–88), both called themselves *Rex Saxonum*. Clay said: 'There is therefore little doubt that the Gewissan kings of the seventh century tended to refer to themselves simply as kings of the Saxons.' Dr Clay advocates the 'Gewissae' name was tribal and linked to a tribe such as those found in the seventh-century Tribal Hidage document, which listed thirty-five different groups across central and south-eastern England.[14]

> *'It is equally plausible that Gewissae had always been a dynastic name or referred to a local territorial grouping of the sort recorded in the Tribal Hidage, albeit one which had achieved exceptional influence over its neighbour.*
>
> *'Indeed Gewissae, should it mean something akin to 'the strong ones', sounds like just the sort of name a band of young mercenaries, newly settled, politically embryonic and tactically vulnerable, might give themselves.'*

The origins of the Gewisse are disputed, and they may have British roots based on a series of admittedly vague but interesting references.

Geoffrey of Monmouth connects the group to four different individuals, including a legendary fourth-century figure from Welsh tradition, Eudaf Hen, who revolts against his brother Constantine's government and wins a major battle outside Winchester against Roman legions. In the account, Eudaf is called a duke of the Gewessei and named Octavius. This name is a Latinized corruption of the Old Welsh/Breton *Outham*, which later became Eudaf.

The wizard Merlin is described as in the 'territory of the Gewisse' at the Galabes Spring, which has been linked to Gwent.

Seventh-century ruler Cadwallader, hailed the last king of the Britons, has a grandmother credited as being from the 'noble family of the Gewissei' according to Monmouth. This could be a product of Monmouth conflating the story of Cadwallader with a near contemporary Wessex king called Caedwalla. It has been suggested Cadwallader was in fact the grandfather of Caedwalla via a daughter who married his father Cenberht, which could be within reason given marriages between Welsh and Anglo-Saxon royal dynasties during the seventh century.[15]

Another ruler, Arvirargus, from the first century is said to have married a Gewissa, the daughter of Emperor Claudius. The infamous Vortigern, the post-Roman ruler who invited the confederates, was also listed as the 'Duke Gewissorum', the same title later held by Cerdic. According to Nennius' *Historia Brittonum*, Vortigern, who he refers to as Guothirgirn, 'came to the northern zone with his wizards and arrived at the region that is called Guennesi and built a city there that is called Cair Guorthigirn after his own name.'

Caerleon in modern-day Newport in Gwent was the home of a Roman legion, Legio II Augusta, which was stationed there between 75 and 300.[16] The II Augusta would often deploy detachments to other parts of Britain, including Hadrian's Wall and as the governor's staff in Londinium.

Some writers have tied the Gewisse, and the unidentified Guenessi, to the Gwent region, where its legendary founder, Caradoc Vreichvras, has been associated with Cerdic. The Welsh names for Gwent are both 'Gwennwys' and 'Gwenhwys' and the people are called Gwynsson, which has led to a theory that 'Gewisse' equals the 'men of Gwent'.

Linguistic expert Richard Coates, an emeritus professor of Onomastics at the UWE in Bristol, begs to differ on this association because he believes the Old English version of Gwenhwys would 'yield something like *Wintis(s)*' rather than Gewis.[17] While agreeing both Cerdic and Ceawlin could not be derived from Old English and are most likely Brittonic, Coates believes the 'Gewisse' is the 'normalisation of an Old English adjective' meaning 'reliable' or 'sure' as commonly suspected and no 'recourse to Welsh is required to explain it'. In a paper, he wrote:

> *'If the first West-Saxon warbands referred to in the chronicle were indeed led by Britons or by men of part-British descent, as has been suggested not un-controversially by numerous scholars over the last fifty years, it would be small wonder if the English had chosen to distinguish good Britons in this way.'*[18]

Searches for any reference to 'Gewis', 'Gewiss', 'Guenessi' or even 'Gewisse' in historic environment records for Wales failed to produce any results.

An expert on the ancestry records of kingdoms in Wales has also dismissed the link. Dr Ben Guy, a researcher at Cardiff University who compiled the comprehensive Medieval Welsh Genealogy in 2020, said:

> *'The Gewisse/Gwent connection is certainly bogus – that idea came about because of the medieval Welsh translations of Geoffrey of Monmouth, which took his Gewisse to be Ewias in south-east Wales just because of the similarity of the names. The G at the start of "Gewisse" is pronounced like "Y".'*[19]

If the association between the Gewisse and Gwent linguistically is dubious, it is interesting to note Coates considers the name of the Hwicce tribe based in modern Gloucestershire to stem from the Welsh word *gwych* and mean something along the lines of the 'most excellent ones'.[20] This mirrors a suggested title for the Gewisse as the 'reliable ones' or the 'trusted ones'. The similarities between the Hwicce, which appears in record after the Gewisse captured the Gloucestershire region, are clear to see.

Moreover, both the Gewisse and Hwicce could fit a pattern of naming among other Iron Age British tribal names, such as Ancalites 'the very hard ones', Catuvellauni 'the battle-excellent ones' or Brigantes 'the high ones'. The name of the Belgae who inhabited Hampshire, which was the heart of Cerdic's kingdom, is thought to mean 'the proud ones'.[21]

A biography of Alfred the Great by the Welsh monk Asser composed during his lifetime in the ninth century suggests the Gewisse title has a British origin as he describes how a 'Gewis' was the great-grandfather of Cerdic but adds immediately afterwards 'from whom the Welsh name all that people Gewis'. With the term 'Welsh' interchangeable with 'Briton' and applied to all Brittonic first-language speakers, it seems strange for Asser to make this distinction in the genealogy for the famed Anglo-Saxon king.

The Gewisse appear to have been important in late-Roman times, possibly as a home civilian force raised in response to the Great Barbarian Conspiracy, which as Clarke suggested may have been stationed at Winchester. Mercenaries were attached to this civilian militia, which evolved into a warband offering protection in Hampshire for residents in the fifth century and earned the moniker of 'the reliable or trusted ones', i.e. Gewisse, mimicking British tribal names as a force that included English-speaking warriors who could be relied upon.

Just as Bede stated, this was the name for this post-Roman warband that emerged in the ashes of Rome. The name stuck until the collective term of West Saxons was born in the later-seventh century, when new regional identities emerged and the kingdom now included Hampshire and the Upper Thames.

Research has shown a gradual shift to an Anglo-Saxon inspired culture in the Upper Thames region, mirroring large parts of eastern England. A large post-Roman cemetery was discovered during quarrying at Queenford Farm near Dorchester-on-Thames in the 1970s.[22] More than 2,000 people may have been buried here, but without grave goods and in nailed coffins, which is more typical of Roman burial practices. Based on radiocarbon studies, the cemetery was in use between the fourth to mid-sixth century, when Cerdic died, and could have served a population of between 200 to 300 people.

Unlike neighbouring cemeteries, Queenford Farm contained a high number of infant burials as a third of the eighty-two excavated in 1981 were children, while twenty-nine of the people laid to rest had skull abnormalities, which can be a marker for disease. Almost every individual over the age of 30 examined displayed signs of osteoarthritis, a form of arthritis causing bones and joints to stiffen, reflecting the intensive manual demands of life. Men at Queenford Farm lived longer than women, but evidence showed they were more likely to suffer fractures and other traumatic injuries.

The site went out of use in the sixth century as the Roman-style administration 'altered and decayed'. Burials then took place within Dorchester-on-Thames at a new burial ground, where a mortuary chapel was turned into a church in the seventh century by St Birinus, the first Bishop of Dorchester. During the fifth century, another cemetery emerged in nearby Berinsfield, which is thought to have contained more than 100 graves and appeared to reflect the more distinctive early Anglo-Saxon culture.

However, a study has shown those buried at Queenford and Berinsfield have very similar teeth, with eleven epigenetic traits, which are little ridges, wrinkles and cusps that are genetically determined, present at nearly the same rate in each cemetery, meaning the people must be related.[23] Scholar Robyn Fleming, in *Britain After Rome, the Rise and Fall*, speculates it appears 'culture rather than population had shifted' and the 'descendants' of people buried at Queenford Farm were now being laid to rest at Berinsfield and using the 'seductive rites and material culture' of their immigrant neighbours. Tests on a sample of tooth enamel from nineteen individuals found just one person was securely confirmed as a 'continental immigrant'.[24]

The 'Origins of Wessex' study analyzed 784 archaeological finds from across nearly 250 parishes in the Upper Thames covering the period from 400 to 750. Researchers discovered most finds along the River Thames, and a 'major concentration of Frankish imports' via Kent from the kingdom of the Franks in modern-day France. However, large parts of the Upper Thames during the fifth and sixth centuries 'produced little or no evidence of early Anglo-Saxon occupation despite having yielded numerous metal-detector finds from earlier and later periods'.

A cluster of post-Roman Anglo-Saxon cemeteries were found in the Abingdon and Dorchester area but none at Brighthampton or between the Evenlode and Windrush, which the study said 'represent enclaves where native forms of settlement and burial persisted into the post-Roman period'.

How much communities took up the culture of migrants depended on the extent their economy and social networks were 'disrupted by the collapse of Roman authority', the report added. Dr Härke notes: 'There is widespread agreement that this situation reflects an early, possibly peaceful settlement of Saxons in Wessex, followed by the conquest by an ethnically mixed warband whose leaders and their descendants had British-sounding names [Cerdic, Cynric, Cædwalla] even though they were later called "West Saxons"'.[25]

Cerdic's power appeared to grow from a militia force in Winchester offering protection to local inhabitants in the post-Roman years and with a taxing administration in the then largely deserted town. At the time of his death, however, Cerdic's kingdom appears to be equivalent to roughly the area of Hampshire, but it is unlikely to have extended to the Upper Thames, 60 miles away from Winchester, during the turbulent years of the foederati rebellion, extreme weather and subsequent plague.

Foederati in Dorchester in late-Roman times would have most probably at first been associated with an authority in Silchester, around 20 miles away and known as Calleva Atrebatum in Roman times, but gradually became independent and possibly in direct conflict as the old Roman Road between the two towns completely fell out of use, and there is evidence of extensive earthworks outside Silchester facing in the direction of the Upper Thames.[26]

The merger with the Upper Thames and Hampshire appears to have occurred during the chaotic reign of Ceawlin, who was recorded as Cerdic's grandson. He was described as the second Bretwalda; a mysterious but extremely powerful title widely believed to signify overlordship of all Anglo-Saxon kingdoms south of the River Humber. This would represent a dramatic expansion from a kingdom confined to Hampshire during the decade of the extreme weather and plague, and possibly including parts of Wiltshire following victories under Cerdic's son Cynric. The merger with or takeover of the Upper Thames in the late-sixth century was crucial.

Gewisse prince Cuthwulf first captured four settlements in Oxfordshire, Buckinghamshire and Bedfordshire, which were part of the former Catuvellauni civitas on the northern side of the Upper Thames. Then Ceawlin and his son Cuthwine seized Gloucester, Cirencester and Bath, which were associated with the former Dobunni civitas. One by one, Ceawlin and Gewisse rulers appeared to be conquering territories based on neighbouring former Roman civitas during warfare in the late-sixth century.

As the dust settled following the plague that devastated communities and cleared post-Roman strongholds, culturally Anglo-Saxon kingdoms were replacing the old order, led by the conquests of Ceawlin, who cemented an alliance with the Upper Thames, or after a takeover through force by intermarriage with tribal leaders. Based on a text from Alfred's biographer Asser, as discussed in the previous chapter, Cerdic's bride had Jutish-Goth ancestry, which means the Gewisse ruling elite already had mixed heritage. The post-Roman authority (led by Cerdic's successors such as Ceawlin) survived by further 'reinventing themselves', just as Iron Age tribes had done centuries earlier by becoming Roman through intermarriage with the immigrants, and Dorchester was the 'most likely setting' for such relationships, according to the 'Origins of Wessex' study.

This seems to have had consequences by creating competing royal factions aligned to either Ceawlin and his nephew Ceol (also called Ceolric), which played out at Woden's Barrow (Adam's Grave) in Wiltshire just a few miles from the East Wansdyke when Ceawlin was driven out after 'great slaughter'. In what sounded suspiciously like a coup, Ceawlin along with Crida and Cwichelm are recorded as dying a year later and Ceol ascended the throne. As outlined in Chapter 4, this must relate to the mysterious Creoda, the 'Crida' from 593, who was mentioned as the son of Cerdic in all but one version of the West Saxon Genealogical Regnal List but seemingly all but erased from the official annals. The reason was likely his apparent role in founding Mercia, where thirteen place names are associated with Creoda in the neighbouring kingdom, including a 'Creoda's Hill' next to Adam's Grave.[27]

The former Dobunni civitas that Ceawlin won was then taken over by the Hwicce, which as a Germanic word where the *hw* could be substituted for a *gw* shares obvious likeness with the Gewisse. By this stage, the kingdom had grown beyond all proportions. Wessex was most likely divided into several sub-kingdoms, ruled by princes or local lords now paying tribute.

The prince Cuthwine, son of Ceawlin, seems linked to Oxfordshire and Buckinghamshire. The Upper Thames became a base for rulers with magnificent halls filled with warriors to combat the growing power of Mercia on the other side of the river, which would become the great rival of Wessex.

In the late-sixth century, settlements with large timber Heorot-style buildings and following Germanic traditions had emerged at Long Wittenham and Sutton Courtenay and possibly, judging from an excavation, at nearby Benson in Oxfordshire.[28]

The Long Wittenham site, excavated in the 1860s by archaeologist John Akerman, revealed 194 burials, several of which included stunning weaponry and imports from northern Gaul, including a late-fifth century bronze-bound bucket or 'stoup' decorated with biblical scenes.[29] This was found in the grave of a young boy who had been buried in a tomb measuring 3ft, 8in and also included a bronze kettle and a small iron knife. The 'remarkable' large stoup was seemingly a drinker container used for holy water and featured an outer metal case stamped with Biblical iconography showing scenes in the annunciation, baptism and the marriage of Cana of Galilee.

One grave included a large set of keys lying next to a woman as these were seen as the 'insignia of the mistress of the household'. Several cremation urns were found during excavations suggesting fifth-century pagan burials. The later graves gradually became east–west in orientation, which means they had adopted Christianity and likely date to the reign of Cynegils around 630. Cynegils was the first Wessex king to be baptized, who legend has it began his mission at a cross in the village.

The site may have then spanned three generations of ten households, each with up to six people. People at Long Wittenham were of a 'large robust race', and men were generally buried with spears, knives and shields.

At Long Wittenham, three rectangular-shaped timber buildings that were identified could possibly have formed a royal Vill, the central settlement of a territory, similar in scale to a nearby great hall at Sutton Courtenay, and along with Dorchester, they were all visible from a trackway connected to all three places .[30]

Hundreds of animal bones were found near the halls and buildings in the Upper Thames, including cattle, sheep, goats and pigs, which were slaughtered for the lavish feasts.

The grand architecture of both royal Vills – Long Wittenham and Sutton Courtenay – matched the complex in Yeavering in Northumberland as part of a desire to 'emulate other kingdoms'. One of the main buildings at Sutton Courtenay, known as Building 500 and described in the 'Origins of Wessex' study as the 'largest Anglo-Saxon great hall ever found', bore a striking resemblance to the halls at Yeavering and Cowdery's Down in its main layout and use of external timber. According to the study:

> *'At all such places, social cohesion appears to have been fostered by a range of communal activities centred on a great hall complex, including feasting, the giving (and probably the manufacture) of precious gifts, and the burial of the dead. In short, great hall complexes such as the one investigated at Sutton Courtenay both expressed and helped shape the more hierarchical society that was emerging in Britain in the later sixth and seventh centuries.'*[31]

Cowdery's Down in Hampshire, which is near a junction of five Roman roads and just 7 miles from Silchester, also featured a massive Heorot-style hall and spectacular courtyard.[32] Excavations at Cowdery's Down have revealed Bronze Age burials, an Iron Age farmstead and then a new complex in the sixth century that featured three wooden structures and a main hall, which can be dated to Cerdic's reign and around the time Silchester was most likely abandoned during the plague.[33]

This grew into a 'high status site' in the seventh century with six timber structures, including three halls each with large enclosures and one of the halls, which featured a central doorway, was roughly 72ft long and just under 29ft wide. These grand buildings were arranged in a perpendicular manner to create a central courtyard, which may have hosted ritual displays on a par with the performances seen at the legendary Anglian complex at Yeavering in the emerging Northumberland kingdom.[34]

Cowdery's Down was then part of several great mead hall settlements in the rapidly expanding kingdom of Wessex, which were headed by kings or princes and subordinate lords who paid tribute. Mead halls staged magnificent banquets, where rulers proudly displayed their authority, honoured ancestors, celebrated triumphs and kept the men fed and entertained. This was real life Beowulf and the masses were lapping it up.

One fascinating link I've found in researching this period, however, is the similarities between the great hall communities of Upper Thames and the post-Roman ones in Birdoswald, South Cadbury and Wroxeter. Surely the premise was not too dissimilar, a powerful warband centred around large halls protecting the locals who paid them in kind with food and supplies they grew and sourced themselves.

Some of the Anglo-Saxon mead halls have the same rough proportions (length to width) as many rectangular Romano-British buildings but have been built of timber and wattle rather than stone.[35] It has been suggested these structures were an Anglo-Saxon adaptation of British wooden halls, which sprung up amid economic constraints after the collapse of the western empire. Long and rectangular timber buildings found across Anglo-Saxon England contained both continental and British traditions.[36] Rather than a new imported invention from the North Sea, although one clearly shared by the Beowulf tribes, the Upper Thames settlements appear more an evolution of the post-Roman communities in old Iron Age hill forts or former garrisons; a grand reflection of culture and ideas merging in central and eastern England.

In the same vein as how the warriors of Beowulf became heroes for Germanic people and appear based on real life individuals and events, despite the obvious blend of myths and folklore, a legendary account developed of post-Roman Britain, with several characters possessing very similar names to Cerdic at the forefront.

As simply the most confusing aspect of this story, I've left this part to the near end. These tales have Cerdic at war with King Arthur in battles that featured armies of thousands of men. They inspired a fascinating theory on Cerdic's identity, which changes everything we know. For this Cerdic was a Welsh king and a famous knight, who sat at the iconic Round Table alongside Arthur himself.

Chapter 12

Monmouth, Caradoc and Arthur

> *Bright were the castle buildings, many the bathing-halls, high the abundance of gables, great the noise of the multitude, many a mead hall full of festivity, until fate the mighty changed that. Far and wide the slain perished, days of pestilence came, death took all the brave men away; their places of war became deserted places, the city decayed. The rebuilders perished, the armies to earth. And so these buildings grow desolate, and this red-curved roof parts from its tiles of the ceiling-vault. The ruin has fallen to the ground broken into mounds, where at one time many a warrior, joyous and ornamented with gold-bright splendour, proud and flushed with wine shone in war-trappings; looked at treasure, at silver, at precious stones, at wealth, at prosperity, at jewellery, at this bright castle of a broad kingdom.*
>
> The Ruin, author unknown, eighth century

The Ruin, one of the most famous poems of the Anglo-Saxon age, recalls a forgotten past now only visible by decaying buildings. Words are tinged with sadness at how yesteryear's splendour has fallen into disrepair. Vibrancy has been replaced by decay. A thriving society has long since departed. Warriors adorned in gold, mead halls packed to the brim and trappings of prosperity are juxtaposed with the present decline. Ruin follows a pestilence almost certainly linked to the devastating Justinian Plague, which killed millions across the world in the mid-sixth century and another outbreak around 120 years later in 664. Towns were stripped of their inhabitants and their once mighty structures left to rot. The inevitability of time and new generations prevails throughout:

> *'This masonry is wondrous; fates broke it, courtyard pavements were smashed; the work of giants is decaying. Roofs are fallen, ruinous towers, the frosty gate with frost on cement is*

> *ravaged, chipped roofs are torn, fallen, undermined by old age. The grasp of the earth possesses the mighty builders, perished and fallen, the hard grasp of earth, until a hundred generations of people have departed.'*

The eighth-century poem evocatively describes the once prosperous Roman town of Bath (Aquae Salis), referencing the 'hot springs' and 'bathing halls'. Its baths remain one of the most spectacular remnants of Roman Britain with its rooftop walkway lined with statues of great emperors, above the massive pool enclosed by grand pillars. Amid the monuments to Rome's

In Bath, statues of Roman emperors line the roof of the iconic Roman baths

military conquests, the former inhabitants seemed to have more mundane concerns. Around 130 curse tablets have been found in the pools, which are the personal prayers of civilians in the form of inscriptions on small sheets of lead and pewter.[1] They were deliberately thrown into the hot springs as a request to Sulis Minerva to get payback on fellow civilians for often petty disputes or crimes: some as trivial as an item of clothing being stolen from outside their house.[2]

According to tales that emerged in the twelfth century, post-Roman Britain was a land of knights, glistening swords, shiny armour, roundtables, warrior tribes and armies of 60,000 men in fleets of 600 invasion ships.

The baths fell into disrepair after the Roman empire abandoned Britain, but it remains a world-famous tourist site

Historians have long sought to work out which accounts and characters were real, muddled up or fictional altogether.

There is an alternative Cerdic who warred against Arthur and was described as a Welsh king, which can be traced to Geoffrey of Monmouth's infamous work *Historia regum Britanniae* (History of the Kings of Britain). Monmouth's British history created the Arthurian legend, but there were doubts about its accuracy around sixty years after it was published. Writing in 1190, one historian, William of Newburgh, said of Monmouth: 'It is quite clear that everything this man wrote about Arthur and his successors, or indeed about his predecessors from Vortigern onwards, was made up, partly by himself and partly by others.'[3]

In his works, Monmouth insisted he had translated a 'very ancient book in the British language that told in orderly fashion the deeds of all the kings of Britain', given to him by Walter, Archdeacon of Oxford, which has never been identified and has become something of a 'holy grail' in British history. William of Newburgh was not having any of it. He was adamant the 'very ancient book' never existed, and Monmouth's account was 'a fiction, promulgated either through an unchecked propensity to falsehood, or a desire to please the Britons'.

While it would seem implausible Monmouth would lie about the book from someone as high profile as the Archdeacon, perhaps William was onto something regarding another motive for the Welsh monk who was possibly a canon of the secular College of St George in Oxford. After all, his patron was Robert of Gloucester, then England's most powerful lord, who was the half-brother of Matilda. As the daughter of Henry, Matilda was the rightful heir to the throne but lost out on becoming the monarch to her brother Stephen.

British history was transformed as Monmouth wrote how Arthur had defeated the Saxons and the Roman Empire affording the ruling Norman dynasty. This was a classical origin myth to match counterparts in Europe, which created perhaps one of the most enduring literary tales in the western world. Such was the clamour for the Latin chronicle, it was disseminated throughout Europe and translated into Middle English and around 215 manuscripts still survive.

Between 1160 and 1180, Chretien de Troyes wrote four long Arthurian romances, which introduced the knights of the round table, Camelot and the quest for the holy grail, and relegated Arthur to an almost supporting role.[4]

In the significant list of kings following Arthur, Monmouth includes four of the five named by Gildas – Constantine, Aurelius Conanus, Vortiporious,

Malgo (Maelgwn) – and then a Keredic, who must have ruled after 547 when Welsh annals record Maelgwn dying from a 'great mortality'. This Keredic could well be based on Cerdic as they ruled around a very similar time, both seemingly employed Saxon mercenaries and fought against the Britons. Monmouth says:

> *'After Maglo, succeeded Keredic, a fomenter of civil discords, hateful to God and to the Britons also. When the Saxons came to understand his fickleness, they sent to Hibernia for Gormundus, the King of the Affricani, who had gone there with an enormous fleet and conquered the people of that country.*
>
> *'As a result of this treachery by the Saxons, Gormundus accompanied by a hundred and sixty thousand Affricani, came over to Britain which between them, the Saxons and the local inhabitants were completely devastating, the former by breaking their oath of fealty, the latter by continually waging civil wars among themselves.'*

So, was there any truth to these events? Dr Miles Russell, who carried out a massive academic study of Monmouth's texts, outlined in his *Arthur and the Kings of Britain* book, explained the Affricani as a tribe known as the Attacotti, which emerged from Ireland and is derived from a term meaning the 'old ones' or 'oldest first inhabitants'.[5] They were first documented in the late-fourth century as part of the infamous Great Barbarian Conspiracy in 367, when tribes joined together and rampaged through the island for more than a year until a Roman relief force sent them packing.

German scholar Rudolf Zenker suggests the 'Gormundus' is ninth-century Viking leader Guthrum, known as 'Gormund' to the English, who was defeated by Alfred the Great, but who had been based with his army in Ireland before invading.[6]

The African origin could be a mistaken misreading of Welsh and Irish descriptions of Vikings as 'black pagans', according to another historian Edwin Pace.

Continuing the tale, Monmouth details how Gormundus made a treaty with the Saxons and drove Keredic to modern-day Cirencester, where he was besieged and eventually captured, with the former second biggest Roman town burned.

'Gormundus then fought Keredic and chased him over the Severn into Wales.

'Next he ravaged the fields, set fire to all the neighbouring cities and gave free vent to his fury until he had burnt almost all the land in the island, from one sea to another. All the settlements were smashed to the ground with a great force of battering rams. All the inhabitants were destroyed by flashing swords and crackling flames and the priests of their church along with them. Those left alive fled, shattered by these dreadful disasters but wherever they went, no havens to safety remained open to them in their flight.'

Accepting Monmouth's version would contradict other evidence but closely mirrors the one provided by Gildas. The reference to 'from one sea to another' has parallels with the infamous Groan of the Britons (below), documented by Gildas, which was a request to the Roman general Aetius for military assistance around 447 in the face of attacks from barbarians. It states: 'The barbarians drive us to the sea, the sea drives us to the barbarians; between these two means of death, we are either killed or drowned.' The terror of 'flashing swords and crackling flames' and of 'all settlements were destroyed' again has parallels with Gildas who remarked:

'For the fire of vengeance, justly kindled by former crimes, spread from sea to sea, fed by the hands of our foes in the east, and did not cease, until, destroying the neighbouring towns and lands, it reached the other side of the island, and dipped its red and savage tongue in the western ocean.'

The idea of Cerdic being in Cirencester is questionable because it was captured several decades later by his grandson Ceawlin, so it seems unlikely the Gewisse king would have been harboured by rivals and even more so that he was pursued by a warring tribe from Ireland.

An explanation can be found in Ceretic from the Yorkshire kingdom of Elmet, who was labelled by Bede as a 'king of the Britons' and is recorded as having died around 616 in the Annales Cambriae, after being driven from his kingdom by Edwin of Deira when he returned to power.

Keredic of Monmouth's world is a conflation of the Elmet and Wessex kings, Gildas' account and barbarian raids two centuries before either reigned.

A narrative comprising and blending fiction, legend and composite characters prevails throughout Monmouth's work, according to Dr Russell, who concluded the *History of the Kings of Britain* had been based on the orally transmitted tales of the pre-Roman Catuvellauni and the Trinovantes tribes, who ruled in the south-east, and the king-lists of post-Roman dynasties in western territories.

In effect, Monmouth created a 'single grand narrative' from a source of folklore, chronicles, king-lists, dynastic tables, oral tales and bardic praise poems of which many had been 'corrupted or garbled with the original meaning lost', according to Dr Russell: 'In doing so he hijacked certain characters and stories from different time periods, rearranging them in such a way that they created a continuous chronology, a line of monarchs stretching from prehistory to the seventh century AD.'[7]

According to Russell, the character of Arthur never existed and his story was inspired by the wars of the Roman emperors Constantine, Magnus Maximus, Togidubnus, Mandrubracius and Cassivellaunus. Even his famous victory at Badon should be attributed to Ambrosius Aurelianus based on analysis of an original tenth-century manuscript of Gildas' sermon, which has no divisions or headings: 'Arthur is the ultimate composite character, inhabiting a world where everything that happens to him has already happened to other people, there is nothing in his story that is truly original.'

Dr Russell was, however, at pains to stress that Monmouth had included 'demonstrable fact' and that everything he wrote at its core stemmed from a historical person or events but had been thrown together to create one sweeping version of British history.

One historian, Rupert Matthews, believes scholars are too quick to dismiss Monmouth. He discovered during research into King Lud, who legend says founded London, how Monmouth correctly lists the names and chronological order of the pre-Roman rulers of the Catuvellauni despite the fact:

> *'they are not named in any written source anywhere – we know about them from 20th century study of coins found in archaeological digs and the stratification of the finds.*

> *'So how did Geoffrey get them so correct? Obviously, he had a written source that has since been lost. What else about early British history was in that source? What else did Geoffrey get correct, but that we cannot corroborate?'*[8]

Three other leaders with very similar names to Cerdic – Cherdich and two named Cheldric – are also prominent in Monmouth's account. They all arrived with huge invasion forces with Saxon soldiers in the confederate war of the fifth century.

The first 'Cherdich' and the sons of Hengist (who supposedly founded Kent) – Octa and Ebissa – are said to have brought thousands of soldiers to aid the British ruler Vortigern, but this is almost certainly linked to the *Historia Brittonum* (attributed to Nennius) and written about 300 years earlier, around 828, which describes how a Ceretic is an 'interpreter' of Hengest.

Then a 'Cheldric' campaigns against Arthur with a fleet of 600 ships but is killed in a later clash involving Cador, the Duke of Cornwall.

It is also thought that Cheldric relates to the near contemporary Frankish king, Childeric, allied with a Riothamus, who was described as a 'king of the Britons' and brought 12,000 men to battle against the Goths.[9]

This could mean Monmouth drew this tale from a real account but turned Childeric into an enemy rather than an ally because he was a Germanic ruler.

Riothamus, which means 'great king', has been associated with Arthur and Ambrosius, but there's confusion over whether he ruled in Britain or Armorica in France, where large numbers of Britons settled in the fifth and sixth centuries.

A third similarly named character 'Cheldric' in Monmouth's history, now backing Arthur's rebellious nephew Mordred, dies alongside 'Elasius' in a list of fallen combatants after being killed in the Battle of Camlann.

While Cerdic had never been named as an opponent of Arthur before Monmouth, the 'Elasius' is an intriguing reference. It is presumably based on an individual named Elafius, described as a 'leader of the region', who met Germanus of Auxerre during his second visit to Britain in the 440s. The later trip has been considered a possible duplicate of his first visit in 429 to combat a Christian theological position known as Pelagianism.

There was no other link between Cerdic and the individual who met Germanus, and whether Monmouth is seemingly implying one or it is just a pure coincidence remains open to debate. Could Monmouth, as Matthews suggested, have been privy to now lost sources of British history?

Some writers have claimed Elafius is a Latinized version of Elesa or Elsa, listed as Cerdic's father and grandfather respectively in the *Anglo-Saxon Chronicle*, and Cerdic has been identified as the Welsh king, Caradoc, whose father is known as Eliavres in Arthurian legend, another possible derivation of Elafius.

Historian Andrew Breeze outlined how academic analysis found the name of Elafius is from the Greek word *elaphos* meaning 'deer', which indicates a 'degree of Romanisation and classical culture' and his role was equivalent to a late senior empire official instead of a local chieftain.[10] Such a name was 'rare even in the classical world' and suggestive of a link with southern Europe, Breeze argued.

Linguistic expert Dr Richard Coates, an emeritus professor of onomastics at the UWE in Bristol, said the association between Elafius with the Elesa and Elsa from the chronicle is problematic: 'A reduction to the English names looks too brutal and involves stress-shifting leading to the loss of the original stressed vowel, in the case of Elsa.'[11] He added the Old English version of Elafius could be something along the lines of 'Elef' if it arrived via Brittonic, while its Norman French dialect form 'Eliavres' is the name from Arthurian legend, which adds to the confusion.

A connection may stem from the writings of Monmouth, which inspired the later French Arthurian tales; however, it is not completely beyond the realms of possibility that the Elafius from the fifth century was an ancestor of Cerdic.

Elafius, who brought the 'whole province' along and whose crippled son was miraculously cured by Germanus, has been tied to the southeast and possibly St Albans, where Germanus visited the shrine of the martyr.

If the second Germanus visit to Britain is accurate it would place Elafius in the mid-fifth century and suggest he was an ally of Vortigern, who welcomed the barbarian foederati before their later rebellion.

Jutish tribes on the Isle of Wight arrived in the late-fifth century and retained close cultural ties with the Jutes in Kent, who are seen as the first confederates. Foederati were stationed at Thanet and the Isle of Wight, where the Saxon Shore forts of Richborough and Portchester guarded the eastern and western maritime approaches to Britain.[12]

The climactic Battle of Badon is likely to have pitted Ambrosius or Arthur against forces from Kent and Sussex led by Aelle, Bede's first

Bretwalda (wide ruler), as the two kingdoms largely disappear from sixth-century chronicle records. Badon was a crushing defeat, but rulers of Kent and Sussex retained a foothold on the east coast. The last entry for Aelle is 491 when his forces attacked the fort of Pevensey and are said to have 'killed every last man' just a few years before the date most scholars traditionally associate with Badon.

The inference of the references in Monmouth to a character named similar to Cerdic aligned with the foederati or his kingdom hosting the foederati in the fifth century appears accurate. Such arrangements were widespread throughout the western Roman empire, as barbarians were given land in return for providing security and manpower in conflict. Mirroring the situation, which sped up Rome's decline from the mid-fourth century, many confederate tribes in Britain rebelled and turned on their paymasters.

Ancestors of Cerdic headed a post-Roman authority in the southeast, but the throwaway line from Monmouth is the only grounds to assume one of these rulers may have been Elafius. His powers may have extended to a much larger area in the immediate aftermath of Rome, possibly the Britannia Prima province, covering south of modern England beyond London given

Aelle of Sussex overran and killed every man at Pevensey Castle, which was once a huge Roman fort (Paul Harper/English Heritage)

the term 'province', but which fractured into territories based on ancient tribal divisions and former Roman civitas by the sixth century.

Cerdic's father alternatively could have been some unidentified post-Roman ruler, whose name Elsa or Elesa featured on the ninth-century Pillar of Eliseg (Elise's Pillar), which was erected in Denbighshire, Wales, by Cyngen ap Cadell in honour of his great-grandfather Elisedd ap Gwylog. Welsh ancestry records show ten different 'Elise' kings, princes and saints from the medieval period, showing its popularity among the ruling class.[13]

There is a consensus that many stories from Arthurian legend are based on historical individuals and traditions. For example, the act of Arthur's Excalibur sword being thrown into a lake is based on Iron Age rituals in which springs, marshes and lakes were seen as a gateway to the other world, between the living and the dead. Hundreds of metal objects including swords have been uncovered from lakes and rivers in Britain and across Europe, which are thought to have been ritual offerings to the gods.[14] Of the 2,500 Bronze Age swords discovered in Britain and Ireland over the past 150 years, the majority have been dredged out of major rivers.[15]

In turn, the Caradoc from Arthurian legend has been identified as Caradoc or Carados Vreichvras, a semi-legendary king, who founded the kingdom of Gwent and is also known as Caradog Friechfras and Cardadoc so Ynwr. The real Caradog is thought to have founded Gwent in the early-sixth century and was based at Caerwent, an important Roman town which was the home of the pre-Roman Silures tribe.

Tradition states Caradog gave the town to Saint Tathyw, who founded a monastery at Caerwent, and relocated his base to a hillfort at Portskewett.[16] Another theory places his new home in Caldicot, a market town near the Severn between Chepstow and Newport. This does appear to be a genuine historical event, with the modern-day Church of St Stephen and St Tathan in Caerwent earmarked as the location of the monastery where a large early medieval cemetery was discovered.[17]

Caradoc is a Latinized version of the name Caratacus, a famous king who resisted the Roman invasion and aligned with the Silures. Fourteen Caradogs and Caradocs and a further eight individuals named Ceredig can be found in Welsh medieval history, many of whom are tied to the same fifth- and sixth-century periods.[18] Winchester's Old Welsh name is believed to be 'Caer Guent', which is similar to the modern Caerwent and could explain how these two kings were seemingly mixed up.

The association between Cerdic and Caradoc rests solely on an ancient Welsh genealogy list involving the seventh-century monk Saint Collen, who gave his name to Llangollen in Denbighshire in Wales and in the tale *Buchedd Collin* (*Life of Saint Collin*) visited many foreign lands and became Abbot of Glastonbury. Some writers believe Saint Collen is Cerdic's grandson, Ceawlin, based on his ancestry in the *Lives of the British Saints*, which was published in 1907 and is reportedly originally taken from a sixteenth-century manuscript known as the Hafod collection.[19]

One genealogy of Saint Collen in the *Lives of the British Saints* is as follows, with the Wessex kings in brackets: Kyriadoc vyraich vyras (Cerdic), Kowrda (his son Creoda), Kydeboc (son or grandson Cynric), Gwynoc, Sant Kollen (grandson Ceawlin).

Dr Ben Guy, a researcher at Cardiff University who compiled the comprehensive *Medieval Welsh Genealogy* in 2020, has poured scorn on the idea that Collen and Ceawlin are the same person as he revealed the original pedigree of Collen in the *Bonedd y Saint* in modern Welsh was 'Collen mab (son of) Padrwn mab Coleddog mab Gwyn'.[20] This was then altered in some later manuscripts of *Bonedd y Saint* surviving from the fourteenth and fifteenth century to the following: 'Collon ap (son of) Gwenog ap Coledog ap Cawrdaf ap Caradog Freichfras'. Dr Guy stated: 'These are all names and characters known from elsewhere in medieval Welsh genealogy and

King Arthur was conceived at Tintagel according to legend, where a monument has been placed in his honour (Paul Harper/English Heritage)

hagiography. I'm afraid that it's really only wishful thinking that would connect this with the Cerdicing dynasty, not least because Cerdic is not quite the same name, etymologically, as Caradog.'

Arthurian legend has become so muddled with fiction and the supernatural I was almost tempted to avoid the subject. Magical swords, monsters and sorcerers are hardly the stuff of serious historical record, but Arthur's name has, however, become synonymous with the post-Roman age. At its core, the notion there was a significant leader of this name in the early sixth century is not as far-fetched as many historians would have you believe.

Medieval Welsh literature and bardic elegies frequently referred to a person of this name. These include *Elegy for Geraint* and *Y Gododdin*, which appear near contemporary and show an 'Arthur', believed to be derived from the Welsh *arth* equalling 'bear' and *(g)wr* 'man' and resonated as a hero for sixth-century Britons.[21]

There remains the possibility both Cerdic and Arthur were active warlords in Britain around the same period, which is truly fascinating. Medieval chroniclers in addition to Monmouth pitted Arthur and Cerdic against each other in epic battles.

In the fourteenth century, the Benedictine monk John of Glastonbury wrote the *Chronicles of the Glastonbury Church*, which drew heavily on the *De Antiquitate Glastonie Ecclesie* by William of Malmesbury and tells the history of the church and draws on Arthurian legend. The author claims Cerdic and Arthur were in frequent conflict:

> *'King Arthur fought mightily against the Saxons and wore them down. He waged twelve battles against them, conquering and routing them in all twelve instances. Often he struggled with Cerdic who, if one Arthur vanquished him, rose up the next fiercer for the fight. Finally, when Arthur tired of the conflict, he accepted Cerdic's fealty and gave him Hampshire and Somerset, which Cerdic called Wessex.'*

Somerset was not fully incorporated into Wessex until the late-seventh century under King Ine, and even then, there is suggestion Wessex forces were driven out in 722 when his wife Queen Ethelburg burned down the settlement in Taunton to stop it being captured by rebels.

One academic paper put forward the remarkable suggestion that Cerdic and Arthur are the same person. Historians John C Rudmin and

Joseph W Rudmin argue[22] Cerdic is identical to Caradoc who in turn is King Arthur, a British merchant in Nantes between 450 and 495, who returned, triumphed at Badon and set up the new Gewisse-Wessex kingdom. Their Caradoc-Cerdic-Arthur would have conceivably been over 80 years old when he died, although most people failed to reach half that age in the fifth and sixth centuries.

It seems highly unlikely Cerdic would have been victorious at Badon against English-speaking warriors and have then become a hero for the Anglo-Saxons. As we've seen, the connection between Caradoc and Cerdic is based on a dubious genealogy, seemingly pulling together famed rulers from Welsh history to add prestige much in the same way the Anglo-Saxon kings were all said to descend from pagan gods.

Historian Philip Jenkins has ruled out the two mystery warriors Arthur and Cerdic being the same person: 'There are no stories connecting Cerdic and Arthur. As we know so little about Arthur and his wars, we have no idea whether the two men would have been allied or hated each other's guts.'[23]

The Hollywood blockbuster *King Arthur*, which claimed to be a more historically accurate version of the Arthurian legend and was released in 2004 starring Clive Wilson, was clear on this subject. Cerdic is Arthur's sworn enemy and depicted as a ruthless Saxon invader who along with his son Cynric leads a reign of terror across Britain In the climatic final scene at Badon Hill amidst smoke and combatants crashing together, the towering and menacing figure of Stellan Skarsgård as Cerdic confronts Arthur after slaying many of his imperious knights.

In reality, Cerdic and Arthur were unlikely to have fought, with the latter having stronger connections to modern-day Wales and the West Midlands and possibly identified as Owain Danwyn, a sixth-century ruler of Powys murdered by his nephew, Maelgwn, based on Gildas' account. This theory stems from how Owain's son Cuneglasus, another of the five kings derided by Gildas, was described by him as 'you bear' and the 'driver of a chariot belonging to a bear's den'. With Arthur known as the 'bear', as the 'Arth' is the old Welsh word for the animal, the 'bear's den' has been deemed to be the stronghold of the legendary warrior. Of all the many candidates for Arthur, which place him from Tintagel to Hadrian's Wall, this would be a more logical theory, matching the suggested timeframe and featuring Maelgwn at its heart, who was the most powerful British ruler in the land.

The character of Mordred, who became Arthur's nephew and arch nemesis, is potentially based on Maelgwn but is thought to have been an ally of Arthur who died alongside him as the Annales Cambriae records a 'Medraut' falling at Camlann. In the Welsh Triads, Medraut (Old Welsh for Mordred) is painted in a favourable light before Monmouth created the Mordred character.

It remains doubtful, therefore, Arthur crossed paths with Cerdic while fighting his own dynastic war in Wales, but the two enduring legends are ultimately connected. Given Cerdic began to reign after Arthur's death at Camlann and the generation of peace after Badon, it would suggest the Gewisse king seized an opportunity to grab power or rebelled as culturally Romano-British kingdoms in former civitas were weakened by civil warfare.

The volcanic winter, famine, Arthur's death and plague swung the balance of power in favour of Anglo-Saxon kingdoms in the sixth century. Unified resistance, which had kept the Anglo-Saxons confined to the east, gradually broke down amid civil war and environmental disasters.

Another ruler, Urien of Rheged, rose to prominence at the end of the sixth century as the head of a British coalition, which fought the Anglian kingdom of Bernicia and stood on the brink of victory until, in the same vein as Arthur, their unity collapsed amid jealousy, internal battles and betrayal.[24] As Gildas prophesied, this was his ruin of Britain.

Hundreds of years later, chroniclers harked back to this golden age – as one did so vividly and mournfully in *The Ruin* – and recalled tales of Arthur, who was immortalized as an enduring symbol of British heroism. In parallel, Cerdic was equally revered as the heroic king who defeated the Britons and paved the way for the political ascendancy of the English. Perhaps unsurprisingly, later medieval historians sought to join up these narratives with the scarcity of sources and resources we have today.

As this book has argued throughout, however, the change was in part evolutionary, circumstantial and considerably more complicated, with wars fought over territory and regional alliances as much as they were ethnicity.

Amid their present-day reality, where cultural divisions were much clearer with Welsh and English kingdoms separated by the mighty Offa's Dyke, chroniclers saw a simpler picture, which overlooked how the majority of the 'Anglo-Saxons' had descended from tribes who arrived long before the Romans.

During my research, amid trying to work out the various conflicting legends, timeframes, vague and questionable accounts, my attention shifted to an intriguing reference which could finally bring the story to life. This was something veritable and identifiable in today's landscape and the reasoning could be explained: a monument of this forgotten and mythical era, much like the ruins in Bath, surviving for centuries afterwards (thousands of these monuments have now been documented and mapped across the land).

Together with excavations and comprehensive academic research, we can begin to build a better understanding of our history and match such findings with the often confusing and vague historic sources. We can begin to shine a light on the Anglo-Saxon age as never before. In the case of Cerdic, one of the most enigmatic figures in British history, this reference could be found in a royal charter from one of his recorded descendants. It potentially reveals his final resting place.

Chapter 13

Cerdic's Barrow

The King's Charter

England will still be England, an everlasting animal stretching into the future and the past, and, like all living things, having the power to change out of recognition and yet remain the same.

'England Your England', George Orwell, 1941[1]

Britain's rich history is held in the hundreds of burial mounds known as barrows dotted across the island. These incredible earthworks remain a feature of the landscape. Many have been ploughed and deliberately destroyed, but traces of these burials can often still be seen from the sky above. The barrows were part of the surroundings for thousands of years as Bronze Age peoples to the Anglo-Saxons buried their loved ones, tribal leaders and kings in these spectacular landmarks.

Often the deceased were laid next to treasures and sacrifices. Mounds were deliberately placed on hills and in prominent positions, so they were visible for miles around to people passing through and enemies from across borders.

According to Historic England, barrows, sometimes described as tumuli on early maps, are mounds of earth and/or stone of various shapes and sizes, which date 3800 to 1400 BC.[2] Construction of barrow mounds, however, on a lesser scale continued until the ninth century, and many feature a mix of timber, turf, rubble, small platforms and enclosures or ditched structures, and they often include stone artefacts, pottery, animal and human bone.

Various types included disc, bell, round and saucer, but the most common one was referred to as a bowl barrow. These were 'inverted pudding' mounds with slopes of varying profile, sometimes with a surrounding ditch and occasionally an outer bank. Bowl barrows varied dramatically in size from as much as 40m in diameter and 4m in height, although small versions measured just 5m or 6m across.

They have contained pottery and stone tools, animal bones, such as cow skulls, and often they were formal burial sites, where an entire skeleton was present or a cremation, which had been placed in pots.

Even barrows that have been ploughed can still be visible from above as they often form a circular vegetation or soil mark, sometimes referred to as a 'ring ditch', although not all of these shapes are the remains of barrows.

Structures under the mounds have included stone platforms, pits, stone cairns or turf mounds, mortuary timber enclosures, wooden and stone chambers, timber or stake circles, pits and post-holes, which might have formed shrine-like features.

Many barrows have been surrounded by up to three ditches, indicating the ground being cut up and reused was an important element.

There was a significant period of reusing Bronze Age barrows in the early Anglo-Saxon times between the fifth and eighth century because English-speaking kingships wanted to stake their claim to land and perhaps pay homage to previous kings and communities by reusing these barrows, which must have been stunning sights. They dug up and buried bodies or ashes in the huge mounds, which were often near existing boundaries

The burial mound on Magdalen Hill Down on the outskirts of Winchester would have resembled Cerdic's Barrow

between rival kingdoms, and there is strong evidence to suggest this is exactly what happened to Cerdic following his death.

When I first began investigating the legend of Cerdic of Wessex, there were several references to a 'Ceardices Beorg' (which translates as Cerdic's Barrow meaning a burial mound) in Stoke, Hampshire, which at first seemed an odd location for Cerdic to have been buried. The capital and heart of his kingdom was believed to have been at Winchester while the earliest elite Anglo-Saxon settlements were linked to the Upper Thames. Groups of Jutes were also documented to have settled in north-east Hampshire and on the Isle of Wight.

Stoke seemed a strange choice for the famed warrior king and one eminent twentieth-century academic, John Myres, suggested Cerdic was engaged in operations at the eastern end of the nearby mysterious Wansdyke when he met an untimely end.[3] If this was the case, where was the exact site located?

Vague references online at first led to a random spot in Stoke, which even included a geolocation placing the burial mound in Hurstbourne Tarrant. There was, however, no reasoning or explanation for why Cerdic was buried there or as to the evidence for this claim.

My search then led to another reference to 'Ceardices Beorg', which attributed a research paper by Professor Barbara Yorke, a leading modern historian on Wessex's history.

Then, I was directed to a massive online database known as Electronic Sawyer, a collection of hundreds of Anglo-Saxon charters compiled by Professor Peter Sawyer and published by the Royal Historical Society. Here, the hunt for Cerdic's potential burial spot began with a truly intriguing ancient charter rubber stamped by Alfred the Great's son.

The King's Charter

Evidence of Cerdic being laid to rest in this spot emerged in a royal charter nearly 170 years before the Battle of Hastings in 1066. This was a turbulent time in British history. While Alfred and Wessex had defeated Viking forces, the island remained divided with large parts of northern and eastern England under Danelaw, where the laws of the Danes held sway.

Andover was first mentioned officially in Old English as Andeferas in 955, which is thought to relate to the Welsh word *onn dwfr* meaning 'ash (tree) water' and shares the same prefix as Wendover, Condover and Micheldever. The 'an' element has also been linked with a Celtic word *annagh*, which means marshy or water. Around the first mention, King Edred, the grandson of Alfred the Great, is recorded as having built a royal hunting lodge in Andover.

King Edred's father, Edward the Elder, drew up a charter in AD 900 to exchange ten hides of land on the outskirts of Andover with Winchester Cathedral for land in Wiltshire.[4] The description of the charter on Electronic Sawyer, which includes Latin and English text, says it was in exchange for land at Chisledon (Chiseldon) and Sparcells.

As the children of Alfred the Great, Edward the Elder and his sister Aethelflæd, the warrior princess known as the 'Lady of the Mercians', were popular leaders who joined forces to defeat the Vikings in Northumberland and began reclaiming parts of the country under Danelaw.

The reason this Winchester Cathedral charter has gained attention among scholars is because it included an intriguing reference to a 'Ceardices Beorg', which translates as Cerdic's Barrow. As it was situated on royal land retained by kings of Wessex, it could conceivably be the burial mound of Cerdic.

This fascinating charter was analyzed by the historian George Beardoe Grundy in an academic paper in 1927 when he mapped out all the different landmarks, including those near and including Cerdic's Barrow.[5] Grundy wrote it was the predecessor for what became the manor of Hurstbourne Priors, which eventually formed St Mary Bourne parish, and he believed the ten hides encompassed a massive area of 11,000 acres, but most of the vast landscape had not been farmed or developed. The hidage, he explained, was taken for purposes of Danegeld, an annual tax paid to Vikings to stop them destroying land, and the area was mainly a 'small clearing from a forest' and 'only a fraction' of the 11,000 acres was under cultivation. Grundy translated the survey of land, including the reference to 'Ceardices Beorg', from the Old English.

This led me on something akin to a treasure hunt as I tried to identify the locality of vague but almost poetically described places such as the Willow Grove on the agricultural landscape. I spent many hours wandering around the tiny roads and fields on the outskirts of Andover in the hunt for the elusive barrow and the relevant landmarks. It was only right that the hunt for the potential final resting place of this mysterious figure in British history would prove to be as puzzling as his poorly documented but ultimately monumental reign.

Grundy's translation was as follows:

1. '*Aerest of Fwyfyrde andlang Weges to Fearn Hlince*' – 'First from the Double Ford along the Track to the Lynch where Ferns grow'
2. '*Andlang weges to Aeses (Aesees) Beorge*' – 'Along the Track to the Barrow of the Ashtree'
3. '*Thanan on ge rihte to thaere Pirigan*'– 'Then straight to the Peartree'
4. '*Thonne andlang Weges on Ceardices Beorg*' – 'Then along the Track to Cerdic's Barrow'
5. '*Thonne on Withig Grafe*' – 'Then to the Willow Grove'
6. '*Thomie on thone Weg the scyt ofer tha Die*' – 'Then to the Track which runs over the Dyke'

According to Grundy's interpretation:

> *'This last point is very clearly marked. To the north of the railway is a dyke called The Devil's Ditch. Along this dyke, and indeed on it, runs an ancient trackway. The previous three points correspond to short turns in the boundary just south of the railway. The Peartree must have been at a sharp bend in the boundary about one furlong west of Faulkner's Down Farm. At this point the boundaries of Hurstbourne Priors and St. Mary Bourne meet. Cerdic's Barrow must have been at the next bend of the boundary 1/4 mile southeast of the southern end of the Devil's Ditch. It is just possible that this may be the grave of the famous Cerdic, founder of the realm of the West Saxons.'*

This last statement alone was mouth-watering. It quickly became apparent the landscape has changed significantly and has been farmed extensively in the past 100 years, so the previous bends and corners mentioned may no longer be relevant. Unfortunately, the large barrows that he referenced have long since been destroyed, but all was not lost straight away. In the 1950s and 1960s, heritage authorities mapped the features of the landscape with aerial photography and traces or the outline of landmarks such as former Bronze Age barrows were still visible even if they had been flattened. There is now a huge open public database, where you can search for historic features, and this innocuous spot on the edge of Andover proved a treasure trove of historic landmarks.

Andover

The town of Andover was still relatively small with around 17,000 residents in the 1960s when a massive programme of house building was launched to provide homes as an overspill for people in London, and the population has since tripled.

For most of its history, Andover was known for being a hugely popular market town. It is just 3 miles from the site of the biggest medieval fair at Weyhill, dating back to the twelfth century, where as many as 100,000 sheep could be traded each day.[6] Many of the livestock had presumably been led there along the historic ancient trackway known as the Harrow Way, which ran through Weyhill and places like the commemorative Ox Drove at the edge of the Picket Piece estate.

These locations would later become key in identifying the potential site of the barrow. Despite its now thousands of new residents, Andover's market remains flourishing, and it retains a distinctly rural character, with huge tracts of ancient woodland and chalk downlands to the northeast.

Head just a few miles from the centre of Andover and you are rooted in the countryside in the Test Valley. An area of vast scenic and rural beauty, centred around the 44-mile Test River, which runs all the way to Southampton. At one stage, a short-lived canal was built through Andover in the late-eighteenth century in which timber sourced from the massive Harewood Forest just outside the town was shipped to Portsmouth dockyard.[7]

This overwhelmingly agricultural and woodland landscape bordering Andover is what makes up the land in the charter that references 'Ceardices Beorg'.

Harewood Forest, around a mile east of the land that became a focus for the barrow's location, is the second biggest woodland in Hampshire, behind the New Forest, covering roughly 8–10km^2 on largely clay soil.[8] Deep inside the forest, there is an infamous site known as 'Dead Man's Plack'. This is a nineteenth-century Grade II statue to Aethelwald, an earl of East Anglia reportedly slain in this spot by his love rival King Edgar of Wessex. According to twelfth-century chronicler William of Malmesbury the story began in 963, just over sixty years after the charter was issued.[9] He wrote how Edgar had sent his 'favourite and most trusted' earl Aethelwald to assess the worthiness of a potential bride Aelfthryth, the daughter of Ordgar, the Earl of Devon. Instantly 'smitten by her beauty', Aethelwald had married the Devonshire woman but kept the union secret from Edgar and told the king she was of 'vulgar and common appearance'. The king learned of the deception and invited Aethelwald on a hunt in Harewood Forest, where he killed him with a javelin near the site of the plaque, which was installed by Colonel William Iremonger in 1825.

However, the validity of this association has been called into question because it is thought the Iremonger family may have found reference to a 'Dudman's plot', as a person of this name lived in the area from the seventeenth century, which they connected with the legend and assumed to be where Aethelwald fell.[10] The story, however, begins to explain why the woodland around Andover was popular among the nobility of Wessex as the fringes of the current town was once part of a massive deer-hunting park.

According to research from the Department of Plant Science at the University of Oxford, deer parks were areas of rough grassland, heath and 'pasture' woodland (woodland not managed for coppicing) in which oak trees dominated.[11] The study found that with the very biggest oak trees in England, some older than 750 years and with girths of 9m and greater, more than 50 per cent are associated with known deer parks.

The existence of the hunting park is evidenced in the charter with numerous references to *hagan*, *haga* in land north of where Cerdic's Barrow was situated. This is an area of extensive woodland as the boundary heads towards Hurstbourne Tarrant. *Haga* was an Old English word to describe a type of strong boundary, typically around a woodland, and often the term for a barrier around the edge of a deer park.[12] In the later medieval period, the word 'hay', which is frequently found in place names and derived from *haga*, is thought to specifically mean an enclosed area of woodland in which deer was stored.

Hunting was a favourite pastime of royals such as Alfred the Great, who was heralded as a talented huntsman. Outlining the education for his children, Alfred said there should be two key areas of focus – literacy and 'manly arts – namely, hunting and other arts appropriate to noblemen'. It is not hard to imagine the young Edward the Elder, son of Alfred, plying his trade as a hunter in forests around Andover, and then in later life, these hunting parks served as places where administrative business was conducted. Hunting was thought to have been ideal preparation for battles, as a popular blog *A Walk in English Weather,* focused on Dartmoor and Devon, outlined in a feature.[13] One academic paper described how: 'Hunting also provided what was thought to be the best possible training in mounted warfare: how to read the country during a high-speed pursuit over varied ground, how to give orders to other riders, and how to use weapons to kill.'[14] During the hunts, a stag was selected and released onto the moor, and this is effectively where the pursuit began with the group chasing a stag on horseback with dogs. Boars could also have been hunted down.

The extent of hunting parks may have been grossly understated in the 1086 Domesday Book as royal Norman hunting grounds, such as the New Forest, were not included because it is thought there was no need to document land already in their possession.

Hunting had also been popular among wealthy Romans. Mosaic art in Roman villas often featured dramatic scenes of hunting involving the property owner, which served to emphasize their masculinity, wealth and prosperity.

The massive Worcester Hunt Mosaic[15], a 140m^2 composition, which featured several individual hunts, was found in a villa destroyed by an earthquake in the sixth century in Antioch, Turkey. This spectacular mosaic showed hunters attacking their prey with spears, and at the centre, a tunic-clad figure stood triumphantly over a dead boar with a spear in his left hand.

At the sixth-century Great Palace of Constantinople, a 20,000ft^2 mosaic, with pastoral scenes alongside animal violence, shows in part a mythical griffin creature, a bird's head on a lion's body, eating a lizard. One academic paper said the 'presence of the legendary creature' made it clear the hunt was an 'extraordinary affair, fit for a man of superior skill and strength'.[16]

Villa owners would turn their estate into a hunting park at places such as the famous Fishbourne Roman Palace in Sussex, where analysis of numerous red deer bones uncovered there suggests they were managed because they were killed during a specific age range.[17] Most were from particularly large deer, and male stags were chosen for slaughter. Some of the bones were of a fallow deer, not native to Britain, introduced after Rome's invasion in 43.[18]

Hunting animals such as deer and boar was a much-loved pastime among Roman, Anglo-Saxon and Norman nobles and kings, and it leads to the possibility Cerdic himself may have roamed the woods and countryside on the outskirts of Andover. This part of Hampshire may well have held a sentimental value for Cerdic himself as a place where he engaged in hunts, along with his descendants – Alfred the Great and Edward the Elder.

As my investigation reveals, there are several other reasons why this site was chosen. It is immediately noticeable how, along with the Harrow Way, two Roman Roads met in Andover, and there was also the Icknield Way, which must have meant frequent visitors passing through on four different ancient pathways.

Andover was known for the spectacular Danebury hill fort, around 5 miles away, which was occupied by a farming community of more than 400 people for nearly 500 years during the Iron Age in Britain.

Excavations between 1969 and 1988 by archaeologist Barry Cunliffe, an emeritus professor at Oxford University, uncovered evidence of seventy-three roundhouses, 500 rectangular buildings and thousands of deep storage pits.[19] While a massive rampart enclosed the fort, which after being extended in different phases was up to 50ft deep to the bottom of the ditch. It is believed to have been deserted around 100 BC, when there was a trend of abandoning the hill forts.

Another hill fort known as Bury Hill[20] was found closer to Andover, which has thrown up Iron Age and Roman finds, and it is once thought to have been a popular site for trading horses.

There is evidence to suggest communities using an Anglo-Saxon inspired culture in Andover when Cerdic reigned, and he was potentially buried on the edge of the town in the middle of the sixth century. Pottery and beads discovered at Foxcotte imply an Anglo-Saxon settlement, while six early Anglo-Saxon huts on the site of an Iron Age enclosure emerged at a place called Old Down Farm. Excavations found these were sunken feature buildings known as *grubenhäuser*, which were built over Iron Age pits, while one irregular building separate from the others included only Iron Age and Roman finds.[21] Archaeologists recorded 7kg of pottery of mainly egg-shaped and globular jars found at other places such as Portchester and Bishopstone in Sussex. Stamped decorations on some of the finds did not come into common use until the sixth century, which could place occupation around Cerdic's age. No human bones were discovered, and the only metal object was described as a Saxon iron spearhead. The 288 animal bones that could be identified, including domesticated animals such as sheep, cows and pigs, indicate a typical country settlement of its age.

There have been other archaeological finds in Andover dating from the post-Roman period with Anglo-Saxon cultural affinities, including a sixth-century cruciform brooch, which was found at Finkley Down near to the modern-day Loom Crescent, along with Roman axes and bone fragments.[22]

Andover along with Portchester, Winchester, around Old Sarum and the Isle of Wight (although with Jutish associations) includes the highest concentration of such Anglo-Saxon discoveries in the former Belgae civitas.[23]

A sixth-century burial ground was found at the Portway Estate in Andover, which is only a few miles from the possible site of Cerdic's Barrow.[24] The cemetery housed sixty-nine inhumation burials and fifty-seven deposits of cremated bones after being excavated by the Andover Archaeological Society between 1973 and 1975. Evidence showed fewer signs of infections and common conditions at the time, such as malignant tumours. Women also outnumbered men, and twenty of the thirty females were buried with necklaces and beads. One girl aged just 12 to 14 was buried with a particularly striking necklace of amber and coloured beads, which suggests she was of high social status. The grave also included bronze toilet instruments and a waist belt with a rectangular iron loop to hang items, and a woman aged 25–30 years old, who was possibly her mother, was found buried alongside.

Another burial site, with a sinister history, emerged during preparation for a new Aldi supermarket store around several hundred metres from Portway Estate.[25] Dated to the seventh or eighth century, this was almost certainly a successor burial site, and its discovery attracted significant media coverage because this was an execution site. In 2009, a study estimated around twenty-seven such places in England where criminals were executed in medieval times, including two in Winchester. Investigations revealed ninety-five graves, which contained some 124 individuals, while bones indicated a further thirty-five people, where a total of 97 per cent (90 out of 93) of those buried being men and 69 per cent aged under 35 years old. Many of the dead had been laid face down and there were twenty-three examples of decapitation, which emerged as the skull was either missing, had been placed in between their legs or there were cut marks to the neck, vertebrae, head or jaw. Another twenty-seven of those buried had their hands or legs bound before being placed in the burial, which in some cases was a sign of hanging. Two of the bodies showed marks of fracture to their second cervical vertebrae indicating such executions.

The dark practice of executing criminals at a designated site, sometimes for petty crimes such as theft or escaping slavery based on medieval law codes, continued until the twelfth century. Many were situated in prominent places, and it is almost certainly the case that this was deliberately situated here because it is positioned near the former old Roman Road between Old Sarum and Silchester.

As I was about to discover, Cerdic's Barrow was placed here with this famous ancient trackway and another even closer one very much in mind.

Chapter 14

Cerdic's Barrow

Land of Ancient Monuments

The hunt for Cerdic's Barrow

Firstly, I needed to avoid a common error with the locality. Sarah Gould from the Hurstbourne Tarrant Historical Society explained how 'Hurstbourne' defined by the boundaries in the charter is the modern Hurstbourne Priors not Hurstbourne Tarrant, which is a few miles further west. According to Sarah Gould, pre-conquest charters do not generally differentiate the two.

With this established, the immediate focus of Grundy's interpretation and starting reference point of this intriguing charter was Faulkner's Down Farm, which lies on the edge of Andover. This is now part of Apsley Farm owned by Henry du Val de Beaulieu, whose great-grandfather, Henry Loebl, purchased the sprawling 1,150-acre estate in 1936 from the Hurstbourne Park Estate, then owned by the Earl of Portsmouth.

Currently, Henry du Val de Beaulieu as director, with his son Edward as operations manager, runs Yelspa Limited, one of the largest anaerobic digestion plants in England, producing biogas, a combination of methane (CH_4) and carbon dioxide (CO_2) from energy crops, such as maize, rye, oats and grass. This plant uses no waste, according to Henry.[26] The feedstock is fed into biodigesters at the plant from which the biogas is extracted and separated with a membrane plant to produce two streams of gases. The methane is injected into the National Grid to heat 8,500 homes continually. The CO_2, after further processing, is supplied to the food and drinks industry. Apsley Farm's plant is now the UK's third largest production site of biomethane and accounts for 2.8 per cent of the UK's biogas.[27] Production of this vital sustainable gas only takes up a small portion of the estate and around 900 acres of the farm's 1,150 acres is arable land and given over to growing rye, barley and maize.

The land boundary from the charter heads up across Apsley Farm (formerly Faulkner's Down Farm) and then west towards the small woodland (Paul Whitewick)

Henry du Val de Beaulieu, who describes himself as 'one of the greenest men in Britain', believes the farm has a rich agricultural history, which dates to pre-Roman times. I had excitedly emailed Henry with what I thought would be a revelation that the Wessex founder may have been buried on his land, but it turns out there had been a previous search. In fact, Henry revealed his farmland estate was a treasure trove for metal detectorists who often turn up in groups of up to forty in the hunt for Roman and Iron Age finds. A medallion belonging to Henry V, who reigned in the early-fifteenth century during the Hundred Years' War against France and achieved notoriety for the famous victory at Agincourt, was found on the farm and later sold.

It quickly emerged Ordnance Survey (OS) maps and HERs make a reference to a tumulus near Faulkner Down's Farm, which is often interchangeable with 'barrow'. Could this be Cerdic's Barrow?

The HERs, overseen by Historic England, are maintained by eighty-five local authorities in England and provide a record of the archaeology and historically built environment for a given geographical location. These records are often based on aerial photography of land, which has documented historical features and landmarks such as barrows.

The record relating to the tumulus states that it is a bronze age bowl barrow some 22m in diameter and 0.5m high with a ditch, which is visible as a cropmark on air photographs from 1955 but 'no trace of a barrow is visible on the ground'.[28] Sarah Gould said the tumulus on Faulkner's

Down Farm is close to an existing parish boundary between Hurstbourne Priors and St Mary Bourne.[29] The barrow, however, appears to have been ploughed over, and this was confirmed by Henry, who said this parcel of land once housed a Roman encampment but has been farmed for years.

When visiting the area of the tumulus, there is certainly nothing visible besides what appears to be a slightly raised bank extending for some 20m. The spot is on the corner of a large field with a small wood cutting nearby, and while nothing can be witnessed in the modern day, a reference by Grundy becomes significant and can be related to this location.

Sarah Gould cast doubt on the interpretation by Grundy because the Saxon boundaries in the charter may have changed significantly and believes 'Ceardices Beorg' may be further west of Faulkner Down's Farm. She explained the modern boundary appears to change from the ancient one west of the farm to a dead straight line up until the Devil's Ditch so the Ordnance Survey boundaries marked by Grundy 'very probably don't correspond to Saxon ones exactly' and his comments on Cerdic's Barrow 'can only be conjectural.'

David Hopkins, a county archaeologist for Hampshire County Council, also agreed the interpretation by Grundy may have been based on boundaries that have altered significantly.

> *'Looking at Grundy's reasoning for locating the barrow where he did is dependent on the parish boundary as depicted not having changed with time. It is possible that the boundaries were subject to some change at the time they were surveyed (last few hundred years), so counting elbows and corners might be misleading.'*[30]

Candidates for Cerdic's Barrow

Remarkably, there were several other candidates in such a relatively condensed corner of farmland. In returning to the HERs maps, the database reveals three other barrows to the west of Faulkner's Down Farm, which were still visible from the air during the twentieth century and could just be the elusive barrow.

One is identified as the 'barrow of the Ash Tree', placed before Cerdic's Barrow in the charter and described as a 'round barrow reduced by ploughing' based on air photography in 1970.[31] It is located further south but on the same Apsley Farm's site, where the parish boundaries of St Mary Bourne, Hurstbourne Priors and Longparish meet. This is in a huge open field with sweeping views of the surrounding landscape. Nothing is visible on the ground in the vicinity of the Ashtree Barrow besides a small mound in this spot, completely overgrown with a collapsing boundary fence, which is noticeable from a short distance but pales in comparison to what was once an enormous mound.

Hopkins believes the records for the barrows may be mistaken and Ashtree Barrow is almost certainly the tumulus near Faulkner's Down Farm. He, therefore, believes the barrow listed as the Ashtree is Cerdic's Barrow, a conclusion supported by Grundy's description of Ashtree Barrow as being close to Faulkner's Down Farm and on land with an 'acute angle', which is certainly an accurate reflection of where traces of a large 22m diameter barrow was once recorded. As previously mentioned, there was nothing for the naked eye, but it is near a distinctive corner, where the field

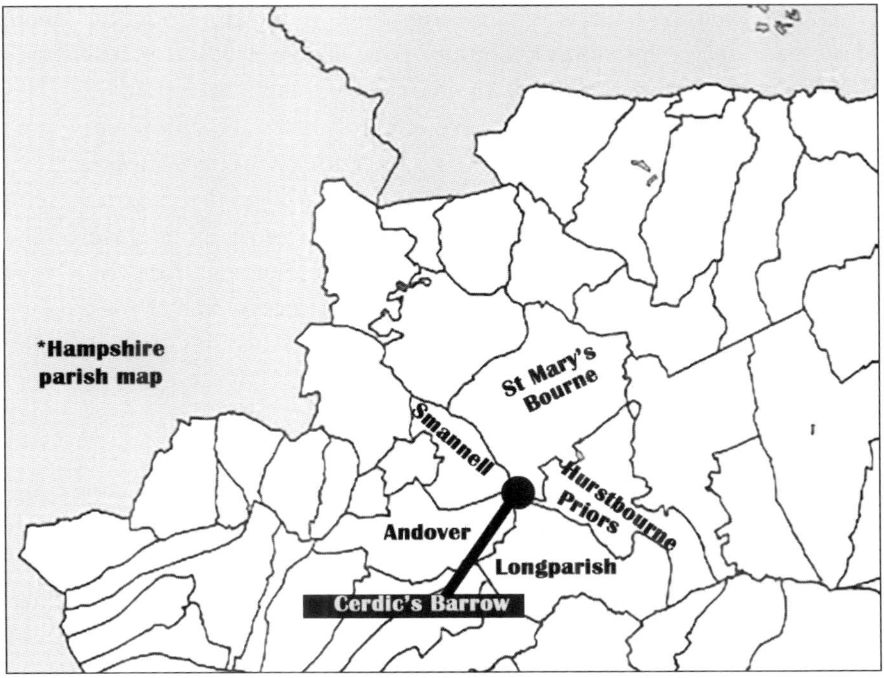

The location of Cerdic's Barrow in relation to Hampshire parish boundaries (Nilfanion, created using Ordnance Survey data/CC BY-SA 3.0)

snakes off west next to a small, wooded area. According to Grundy, the boundary of the land began further east, where the Test River splits into two near Hurstbourne Priors.

In email correspondence, Hopkins stated this means all the first six landmarks on the boundary, including the two barrows (Ashtree and Cerdic's Barrow) are between the double river crossing and the Devil's Ditch (dyke), around 2.5 miles west:

> *'There are two burial mounds in the charter and two burial mounds on that boundary between the river and dyke. The first is therefore by implication Ashtree Barrow and the second is Cerdic's Barrow.*
>
> *'If so the one now called Ashtree Barrow is Cerdic's Barrow and Ashtree Barrow is the other unnamed mound to the east between Cerdic's Barrow and Twyford. That surely would solve the mystery?'*

Hopkins revealed a geophysical survey had taken place around Ashtree Barrow in 2005 to find traces of this barrow and a spot nearby for Cerdic's Barrow, which was carried out by Vaughan Roberts and Jim Gunter, who were both MA Landscape Archaeology students at the University of Bristol, on behalf of archaeologist Mark Godwin who was researching Cerdic of Wessex.[32] These surveys use detection methods to map the contrast between archaeological remains and the surrounding soil. Their report states that in the spot of Ashtree Barrow they discovered evidence of 'the ring ditch of the barrow with at least two burial pits near the centre', which they added was also indicated by a 'difference in the wheat crop height' and there was also some suggestion a stone wall once stood there.

This large barrow must have been an awe-inspiring part of the landscape as it measured approximately 22m in diameter, which is equivalent to around 72ft. The investigation confirmed the barrow identified by Hopkins as Cerdic's Barrow from the ancient land boundary appears to have been used as a burial site for two individuals at one stage.

Just north of Ashtree Barrow, another spot was examined in the belief it was Cerdic's Barrow. This search had been influenced by Isaac Taylor's inch to the mile map of Hampshire produced in 1759, which pointed to another

The spot on Faulkner's Down Farm of a former tumulus and potentially Cerdic's final resting place, which showed signs of two burial pits

barrow near Ashtree Barrow. No traces of a barrow or any archaeological finds were discovered in the spot earmarked as Cerdic's Barrow and the survey report stated, 'as nothing was found, this suggests that either the complete barrow and ditch have been destroyed or, more likely, the location is wrong'.

The report also mentioned suggestions of an unmarked barrow north of Walworth Road, which could be located where Peter Read, owner of the Wyke Down Farm that runs adjacent to Apsley Farms, told the archaeologists a crop mark appears on his golf range every year. Traces of a large barrow have been visible from the air near a site called Lower Wyke farm just north of Walworth Road. Records state this 'heavily ploughed' mound was a Bronze Age barrow, which once measured around 28m in diameter but based on air photography in 1967 was now just 0.2m in height.

Hopkins, however, remains convinced the spot recorded as Ashtree Barrow – where a barrow was located – is the most likely candidate for Cerdic's burial mound:

> *'The site of Cerdic's Barrow is uncertain. Although identified as such in the Saxon charter (although we should not take at*

face value such named associations, I recognise oral tradition can indeed be powerful) the exact location is not known.

'Ashtree Barrow is at the junction of three parish boundaries and as a remarkable element of the landscape might well have acted as the focus of the land divisions layout.

'I favour Ashtree Barrow where the three parishes meet as this is less likely to have been moved and most likely to have been a remarkable feature that the neighbouring communities could refer to.'

Fittingly, as with the legend, the exact site of the Cerdic's Barrow is proving mysterious and open to considerable interpretation. There appears to have been folklore Cerdic had been buried locally in St Mary Bourne or certainly this part of Hampshire. Archaeologist Jim Gunter, who carried out the geophysical survey for Cerdic's Barrow in 2005, examined a second spot ten years later also known as 'Ceardices Beorg' in nearby St Mary Bourne.

I wondered whether this was related to the Cerdic's Barrow mentioned on a random website as being in Stoke, Hurstbourne, which included a geolocation for Cerdic's burial, but investigations showed this proved to be without foundation.

This led me to return to Gunter who supplied more details in the shape of the report.[33] Gunter undertook the survey on behalf of the Wiltshire Archaeology Field Group with colleague Mike McQueen and researcher Mark Godwin. It took place in January 2015 in a field to the north of the B3048 located between the villages of Stoke and St Mary Bourne just over 2 miles north-east from the land around Faulkner's Down Farm. According to the report, the roughly circular barrow was still an impressive site in the field at 33m in diameter and 1.3m high, which represented 'an unusual survival in a relatively low-lying location, which has otherwise been subject to intense agricultural usage'. A ditch also still surrounds the barrow where earth was excavated to create the mound, which was 10m wider than those 2 miles away near Andover, indicating it was built by a different Bronze Age tribe. The barrow is still visible as an unusual mound in fields fenced off for horses in the tiny village. From Gangbridge Lane on the other side, a mound can clearly be made out.

Unlike the other barrow that originates from a royal charter, it is unclear as to how this barrow became known as a potential final resting place for the first king of Wessex, but there was a clue. Intriguingly, a 'Willow Tree Farm' had once been located nearby when a 'Willow Grove' is the next significant landmark in the royal charter. Perhaps, there was a local tradition of Cerdic being buried in this corner of Hampshire near a cluster of willow trees or it resulted in the mistaken association. The second one was also located very close to the Bourne rivulet, a seasonal chalk stream, which rises normally in January and flows until around August.

The geophysical survey aimed to identify any archaeological features, discover the shape and positioning, and whether this was a Bronze Age or later mound. Two other barrows nearby at Blagden Copse and Doles Wood did not produce Saxon finds so this has become the 'only visible' choice for Cerdic's Barrow and to prove he existed, the report added. As the barrow is listed as an ancient monument, they needed permission beforehand from Historic England to undertake the work. The team used resistivity and magnetometry surveys to search for ground anomalies, but nothing was found and the report concluded that neither survey identified any archaeological features. Asked about the survey, Gunter stated it showed 'nothing other than it had been robbed sometime in the past'.

Gunter, who has studied the history of Wessex extensively, believes it is likely the barrow had simply been named after the legendary king: 'There is a problem with these barrows being named after long-dead people for whom there is very little evidence for their existence nor where and what they did.'

The question must be asked whether this huge barrow housed the legendary founder of Wessex or was another fictional aspect of a myth that grew after the story of Cerdic as a great English leader who conquered the natives emerged in the chronicle. There is, of course, the possibility Cerdic's Barrow in the charter was simply a prominent local landmark named after a famous figure. One factor that could support such a conclusion was that the *Anglo-Saxon Chronicle* was first produced during the reign of Alfred the Great in the late-ninth century, just before this land charter was drawn up in 900 by his son Edward the Elder. This was the first time the story of Cerdic of Wessex was put to paper, and it must have been a huge influence on the serving nobility, who could then have renamed a significant feature of the landscape after the famous king to honour him.

Certainly, all the Wessex kings were desperate to show their blood line could be traced back to Cerdic, so his impact was clearly monumental. As Dumville observed, descent from Cerdic was the 'crucial legitimising factor' for future Wessex kings.[34] Perhaps Edward the Elder wanted to go a step further and proclaim a significant landmark as Cerdic's final resting place. According to the scholar Professor Barbara Yorke, one of the foremost authorities on Wessex's foundation, these 'features were often named after heroes and quasi-legendary people'.[35] Hopkins also suggested the name of Cerdic's Barrow 'was used to explain its presence' such as other Iron Age landmarks in Hampshire, namely Oliver's Battery (later reused as a civil war battery) and Caesar's Camp: 'There may have been a local folklore that Cerdic was buried locally but that as time went on a prominent existing burial mound became known as Cerdic's Barrow tying the folklore into a feature prominent in the landscape.'[36]

Historians often avoid the Cerdic legend because of the lack of contemporary evidence and issues with the chronicle, which include folk mythology characters and a backdated timetable. Scholars who base their findings on archaeology are more inclined to avoid the debate around Cerdic because of the discrepancies with the historical record.

It could be the case that Cerdic's Barrow was named after the mysterious king after the legend emerged and was the talk of communities across the land, particularly elite families in Wessex. Naming parts of the landscapes after fictional mythical figures was not unusual. The report into the second 'Ceardices Beorg' stated:

> *'Saxons often named landscape features, including barrows, after famous or mythological personages e.g. the frequent use of the name 'Woden' for many features such as Wansdyke stretching across Somerset and Wiltshire,*
>
> *'However, to date, no examples of barrows that were named after a specific king or leader have actually proven to be the burial site of the said person.'*

This reference to Cedric's Barrow was, however, something real on royal land indicating he was buried there. As it turns out, there were six large burial mounds in a relatively small parcel of land, about 2 square miles, on the outskirts of modern-day Andover but only one was named after the Wessex king. This is an interesting facet as the research into fifty-one place names linked to Mercian kings discussed in Chapter 4 did not link any to barrows or burial sites. It suggests the association with barrows was, not without reason, compared to how the rulers were associated with hills, streams and other landmarks.

Further evidence emerged to support the location of Cerdic's burial because research has shown this act of reusing large Bronze Age barrows for burials was also commonplace when Cerdic reigned. Howard Williams, a professor at the University of Chester, documented 334 examples of ancient monuments and structures being reused for burials between the fifth and eighth centuries.[37]

The prehistoric round barrows, similar to the barrows located in the area of Grundy's charter, were the most popular because they accounted for 61 per cent of the monuments reused – from 202 cases, fifty-seven were certain to have been used for a secondary burial. Notably, one reused prehistoric round barrow occurred in Abingdon Saxton Road in Oxfordshire in the late-fifth or early-sixth century in the heart of the Upper Thames region associated with the Gewisse. In addition, Williams noted 'around Dorchester and Abingdon in the Upper Thames valley, round barrows, long barrows, henges, hillforts, valleys and Roman villas were reused as burial sites'. His research suggests the practice of monument reuse was not more common among certain statuses, despite suggestions it was favoured among poor social groups as it was cheaper to reuse barrows instead of creating a new one.

Monument reuse for burials was also common before, during and after the rise of Christianity in Anglo-Saxon England, which implies it was 'not a Christian or Pagan' practice, according to the research. Williams believes culturally Anglo-Saxon communities were attempting to connect with the past and supernatural world by reusing ancient monuments. He believes 'ancient places' may have also been timeless places, which existed in both the past and present, the world of the living and supernatural. According to Williams, monuments could have been associated with 'imagined ancestors, land spirits, heroes or gods' and each new burial would have re-inscribed such meanings on old monuments: 'In short, early Anglo-Saxon communities were constructing and reproducing their idealised visions of past and present, their mythical origins and their social identities, through the placing of the dead at old monuments.'

Wessex and the Upper Thames, which were the heart of Cerdic's kingdom, contained more examples of monuments being reused than any other regions in England. In Wessex itself, forty-four round barrows, the type in which Cerdic was most likely buried, were reused during the early Anglo-Saxon period, which was the highest, followed by thirty-two in both the south-east and Yorkshire and Northumbria, thirty-one in East Anglia and twenty-seven in the Upper Thames. The placing of the barrow near a significant landmark such as the Devil's Ditch, which most likely formed an old Bronze Age boundary, also ties with tradition.

While you would assume Cerdic would be laid to rest in Winchester, which had been the stronghold of his kingdom, a location in Andover is more fitting with how Wessex buried its chieftains. In post-Roman Britain, many kings and those from elite families were buried in reused barrows on the boundary of estates, which were visible for miles around. Williams said: 'for elite groups in the 7th century this exclusive reuse may have been a deliberate symbol of status and power with reference to the past'.

One such Bronze Age barrow on Swallowcliffe Down in Wiltshire, around 30 miles away from Andover, became known as Posses Halaewe or 'Poss's Mound' and could be seen for many kilometres by those passing through the neighbourhood on an ancient trackway.[38] It was reused in the seventh century and replaced with the body of a young, well-dressed woman who lay on an elaborate wooden bed surrounded by objects including iron and bronze-bound buckets, a small wooden casket and blown-glass palm cups.

Another seventh-century burial at Oliver's Battery just outside Winchester was an example in the Hampshire region of a 'rich isolated grave in the late 6th and 7th century which re-used a prehistoric burial mound', according to a report.[39] The burial, which was accompanied by a dagger, spear and bronze hanging bowl, was situated in an elevated position overlooking the River Itchen and a nearby settlement at Twyford.

The report for the second 'Ceardices Beorg' acknowledges that: 'Many Bronze Age barrows were re-used in the early Saxon period, particularly where they lay adjacent to boundaries. Charters frequently noted barrows in delineating the bounds of a grant of land. It is clear that barrows were significant places for pre-Christian Saxons.'

Historian and archaeologist Max Adams in his book *Land of the Gods* in which he travels across Dark Age sites of the British Isles surveyed some of the thousands of barrows on the Wolds in Yorkshire noting how they 'reinforce ties with the mythological past landscape' and were deliberately positioned.

> *'Joining up the dots of these blips on the map reveals they functioned as markers, for they often lie on the edge of territories that later became our parishes. They took the natural watershed of the land, its watershed and ridges, and drew onto it an idea of owning and belonging, they are proprietorial.'*

Academic Robin Fleming explained in her book *Britain After Rome* that elite burials in reused barrows 'promoted the connection between power and territory' and showed 'the extent or boundaries of the territories they claimed'. She said:

> *'In Wessex and the Upper Thames Valley alone, eleven reused barrows have been identified, all of which lay on the boundaries or 'natural frontiers' and all were visible from a distance or from some major trackway. Barrow burials fit neatly into the project of the genealogies and the origins myths. Some for example may preserve the names whose bodies lay beneath them.'*

Fleming added that the barrows broadcast 'rights over the labour of others and claims to territory to very wide audiences…and spoke not just to like-minded elite minded households but all those moving through the landscape.'

It is unlikely the barrow near Faulkner's Down Farm given its topography in the middle of a sloping fields system would have been visible from afar, which makes me slightly doubtful this was Cerdic's Barrow. As it stands, however, this is the prime candidate and with the preceding landmarks it could match Grundy's interpretation, while an initial survey suggests people had been buried there.

Chapter 15

Cerdic's Barrow

The Mysterious Ditches

Devil's Ditch

The Devil's Ditch, which was also called Grim's Ditch, is referred to in the charter as the second point on the land boundary after Cerdic's Barrow. Traces can still be found, and it is described as an earthwork running for over half a mile southward from the Silchester to Old Sarum 'Portway' Roman Road to Tinker's Hill.[40]

The west-facing bank defends a pass against an enemy coming from Southampton, where it is 'most formidable', but it is completely ploughed except near a railway plantation where evidence shows it was originally 9ft deep. It is still visible for around 300m behind the railway and up to a small woodland.

Although one bank has been significantly reduced, you can begin to appreciate its scale and how it must have been a major point of reference. It would have been a hugely impressive sight for travellers on the Portway, not to mention the logistics of creating such a man-made earthwork, which ran for more than a mile. It surely speaks of a tribe or significant group that had the necessary manpower.

Historic England states how the ditch in Andover has similarities in how it traverses ridges and crosses summits to late Bronze Age landmarks in Quarley and Snoddington Hills, around 10 and 15 miles west respectively. These defences could have been extended and used by the Atrebates.

These defences could also have been intended as a barrier or border with the rival Dobunni and Durotriges tribes who controlled neighbouring Wiltshire and Dorset respectively. Interestingly, the part of the ditch beyond the railway line still marks the boundary between the present-day districts of the Test Valley and Basingstoke and Deane.

Mike Farrell, who is 6ft 2in to give perspective, stands in the ancient Devil's Ditch, which had banks as deep as 9ft

As my investigations delved deeper into Cerdic's battles around Southampton Water and near Charford, which appeared to be the scene of a great victory, while Winchester the later capital of Wessex seemed to remain the centre of a tax collecting administration, it led to questions why Andover was chosen. It then became evident I had underestimated the significance of the Devil's Ditch.

A Hants Field Group paper on the Belgic advance through Hampshire suggested it may have extended for another 8 miles north from Tinker's Hill towards a place called Chute Heath, which is on the boundary between Wiltshire and Hampshire.[41] It claimed the ditch headed northwards past Doles Wood and remained 2 to 3ft deep as it crossed the Andover to Newbury Road and marked the extent of an advance by Belgic tribes. This placed the construction of the ditch to as late as 1200 BC, during the late Bronze Age, and as early as 50 BC, around when the Belgae arrived.

Roughly 0.75 of a mile north lies a historic small woodland called Blagdon Copse, where an 'important' first-century Belgic burial was found, along with enclosures, ditches and a pit, which included the burial of an infant and a horse skull.

According to HERs, the ditch is visible around Tinker's Hill where although it has been filled the 'rampart stands up well and the curve of the hill implies command of the flats lying towards Andover'.[42]

As I found when visiting, the dyke is bigger than anywhere else in the woods behind the railway line, on the other side of Walworth Road, where it is believed to have once had a width of 32ft and a bank 12ft high. Traces disappear as it crosses the Roman Road, and after Rag Wood, it 'becomes difficult to trace', according to the records. It then supposedly joined up with another dyke and continued for another 5 miles west to the Wiltshire border.

The existence of such a dyke has been recorded near a place called the Chute Causeway, which formed part of another Roman Road between Winchester and Cirencester and joins up with the Portway in Andover. According to Wiltshire's ancient monument records, a bank and ditch runs for 3 miles and has also shaped local parish boundaries.[43] Remarkably, it appears the same ancient tribal divisions have stood the test of time.

Another dyke has also been detected in Wherwell Wood, around 2 miles east of Andover, where it meets the Roman Road from Winchester and could form part of the same dyke. Given records state it may have begun at Branbury near Wherwell Wood, which is some 15 miles east of Chute parish, this would make it even longer than the East Wansdyke.[44]

A more cautious estimate would suggest the Devil's Ditch ran for at least 8 miles between Tinker's Hill near Andover and Chute parish and, even more conservatively, for nearly 3 miles between the hill and Rag Wood, which is still a considerable earthwork in any age.

I resolved to investigate whether traces of the ditch could still be found. Soon enough, it became apparent the ditches had been recorded in Rag Wood near Hurstbourne Tarrant, which is around 2.5 miles from Tinker's Hill on the outskirts of Andover.[45]

An earlier excavation revealed two banks, one facing north and the other 150m away facing south, which implies it is a boundary marker rather than a defensive structure. Evidence of a bank and ditch is also found nearby on the other side of the A343 Newbury Road, and it reappears in Rag Wood, having snaked round extensive nearby woodland. The charter boundary follows roughly the same course before heading towards Hurstbourne Tarrant and coming back on a loop to the starting point of the Test River near Hurstbourne Priors.

Rag Wood looked enchanting from a distance, almost like something from a fantasy film, awash with vibrant colours, such as orange and

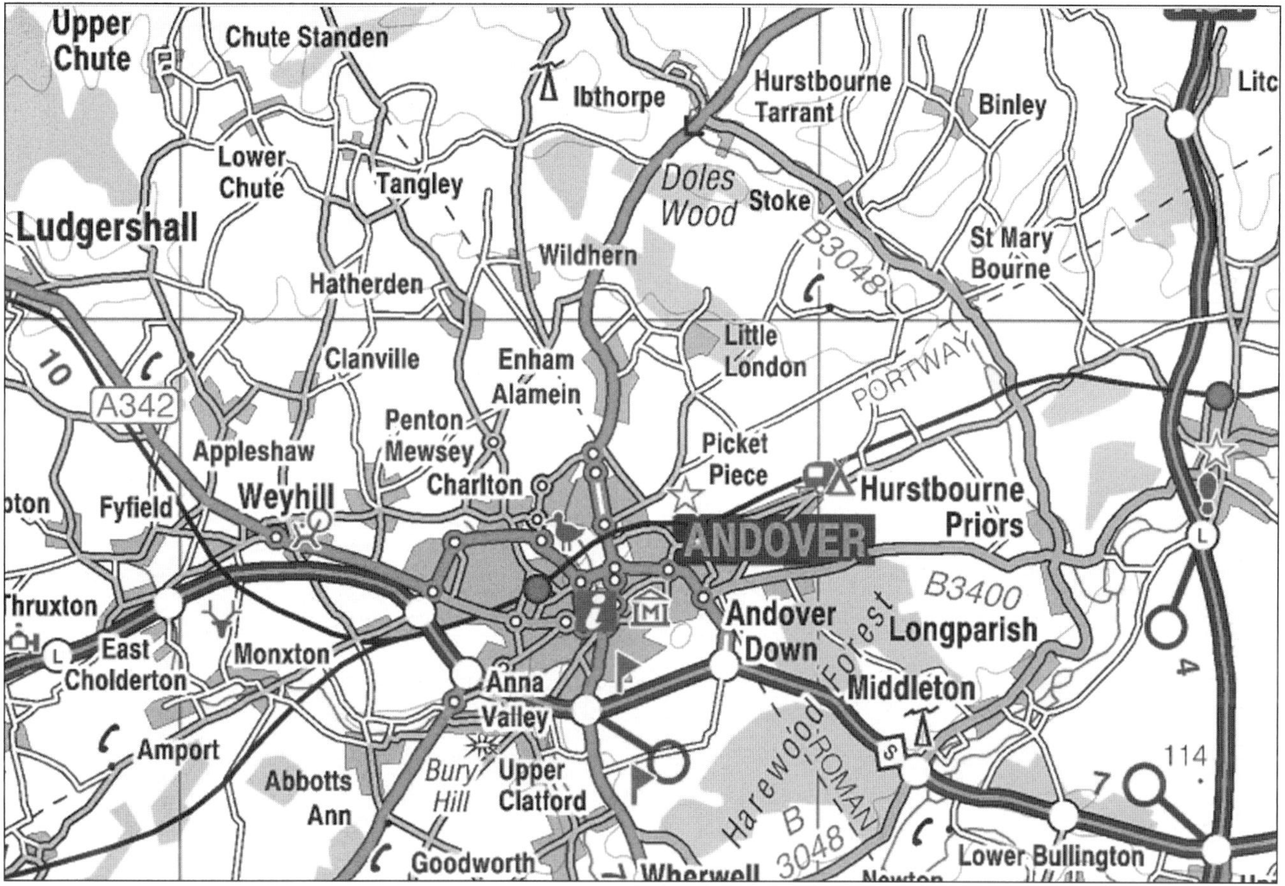

The Devil's Ditch is believed to have run from the edge of Andover to near Doles Wood and then onto Chute parish on the Wiltshire–Hampshire border (Contains Ordnance Survey data ©Crown copyright and database right (6-June-2010))

yellow, during my visit in autumn. I had picked a perfect day when the small woodland was an almost magical sight to behold. The public path on private land takes you around the edge of the wood, and I was unable to head through the centre because of warning signs, which prevented seeing where the ditch is supposed to cross a path. I managed to find an entry at the far side of the woods, where a series of criss-crossing paths shot off in every direction, but I decided against venturing beyond the blocked-off routes, despite a couple of dog walkers and hikers, and a group of rabbits playing in a field, being the only company I saw for the best part of two hours at this isolated spot 4 miles outside Andover. Instead, I headed to the other side of the road, where traces of the ditch in a small parcel of vegetation could be seen between Doles Wood and Rag Copse.

Although filled with several fallen trees, a north-facing bank, which was a few metres high, could be traced for roughly 100m in this vicinity. Picturing the remaining bank and showing its scale proved difficult, but it was an odd feature of the now agricultural and woodland landscape. OS maps dating from the nineteenth century revealed it had formed an ancient municipal boundary. I began to suspect the boundaries in this historically rich corner of Hampshire had been based on this original tribal ditch. Perhaps this was a marker towards the westerly corner of a kingdom and a spectacular mound greeted enemies who had traipsed to the southern side. The tribe that had dug the earthwork must have had the same idea in mind.

While doubtful this was a definitive border, as further south in Andover there were settlements dating to the sixth century period, the ditch now seemed crucial to this section of the land charter.

Across Britain, there are more than 100 possible early medieval linear earthworks commonly termed dykes that stretch further than 400km and vary in size from those just 100m in length to the famous Offa's Dyke, which is more than 95km long and runs between England and Wales.[46]

The Wansdyke

In the heart of Cerdic's kingdom lies another spectacular earthwork that has remained a mystery. I had planned to cover this remarkable dyke separately but instead thought it would be best to explore the origin and link to the Wessex founder in this chapter given its similarities with the earthwork

The massive East Wansdyke ditch on Tan Hill, which runs between Savernake Forest and Morgan's Hill in Wiltshire

near Andover. Were the two built at the same time and how did they begin to create such mammoth earthworks?

The Wansdyke, which translates as 'the dyke of Woden', is a series of ancient defensive earthworks running from east to west between Savernake Forest in Wiltshire and the Iron Age hillfort Mae Knoll in Somerset near Bristol. In total, the East Wansdyke runs for 12 miles between Savernake Forest and Morgan's Hill in Wiltshire, while the middle section is an Old Roman Road, which runs for 15 miles, and the West Wansdyke is the same length from Odd Down to Mae Knoll.

To appreciate the scale of the Wansdyke, I headed to the incredible Tan Hill in Wiltshire, which at 294m high offers spectacular views of the surrounding chalk downlands. Here, the East Wansdyke can still be seen in its full glory. Offering sweeping views on a sunny day, you can see as far as the Brecon Beacons and the Black Mountains in Wales. After a spell of Covid-19, it was perhaps not the best time to face the daunting slopes.

Tan Hill is set in the middle of the countryside, 1.5 miles from the nearest road, 5 miles from Devizes and 19 miles from Swindon. Accessing the site can be done via a Wansdyke trail and taking a shortcut from Horton Road is ill-advised as cows and sheep are residents in fenced-off sloping fields.

At one spot just west of Tan Hill, below an adjacent spot called Clifford's Hill, which itself stands an impressive 242m high, there is a huge drop in a small valley, which is intimidating to say the least, and a path around the brow of the steep hill.

As I trudged closer to Tan Hill, the Wansdyke was still not visible until I finally reached the summit, where the incredible feature finally emerged after a steep walk up a lane on the other side of Clifford Hill and it was worth the trek. The Wansdyke has been almost perfectly preserved on Tan Hill, and you could instantly see how when, facing north, this would have been a vital defensive structure. Behind a north-facing bank, forces could have been hiding in wait ready to pounce on the invaders who were at their most vulnerable. As the Wansdyke snakes around the top of Tan Hill from Milk Hill towards Morgan's Hill around 4 miles away, it becomes spectacularly deep – thought to be as much as 13ft in places. Stunning views of the surrounding countryside, which include the Mendips, Cotswolds and Salisbury Plain, ensured enemies could have been spotted in all directions.

Woden or Odin, who the dyke is named after, is a chief god in Germanic paganism and Norse mythology, who was also the god of boundaries. His origin may have been related to the Anglo-Saxon foundation myth in which all the founders of English kingdoms – aside from Essex – were recorded as being descended from Woden. References to the earthwork as 'Wodnes dic' are common throughout Anglo-Saxon charters of Somerset and Wiltshire but can all be dated to the tenth century.[47] Three instances deal with the same section of the Wansdyke around Tan Hill in 903, 957 and 960.

As the bank faces north, many, including eminent historian John Myres, have speculated the invading force were the Germanic confederates described by Gildas who wreaked havoc across modern-day southern and eastern England in the mid-to-late fifth century.[48]

The East Wansdyke faces and is near an ancient trackway known as the Ridgeway, which leads directly from the Upper Thames to Wiltshire, and leading landscape archaeologist Peter Fowler believed the two were interlinked. Fowler identified ten original openings through the Wansdyke, most of which could be linked to ancient through routes connecting the Ridgeway to the Vale of Pewsey, which are 0.5 Roman miles apart.[49]

The earthwork was constructed by excavation of pits along a marker line with the spoil thrown southwards to form a bank created by a series of dumps. Joining up the pits and deepening the trench formed a steeply inclined ditch, which ran to the top of the bank, completing the structure.

Paraglider hangs above livestock on Tan Hill, which is among a series of huge rolling hills in Pewsey Downs

Fowler believed the East Wansdyke followed a military design layout comparable to Hadrian's Wall and made use of local topography and places with excellent field of vision, such as at Tan Hill. However, Fowler concluded that the earthwork was unfinished as the threat disappeared. One suggestion could be the earthwork was constructed under the stewardship of a Romano-Briton type military leader such as Ambrosius Aurelianus, who was still in control of the southwest during the confederates war and then its construction was later abandoned after the victory at Badon. The landmark is believed to follow the southern corner of the former Dobunni civitas.

Interestingly, contenders for Badon include Liddington Castle, which is part of the Ridgeway. This huge Bronze and Iron Age fort is on the top of a hill above Badbury in Wiltshire, which is known as Baddan Byrig in Old English.[50] Alternatively, the famous conflict has been associated with Bath and Solsbury Hill, which is close to the western end of the Wansdyke. Certainly, whoever constructed the Wansdyke, wielded considerable authority, and had access to a large army or workforce.

In his book *Warfare, Raiding and Defence*, based on his PhD thesis, academic Dr Erik Grigg carried out an in-depth study of the thousands of medieval dykes across the country, including the Wansdyke. He estimates between 1,100 and 2,300 labourers constructed the east and west sections of the dyke during a working season of 100 days. A previous study by John Reynolds in 2006 theorized up to 15,000 workers were required.

Standing atop Tan Hill gives you the distinct impression a great deal of planning and surveying had gone into the construction of the Wansdyke. There are countless slopes as far as the eye can see yet the course of this earthwork was deliberately aligned with the highest points of Tan Hill and Milk Hill. Moreover, the increase in depth of the dyke around this specific point, speaks of this being a location that may have been manned to some degree, if sporadically, during times of danger.

Research has shown an engineer surveyed how the Wansdyke would cross valleys and streams during its construction.[51] Marker pits were dug in front of a small trench to show the line of the dyke, before large groups of workers began digging deep pits at timed intervals, which were enlarged and connected. Soil was heaped up behind the ditch to form the bank, and it was deepened to as high as 13ft in some places creating the earthwork.

The mass organization and planning required for the Wansdyke leads me to believe it was not constructed originally during Cerdic's reign, when battles were clustered between Southampton Water and near to Old Sarum. The kingdom at the time probably began about 20 miles away near Andover from the starting point of the dyke at Savernake Forest. Moreover, Cerdic most likely reigned during famine and plague when the task of recruiting hundreds of workers to dig and construct the Wansdyke would logically have not been possible.

This mysterious earthwork could, however, be linked to his warlike grandson Ceawlin, who was defeated in 592 at Woden's Barrow (Adam's Grave), a tumulus at Alton Priors in Wiltshire, just a few miles from Tan Hill. After Ceawlin's defeat, the Wansdyke is suspected to have become a boundary marker, which was possibly enlarged or defended in sections, between a British-speaking kingdom further west and the rapidly expanding Wessex.

Only later into research had I realized how significant this place had been in Wessex's early history. As discussed in Chapter 4, Golden Boot Hill, just 0.5 miles away from Adam's Grave, was once known as 'Creoda's Hill', which is linked to Cerdic's illusive son who is also thought to have been the 'Crida' who died alongside Ceawlin a year after he was driven out.[52] During my visit, I had walked to Alton Priors for refreshments not realizing

Some believe the Wansdyke was built to stop rebelling Saxon confederates from reaching the south-west

the significance of this now tiny village in the Wiltshire countryside. The western section of the Wansdyke was thought to have been a similar marker after Ceawlin's victory at the Battle of Deorham in 577 near Bristol.

General Augustus Pitt Rivers, a former British army officer and an acclaimed nineteenth-century archaeologist, believed the pre-existing Roman road was made use of by Wansdyke creators as it is joined near Morgan's Hill on the south side, where there is a deep ditch and rampart up to 27m wide combined. Pitt Rivers' investigation unearthed pieces of Samian ware embedded in the Wansdyke near Morgan's Hill, a luxury item used in Roman tableware pottery, and he concluded the earthwork could be dated to during or just after the Roman period.[53]

The Wansdyke could be linked to another similar earthwork known as Bokerley Dyke in Dorset as they both face north and include a ditch with a small external mound and a higher rampart.[54] Bokerley Dyke was reinforced in the mid-fourth century, as coins of the Roman emperor Valens, who reigned between 364 and 378, were found at a spot where a Roman road from Old Sarum to Badbury Rings, which cut through the earthwork, was blocked off. This is notably around the same time as the Great Barbarian Conspiracy in 367.

Construction and development of the Wansdyke can be tied to three different phases, but part of its route may date to the Iron Age, as with other dykes. Work began on strengthening the East Wansdyke following the Great Barbarian Conspiracy and it was then reinforced and possibly extended under the leadership of Ambrosius Aurelianus in the fifth century. From the words of Gildas, the Britons 'regained their strength' under the post-Roman ruler who may have had the resources and influence to oversee a building project on this scale. Finally, the Wansdyke may have again been extended and strengthened following the expansion of Wessex under Ceawlin, particularly the western section, which appeared to mark a boundary with the culturally Romano-British settlements further west.

Cerdic was not involved in the building of the Wansdyke despite its eventual significance and prominence in the expanded Wessex, but my investigations were beginning to show that the other huge ditch near Andover could be vital in establishing the whereabouts of 'Ceardices Beorg'.

Chapter 16

Cerdic's Barrow

Final Resting Place

Willow Grove

In returning to the Grundy charter, the next landmark after Cerdic's Barrow is a 'Willow Grove', which he believed must be 'somewhere close to where the Devil's Ditch impinges on the railway' north of Walworth Road on the edge of Andover.

No records of significant trees are recorded in this spot among the thousands in the Ancient Tree Inventory logged by the Woodlands Trust

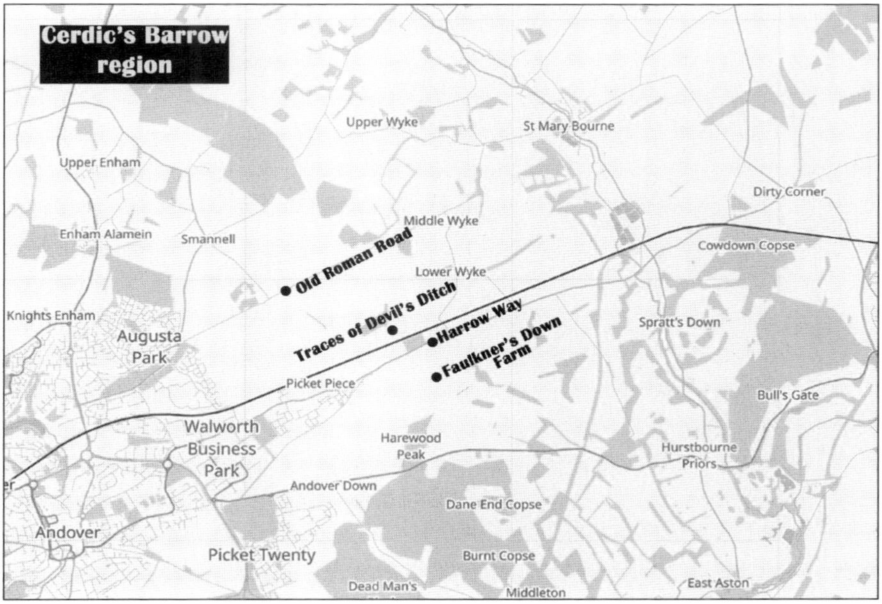

Key sites in the region of Cerdic's Barrow on the outskirts of Hampshire (Maps ©Thunderforest, Data ©OpenStreetMap contributors)

or near to the railway line, which runs adjacent to Walworth Road around 200m away. As mentioned previously, the ditch was once identifiable near Tinker's Hill and traces are still visible behind the railway line.

The next landmark after Willow Grove can be easily located, as it mentions how the former Devil's Ditch crossed the ancient trackway, which was the old Roman road known as the Portway. This ancient road ran for 36 miles between Old Sarum and Silchester and may have been in existence even before the Romans arrived and continued to form part of what was known as the Devil's Highway between Silchester and London.

Notably, Cerdic's successor and son Cynric is recorded as having fought a battle at Old Sarum in 552, which had been a famous Iron Age hillfort established about 400 BC and continued to be occupied after the Roman invasion. The context and dating of Cynric's victory at Old Sarum had been thrown into question as there were settlements using a Germanic-inspired culture close to the fort fifty years before. I'm convinced the account of the

View from the old Roman Road (now Finkley Road). It is believed the land boundary and the Devil's Ditch followed a similar course to the existing hedge bank towards the Portway. The patch of land was the site of a Roman villa (Paul Whitewick)

chronicle was based on real events and Cynric, or possibly even Creoda, appears to have won a battle at the fort as stated, most likely in the aftermath of the plague between 555 and 570. One of Cerdic's final battles has been placed at a spot just 3 miles from Old Sarum called Odstock Copse.[55]

In Andover, the modern-day Finkley Road, around a mile north of Walworth Road, has been built over the Portway. Identifying the Willow Grove was a less straightforward task than matching the trackway from the charter with the old Roman road. One local tree surgeon was unaware of any significant willow trees, but instead directed me to speak with two long-serving employees of the sprawling 1,600-acre Trinley Estate, which is situated north of the railway line and is taken up largely by arable land where crops such as wheat, barley, rye and oilseed rape are grown, with a small portion occupied by woodland and grassland.

Former estate workers Ron Holdway and Daniel Burgess, who are both in their 80s, filled me in on the history of the landscape, which contains numerous Bronze Age and Roman finds. They described how just behind the estate building were once two 'huge' burial mounds, which have been ploughed extensively. This section is now being protected on the advice of Historic England, which has identified two former Bronze Age bowl barrows, the same type of mound as on Faulkner's Down Farm. Historic

The huge banks surrounding Old Sarum, which was a powerful Iron Age and Roman fortress

England describes both barrows as 26m in diameter and 0.8m high, which is a similar size although slightly higher.[56]

Traces of the huge mounds have all but disappeared; however, two slightly raised areas where the tumuli were located are detectable within the patch of land now sectioned off. Mike Farrell, the Trinley Estate's manager, who arranged the meeting with Ron and Daniel, said it's a 'great shame' more care wasn't taken to protect these sites of enormous historic interest. He believes two massive pits on the other end of the estate were potentially dug up for chalk to create the barrows.

These are not the Cerdic's Barrow from the charter because they are later referenced as landmark no. 11 ('Ceardices Beorg' is no. 4). The description reads: 'Utt with Feld Beorga', which Grundy translates as 'Out over against the Barrows of the Moorland.'

The barrows are just west of where the Devil's Ditch would have crossed the old Roman Road and then the route of the land boundary heads towards Hurstbourne Tarrant. The boundary diverted from the ditch, according to Grundy, and then came back to a similar position near the two barrows, before following the existing boundary of St Mary's Parish and Basingstoke and Deane up to Doles Wood and then to Hurstbourne Priors. This section had proved puzzling as the descriptions of features such as a 'pollard oak tree' and 'wooded slope' are hard to detect on a much-changed landscape.

County archaeologist Hopkins suggested there are small, incised valleys to the west of the boundary line, which presumably included the wooded slope.[57] Traces of a prehistoric field system are found west of the boundary near the village of Smannell, which could explain why the boundary was diverted to include this land.

Farrell reveals another site of significant historic interest is located on the estate – a former Roman villa. The Historic England record states the flint-built Roman building was excavated in 1871 and featured an irregular floor plan with five large rooms, a big central area, while a 'Roman cremation burial' was discovered in a cist beneath the doorway of the building, which was accompanied by four Romano-British pottery vessels and a small iron knife.[58] Employees also claim sections of a Roman mosaic in the villa were stolen during the night while archaeological excavations took place, and as with the two barrows, the area has been sectioned off now to prevent any damage from farming. Historic England also revealed how their investigation found that in the late-Roman era, the site consisted of a workshop, a villa and inhumation space along with several rubbish pits.

Intriguingly, Historic England stated how it was once thought that this could be the mysterious lost Roman settlement known as Vindomis, an association which is even referenced in nineteenth-century Ordnance Survey maps. The town of Vindomis, which could translate as 'mansion of the wine country', may have once had a population of some 2,000 people and have been the centre of a large estate where pottery was produced. It is now believed Vindomis was located at Neatham near Alton in east Hampshire, where the Old Roman Road from Winchester to London and Chichester to Silchester would meet.

Both the ditch and the villa are now scheduled monuments. Excavating either site would require a licence from English Heritage, which would be costly and any attempt to carry out work without one would incur a massive fine. It is a criminal offence to damage the site of a scheduled monument without consent, which would be subject to an unlimited fine or up to two years' imprisonment. Any excavation would have to satisfy English Heritage that the work would be justified against the benefits of preservation, a process described as 'closely scrutinised', which can be 'quite a hurdle to achieve', according to Hopkins.[59]

Evidence suggests the ditch may have extended all the way to the Hampshire-Wiltshire border in Chute

Just a few hundred metres from the villa lies a small parkland and wooded area known as Pepper Hill Firs and locally as Dyke Wood because the Devil's Dyke ran alongside. The small woodland houses between fifteen and twenty yew trees, which have deeply religious significance and were sacred to the Druids in Britain before the Roman conquest. In the pagan tradition they were considered symbolic of the regeneration of the natural world and spirit.[60] As the drooping branches of old yew trees can root and form new trunks where they touch the ground, the trees came to symbolize death and resurrection in Celtic culture. These types of trees have often been associated with old churches and can be found in graveyards across the country.

Farrell took me on a tour of the woodland and said they are a 'very unusual feature of the landscape' and believes they must have been planted. He is adamant a waterway of sorts once ran past the Roman villa and in front of the woods, which followed the valley contours. He asked:

> *'The villa would have been about two miles from the nearest rivers in either direction that we know today so how else would they have been regularly supplied? I'm convinced that there must have been a waterway nearby somewhere as it would make sense that the Romans would have chosen the location for the villa. The closest water that we currently know of is the Bourne Rivulet or the river in the middle of Andover. Both would have been quite a hike in my opinion to cart water.'*

It is theorized that Finkley Road may have altered the hydrology at the head of the valley next to the villa site. Modern drainage may mean the valley is dryer than in the past. The supply could conceivably have come from a well or a winterbourne (also known as rivulet), which is a stream or river that is dry through the summer months and generally forms in areas that contain downland clay deposits in vales and valleys. Chalk holds water when it rains and releases it at a steady rate. During dry seasons the water table could fall below the stream's bed causing it to dry out. Farrell alluded to how 'tonnes of chalk' were dug up nearby and possibly used to create the two burial mounds. Nearby, St Mary Bourne is an example of a 'bourne', which stems from the Old English word to describe a river flowing from a spring.[61]

The potential presence of a waterway near the villa is pivotal in the quest to identify the Willow Grove. Willow trees are traditionally found on moist soils and near waterways and include some 400 different species.

The Willow Grove, the next landmark after Cerdic's Barrow, was most likely at the end of a small woodland close to an old Roman villa

They are fast growing with an average lifespan of only 30 to 50 years. Farrell believes at one stage, with the potential stream running past the former Roman villa and woodland, a cluster of willow trees stood nearby, and this could conceivably be the spot of the 'Willow Grove'.

Fascinatingly the other *Ceardices Beorg* between St Mary Bourne and Stoke is also located near the Bourne rivulet, a seasonal chalk stream and close to a 'Willow Tree Farm'. As suggested earlier, this implies there was a legend of Cerdic not only being buried in this corner of Hampshire but also close to willow trees, which is perhaps how both burials shared the same name.

The final 'Ceardices Beorg' candidate

The location of the Willow Grove would align with another strong candidate as the prime spot for Cerdic's Barrow in the HERs database.[62] This barrow, which was first documented in the 1950s and then a decade later from aerial photography, is of great interest and around 0.5 miles west from the one on Faulkner's Down Farm.

Traces were discovered close to the southern side of the Devil's Ditch landmark feature referenced by Grundy and an area known as Tinker's Hill, which reaches 120m high, where a large circular raised mound on this scale – around 72ft in diameter – would have been a massive focal point. It is possible to speculate the mound was at least 5ft in height because another famous Iron Age barrow, the Lexden tumulus[63] described in Chapter 2, was this height and almost the exact same diameter which speaks of some established method for the burial creations.

Records describe it as a ploughed, low-mound Bronze Age bowl barrow, which is surrounded by a dark green circle ditch, but unfortunately it was only visible from air photographs in 1966 and the ditch now shows as a crop mark.

An Iron Age trackway and brooch was found just west of the site. Notably, the barrow is also the exact same size in diameter as both the barrows near Faulkner's Down Farm, indicating a connection between the historic landmarks and how the same tribe of Bronze Age people created all three burial mounds for their dead.

When I reached this barrow after traipsing around the back of the Picket Piece development, I did feel a rush of excitement. Fortunately, the new housing estate was not built over the land which is now a private field. This fact alone made me curious as such burials were often thought to be sacred and not built over, so it remains a possibility the barrow has influenced the layout. There is no longer any sign or traces on the ground of the mound or the Devil's Ditch near Tinker's Hill and a resident was aware of the former dyke but not a potential barrow. I paced around the hill in circles in a daze at the prospect this could be the 'Ceardices Beorg'. Admittedly, the resident did look on in slight bemusement at a random person walking head down intensely analyzing the ground, claiming the founder of what became England might have been buried here on what is an essentially innocuous spot with no visible landmarks on the edge of Andover. Standing at the site, however, you can instantly see how it offers a commanding view of the surrounding landscape towards the old Roman Road.

Grundy placed the barrow south of the ditch, whereas this mound is just north-west of the landmark, but it remains the most likely candidate given its scale, location near the ditch and on a hill overlooking the surroundings in keeping with elite burials at the time. This would have been an inspiring and prominent burial mound.

One factor worth considering is also how hundreds of these barrows could be found across the British Isles, with the presence of six former

Willow Grove was most probably located at the front of the woods next to a possible winterbourne and the Roman villa (Paul Whitewick)

Bronze Age barrows in a small corner of Hampshire indicative of their popularity. On the Isle of Wight alone, there are thought to have been around 240 Bronze Age barrows of various shapes and sizes.[64]

Surely, if one barrow had been named 'Ceardices Beorg' and, in fact, the final resting place of the Wessex king, it would have possessed something unique, and this must have been the huge ditch running nearby.

Another element supporting the conclusion is the other descriptions of the land boundary, which each have a noticeable feature, such as the 'Ashtree Barrow', the 'Peartree', the 'Willow Grove', where the 'Dyke crossed the track (Roman Road)' and the 'wooded slope'. Someone walking the possibly boundary route would have clearly noticed these trees and landscape markings.

It is unlikely there would have been a plaque stating Cerdic's Barrow, unless it has long since been removed or destroyed, so this would suggest possibly widespread knowledge this barrow was related to Cerdic and not the five nearby, one of which is roughly 600m away.

A legend based on Cerdic's reign in the *Anglo-Saxon Chronicle* in 893 would have had to develop within just seven years before the charter was composed. This would support the tantalizing prospect it was called Cerdic's Barrow because this is where Wessex's founder was laid to rest as Grundy speculated.

Noticeably, the distance between the spot of this former barrow and the Willow Grove hints at a method of working out this land boundary because it could be roughly 0.5 miles based on five of the six first points.

Based on this premise, the position of the Peartree was near where the parish boundaries converge. Pear trees were introduced to Britain by the Romans but it is believed they did not become widespread until the late-tenth century, around 100 years after the charter.[65] They would have been unmissable at heights of up to 30ft and grown in less sheltered areas for maximum sunlight.

The existing landscape hints at how small woodlands may have dictated the course of the boundary.

The mile marker stems from the Roman word 'mile passus', which meant 'thousand paces', and consisted of a thousand paces as measured by every other step or equivalent to the total distance of the left foot hitting the ground 1,000 times.[66] A modern-day mile is 1.6km but the Old English mile, which would be most relevant to the tenth-century charter, ranged in size from 1.23 to 1.3 miles, but it was based on the Roman concept of a mile equalling 1,000 paces and 5,000 feet. The precise common length of a mile may have varied, but it appears a notable feature was mentioned at roughly every half mile as they mapped out the land boundary. And, as mentioned earlier, research into the East Wansdyke found openings every 0.5 Roman mile, which hints at a similar system.

There was no indication of a long track on the ground leading up to the barrow, as stated in the charter, however around 20m away a track running briefly alongside is indicated in the HERs database.

I returned to the investigation into the barrow on Faulkner's Down Farm carried out by archaeologists in 2005 and was stunned by a detail on a map in the report.[67] There was, in fact, a track leading alongside and close to the barrow over the hill near where I suspect the preceding Peartee was situated. This track, which is now a field boundary, was displayed in a map within the report by English Heritage highlighting the various archaeological features on the landscape. It fits the description of the charter, which stated all the way back in 900: '*Thonne andlang Weges on Ceardices Beorg*' ('Then along the Track to Cerdic's Barrow'). This seemed hugely significant.

Trackway on Faulkner's Down Farm which may have formed part of the land boundary in the ancient charter

Returning to the HERs database, there are signs recorded of an Iron Age and Roman field system in the presence of ditches along where the track would have run.[68] This section of the boundary was seemingly shaped around two wooded areas before heading towards the unmissable ditch and then the Portway.

And there was another – and perhaps the most – compelling reason why the barrow could have been reused for Cerdic's burial: it was close to an ancient road known as the 'Harrow Way', dubbed the 'oldest road in Britain'. This route dates from the Stone Age and ran between modern-day Seaton in east Devon and Dover in Kent and was believed to have once been used by tin traders.[69] The Harrow Way has been traced through modern-day Andover and just east of St Mary Bourne and is now the modern-day Walworth Road, which runs through Picket Piece, having been renamed in the 1960s when the current Walworth Industrial Estate was built.

Ordnance Survey maps dating back to the nineteenth century confirmed the old route. Perhaps the track alongside the barrow connected the old trackway to the edge of Harewood Forest, known as Harewood Peak. The Harrow Way was also used to lead cattle, which explains the current Ox Drove from Walworth Road at the end of Picket Piece. There is also a Harrow Way Community School in a street of the same name further west

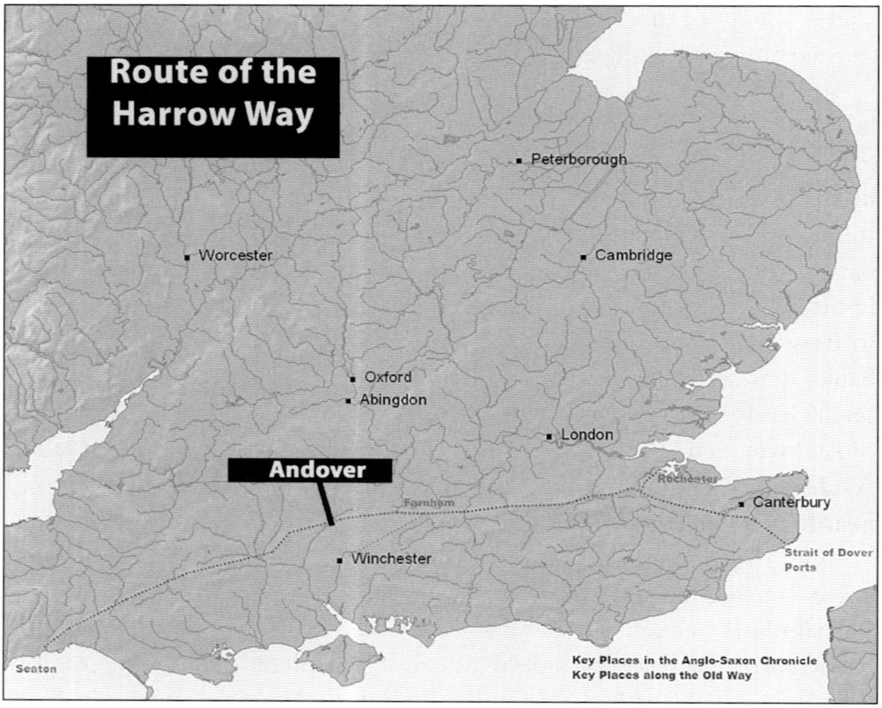

The route of the Harrow Way trackway dating to the Stone Age, which was also known as the 'Old Way' (Adam37/CC BY-SA 3.0)

in Andover, which has an Upper Drove leading from it, indicating again the connection between the Harrow Way and cattle.

The name could stem from the Old English word *hereweg* for an 'army path' and relate to the reign of Alfred the Great when the king ordered a series of connected burghs via similar ancient trackways that could be quickly defended in a Viking raid.[70] Some suggest the Harrow Way could have influenced the siting of Stonehenge as it ran alongside the monument. 'Harrow Way' could also be derived from the Old English word *here weag*, which translates as the 'path to a holy place or shrine'.[71] When the ancient trackway was named by Old English speakers, it was clearly still of considerable importance for both religious and military purposes.

For thousands of years, this route has, therefore, been well trodden by tin traders, armies and cattle drivers. This means the barrow near Tinker's Hill was sandwiched between the ancient trackway and the ditch. In the sixth century such a large mound would have been completely unmissable to anyone travelling along the Harrow Way. And there was a further discovery.

Around 12 miles south of Andover lies the village of Cholderton, which is situated on the current boundary between Wiltshire and Hampshire. Running through Cholderton is another Devil's Ditch, which according to Historic England dates to the Late Bronze Age and early Iron Age and follows the boundary of the two counties passing through the Wiltshire parishes of Cholderton, Figheldean and Tidworth, and then Shipton Billinger in the Test Valley district of Hampshire.[72] Much of the ancient dyke is said to be wooded and damaged by tracks, but the northern section features banks that could have been as much as 20m (65ft) wide.[73] Notably, the ditch also features two associated barrows, such as the one on the outskirts of Andover, and has been listed as a scheduled monument for preservation. As discussed earlier, the ditch in Andover could join up with another one near Lower Chute, which is also on the Hampshire–Wiltshire border.

Cholderton was recorded in the 1086 Domesday Book as 'Celdrinetone' twice and has been associated with either Ceolred, a Mercian king, or the similarly named Ceol (also known as Ceolric) whose grandfather was Cynric, the recorded son of Cerdic.[74] The name Cholderton could be translated as 'the village of Ceol' as the word 'ton, tun' which is found throughout England, was an Old English word for 'enclosure, hamlet or village'.[75]

Two ditches just 12 miles apart are linked to the Wiltshire–Hampshire border and potentially Wessex kings Cerdic and his great grandson Ceol. In the scheme of things this is hardly surprising that such prominent landmarks that shaped land boundaries were associated with kings, but it is particularly relevant in the context and given one barrow was so closely positioned next to a ditch.

It is remarkable that this small patch of Hampshire farmland once housed such a cluster of historic features, including no less than six large Bronze Age barrows. One of these was the 'Cerdic's Barrow' from the charter. Two near Trinley Estate can be ruled out as they are beyond the former Roman Road past the point marked Cerdic's Barrow, while the Ashtree Barrow now placed near Faulkner's Farm was situated before. That leaves three, of which the one south of Lower Wyke Farm is less favoured than the ones near Tinker's Hill and west of Faulkner's Down Farm. The latter cannot be completely ruled out because it is located where significant land boundaries may have converged. It could fit the charter description and investigations have shown two burial pits underground. The preceding Peartree would seem to be in a similar position and the parish boundaries, which have been subject to change, also run a few hundred metres away from the Tinker's Hill barrow. The barrow near Tinker's Hill was the more striking of the two burial mounds, visible to those traversing the Harrow Way and the old Roman Road, a mile west. You can imagine travellers walking along the Harrow Way and being awestruck with the mound on a hill. This must have been the barrow. Even today with a train line in a small valley between the two points, if you stand on the old Roman Road, this site can also be seen from a distance. Surely, a 72ft-wide burial mound, and some were as much as 13ft high although this varies significantly, would have not gone unnoticed.

Ultimately, where Cerdic's Barrow was 'located' in the tenth-century charter by Alfred the Great's son, there was a spectacularly large barrow. Battles around Hampshire's borders speak of clashes with rival kingdoms as Cerdic appears to be either defending or slowly expanding his territory, against rivals in modern-day Wiltshire, which was not part of his realm. The choice of his burial place facing west towards Wiltshire was twofold: aimed at travellers on the Harrow Way and old Roman Road and deliberately

The most probable final resting place of Cerdic near the former Harrow Way (Walworth Road) and with the old Roman road in the background beyond the hedge

placed near a massive ditch, which acted as a long running boundary. The message with reusing the huge mound near Tinker's Hill was clear: 'This land belongs to the Cerdicing dynasty, enter at your own peril.'

Almost 75 per cent of barrows have been destroyed by development and ploughing in Hampshire and just 5 per cent remain intact.[76] We should be thankful that such a comprehensive mapping of the island's historic landmarks took place from the skies during the twentieth century, and such a rigorous process protects the monuments and ensures they were not lost forever. Thousands of dykes, ancient trackways and barrows have been mapped out across the countryside, towns and villages as Britain's population has increased by more than 20 million in the past century.

As with the Prittlewell Prince, which could be dated to as close to thirty years after Cerdic's death, the body may have dissolved or have been targeted by grave robbers as the St Mary Bourne barrow associated with Cerdic may have been. At some point between the tenth and nineteenth century, the barrow had been destroyed.

After the Norman Conquest and the comprehensive seizure of land from Anglo-Saxon lords, the significance of this barrow may have gradually diminished and eventually become confused with the second one near St Mary Bourne.

Up until the landing of William the Conqueror, some 500 years after Cerdic was buried, this could have been an infamous feature of the landscape. Wessex kings including Alfred the Great were almost certainly hunting in the area and would have stopped to admire the sacred spot of their famed ancestor.

The barrow begins to support the existence of a powerful king in the mid-sixth century known as Cerdic in Old English and has brought the legend to life. This is proof Cerdic was not simply a product of fantasy in the chaotic aftermath of Roman Britain but a real king whose victories against neighbouring warlords spawned one of the most powerful nations in the modern world.

Further investigation needs to take place, but I believe in this small part of Hampshire the body of Cerdic of Wessex was laid to rest. Here, on royal land and the borders of his kingdom, which was roughly equal to Hampshire, a reference was made to the burial mound of Cerdic of Wessex. A sacred final resting place, which was part of the royal estate of Wessex kings, who had ensured it was protected for generations. The same kings who were desperate to trace their ancestry to their kingdom's legendary founder hundreds of years after his death. Devoted followers placed Cerdic's body in a Bronze Age barrow. Their reuse was happening across the country, and none so more than in Wessex, around the age he ruled. Situated on a hill next to a famous ditch, which ran for miles, and an ancient road dating back to the Stone Age, this mound must have been a famous local landmark.

With English-speaking warriors and native Britons, reflecting the migration and cultural transformation after Roman troops departed, Cerdic had forged a powerful new kingdom. Tales of his epic defeat of Natanleod, the victory at Portchester over the 'noble man' and the Isle of Wight were spreading through the land. Memories of these famous victories during extreme hardship would immortalize his reign and he deserved a glorious send-off befitting a warrior king. Kinsmen decided to honour the legendary king by reusing an imposing monument near a spectacular earthwork and old trackways, which his rivals could not miss. A powerful statement of how Cerdic was dead, but his kingdom lived on. The kingdom which grew into England.

Special thanks

I am indebted to David Hopkins, the county archaeologist for Hampshire County Council, for his time and enthusiasm, which really helped kickstart this project.

Mike Farrell, Henry du Val de Beaulieu and another resident for kindly allowing me to search for the ancient barrow. Rupert Matthews, Andrew Breeze, Barbara Yorke, Jillian Hawkins, Jim Gunter, Sharon Gedye and Helen Gould for their insight and assistance.

Above all, I'm thankful to my mum, Julieann, for all her support over the years.

In memory of my dad Norman Harper.

References

Preface

1. www.kongeaastien.dk/en/content/gredstedbro-ship
2. http://early-med.archeurope.com/migration-period/the-nydam-boat
3. https://christhorndycroft.wordpress.com/2015/09/19/anglo-saxon-ships
4. Nicolle, David and McBride, Angus (1984), *Arthur and the Anglo-Saxon Wars*, Osprey Military

Chapter 1: Winchester

1. Historic England website, Round barrow cemetery on Magdalen Hill Down (https://historicengland.org.uk/listing/the-list/list-entry/1016746)
2. Cherryson, Annia (2005), *In the Shadow of the Church, Burial Practices in the Wessex Heartlands*, University of Sheffield, p.87 (Winchester Museums Service History File – Saxon discoveries from St. Giles Hill 1905)
3. Historic Environment Record (Hampshire HERs) 27078, Anglo Saxon burials from St Giles Hill
4. Ekwall, Eilert (1936), *The Concise Oxford Dictionary of England Place Names*, 4th edition, Clarendon Press, p.101
5. Shurlock, Barry, 'Hampshire's horrible history': (26 December 2021), *Hampshire Chronicle*
6. Hawkes, Sonia, Grainger, Guy and Biddulph, E (2003), *The Anglo-Saxon Cemetery at Worthy Park, Kingsworthy, near Winchester, Hampshire*, Oxford University School of Archaeology Monograph
7. Leggett, S. and Lambert, T. (2022), 'Food and Power in Early Medieval England: A Lack of (Isotopic) Enrichment', *Anglo-Saxon England*, Vol 49, pp.155–96

8. Levick, Ben (2002), 'Food and Drink in Anglo Saxon England, Regia Anglorum' (regia.org)
9. Williams, Thomas (2022), *Lost Realms, Histories of Britain from the Romans to the Vikings*, William Collins, p.195
10. Hampshire HERs 32037, Late Roman Early Saxon Cemetery at Itchen Abbas Primary School
11. Cunliffe, Barry (1993), *Wessex to 1000 AD*, 'Regional History of England', Routledge, p.206
12. Email correspondence (2 February 2023)
13. Historic England Research Records, Neatham Roman Settlement, 244074
14. Hampshire Cultural Trust (object no: HMCMS:ACM1967.114.1)
15. Evison, V. I. (1988), *An Anglo Saxon Cemetery at Alton*, Hampshire Field Club & Archaeological Society Monograph (www.hampshirearchaeology.wordpress.com)
16. Anglo Saxon Cemetery at Chalton Peak, 1021292, Historic England National Heritage List, Scheduled Monument
17. Cotswold Archaeology, 'A Research Strategy for the Later Iron Age and Roman periods in the New Forest National Park and surrounding areas', seminar held at Lyndhurst (29 January 2016)
18. King, Anthony (2020), 'Venta Belgarum: What is in the Name for Roman Winchester?', *The Land of the English Kin: Studies in Wessex and Anglo-Saxon England in Honour of Professor Barbara Yorke*, edited by Alexander Langlands and Ryan Lavelle, Brill
19. Biddle, Martin (1971), *Excavations at Winchester*, Tenth and Final Interim Report, Winchester Excavations Committee
20. Rivet, A. L. F. and Smith, Colin (1979), *The Place-Names of Roman Britain*, Batsford, p.267
21. Adams, Max (2021), *The First Kingdom: Britain in the Age of Arthur*, Head of Zeus, p.15
22. Pace, Edwin (2015), 'Walls and Withdrawals: Gildas' Version of the End of Roman Britain', *Journal of the Australian Early Medieval Association*, Vol 11, pp.17–40
23. Guest, Peter (2005), *The Late Roman Gold and Silver Coins from the Hoxne Treasure*, British Museum Press
24. Biddle, Martin and Keane, Martin (2017), *The British Historic Towns Atlas*, Volume VI, Winchester Studies Volume 11, Winchester
25. Chris Catling (1 April 2017), 'Rome's homes on the range: Revealing the Romano-British countryside' (www.archaeology.co.uk)

26. *Excavations at Winchester*
27. Pryor, Francis (2005), *Britain AD: A Quest for Arthur, England and the Anglo-Saxons*, Harper Collins
28. Adams, Max (2021), *The First Kingdom in the Age of Arthur*, Apollo, p.175
29. Biddle, Martin and Keene, Derek (2017), *The British Historic Towns Atlas, Volume VI, Winchester Studies Volume 11, Winchester,* Winchester Excavations Committee
30. Meaney, A. L. and Chadwick Hawkes, S. E. (1970), *Two Anglo-Saxon Cemeteries at Winnal, Winchester, Hampshire*, Society for Medieval Archaeology
31. Dinwiddy, Kirsten (2011), *An Anglo Saxon Cemetery at Twyford near Winchester*, Hampshire Field Club Report
32. *The First Kingdom in the Age of Arthur*, pp.184–85

Chapter 2: The Anglo-Saxons

1. History of Hadleigh Castle, English Heritage website (www.english-heritage.org.uk/visit/places/hadleigh-castle/history)
2. Adams, Max (2015), *In the Land of Giants*, Head of Zeus, p.117
3. Hooke, Della (1998), *The Landscape of Anglo-Saxon England.* Leicester University Press, p.46
4. Museum of London Archaeology (MOA) website (www.prittewellprincelyburial.org)
5. https://archaeology.co.uk/articles/features/new-secrets-from-prittlewell-reconstructing-a-burial-chamber-fit-for-a-prince.htm
6. Smith, Roth (9 May 2019), 'New research questions famed burial of "first" Christian Anglo-Saxon king', *National Geographic*
7. Benham's (1946), *Benham's Colchester — a history and guide*, Benham and Company Limited, Colchester
8. Foster, Jennifer (1986), *The Lexden Tumulus: A Re-appraisal of an Iron Age Burial from Colchester, Essex*, British Archaeological Reports British Series
9. Crummy, Philip (1997), *City of Victory; the story of Colchester – Britain's First Roman Town*, Colchester Archaeological Trust
10. Telephone conversation (23 March 2023)

11. Thomas, Mark, Stumpf, Michael and Harke, Heinrich (2006), 'Evidence for an apartheid-like social structure in early Anglo-Saxon England', *Proceedings of the Royal Society B – Biological Sciences*, Vol. 273 (1601), pp.2651–57.
12. Morris, Marc (2021), *The Anglo-Saxons: A History of the Beginnings of England*, Penguin, p.50
13. Harper, Kyle (2017), *The Fate of Rome: Climate, Disease, and the End of an Empire*, The Princeton History of the Ancient World, Princeton University Press, p.232
14. West Stow Anglo Saxon village (www.weststow.org)
15. Adams, Max (2021), *First Kingdom: Britain in the age of Arthur*, Apollo, p.123
16. West Stow Anglo Saxon Village Museum
17. Gretzinger, Joscha et al (2022), 'The Anglo-Saxon migration and the formation of the early English gene pool', *Nature*, Vol. 610, pp.112–19 (www.nature.com/articles/s41586-022-05247-2)
18. Hills, Catharine (1977), *The Anglo-Saxon Cemetery at Spong Hill, North Elmham, Part I: Catalogue of Cremations*, East Anglian Archaeology 6
19. Hills, C. (1974). 'A runic pot from Spong Hill, North Elmham', *Norfolk Antiquaries Journal*, Vol. 54(1), pp. 87–91.
20. Flowers, Stephen (2006), 'How To Do Things With Runes: A Semiotic Approach To Operative Communication' in Stocklund Marie (chief editor), *Runes and their Secrets: Studies in Runology*, Museum Tusculanum Press
21. Eagles, B. and Briscoe, D. (1999), 'Animal and Bird Stamps on Early Anglo-Saxon Pottery in England', *Studien zur Sachsenforschung*, Vol. 13, pp.99–111
22. Palmer, Lyn and Richardson, Andrew, 'Anglo-Saxon Kent AD 410 to AD 1066', www.kent.gov.uk
23. Fleming, Robin (2011), *Britain After Rome: The Fall and Rise, 400 to 1070*, Penguin History of Britain, pp.75–78; Hines, J. (1984), *The Scandinavian Character of Anglian England in pre-Viking period*, BAR Publishing; Brugmann, B (1999), 'The role of Continental artefact-types in sixth century chronology', in Hines, J., Nielsen, K. H. and Siegmund, F. (editors). *The Pace of Change: Studies in Early-Medieval Chronology*, Oxbow Books, pp.3–64
24. Evison, Vera (1987), *Dover: the Buckland Anglo-Saxon Cemetery*, English Heritage Archaeological Monographs

25. HS2 website (www.hs2.org.uk/building-hs2/archaeology/uncovering-wendover-burial-ground)
26. Adams, Max (2001), *The First Kingdom, the Age of Arthur*, Apollo, pp.127–28
27. Hughes, Susan S. et al. (June 2018), 'Isotopic analysis of burials from the early Anglo-Saxon cemetery at Eastbourne, Sussex, UK, *Journal of Archaeological Science*, Vol. 19, p.302
28. Oosthuizen, Susan (2019), *The Emergence of the English*, Past Imperfect
29. Timofeeva, Olga (2013), 'Latin Loans in Old English and Finnish Loans in Modern English: Can We Distinguish Statistics from Myth?', University of Zurich
30. Fleming, Robin (2011), *Britain After Rome: The Fall and Rise, 400 to 1070*, Penguin History of Britain, p.58
31. *The Emergence of the English*; Gelling, Margaret (2010), *Signposts to the Past*, Phillimore, p.85. Halogen Geospatial Search Facility
32. Williams, Thomas (2022), *Lost Realms, Histories of Britain from the Romans to the Vikings*, William Collins, p.58
33. Callaway, Ewen (2015), 'UK mapped out by genetic ancestry', *Nature* (study uses data from Wellcome Trust-funded People of the British Isles study, an Oxford University project)
34. Crossley-Holland, Kevin (1984), 'The Battle of Brunanburh', *The Anglo-Saxon World, OUP*

Chapters 3–4: Gildas and the *Anglo-Saxon Chronicle*

1. Breay, Claire and Story, Joanna (2018), *Anglo-Saxon Kingdoms: Art, Word, War*, British Library
2. Harper, Paul (2018), 'Medieval British king had ARABIC gold coins praising Allah', 20 October, *Daily Star* online
3. Medieval Manuscripts Blog (23/10/2016), British Library website (www.bl.uk)
4. Phillimore, Egerton (1888), *The Annales Cambriae and Old Welsh Genealogies from Harleian Ms. 3859*, British Library
5. Woods, David (2010), 'Gildas and the Mystery Cloud of 536–37', *Journal of Theological Studies*, Vol. 61 pp.226–34
6. Breeze, Andrew (2020), *British Battles 493–937: Mount Badon to Brunanburh*, Anthem Studies in British History, Anthem Press, pp.1–6

7. Morris, Marc (2021), *The Anglo-Saxons: A History of the Beginnings of England*, Hutchinson
8. Tacitus (2004), *The Annals*, translated by A. J. Woodman, Hackett Publishing
9. Jenkins, P. (2013), 'Maurice, Son of Theodoric: Welsh Kings and the Mediterranean World AD550–650' North *American Journal of Welsh Studies*, Vol 8, pp.4–5
10. Phillips, Graham (2016), *The Lost Tomb of King Arthur*, Bear & Company, pp.190–91
11. Laycock, Stuart (2009), *Warlords: The Struggle for Power in Post-Roman Britain*, History Press, p.154
12. Fleming, Robin (2010), *Britain after Rome: The Fall and Rise, 400–1070*, Allen Lane, pp.86–88
13. *The Lost Tomb of King Arthur*, p.191
14. *Britain After Rome*
15. Matthews, Rupert (2012), *Ceawlin, the Man Who Created England*, Pen and Sword
16. Koch, John (2006), *Celtic Culture: A Historical Encyclopedia*, ABC-CLIO
17. Whitehead, Annie (2020), *Mercia: The Rise and Fall of a Kingdom*, Amberley Publishing
18. Schrijver, Peter (2014), *Language Contact and the Origins Of The Germanic Languages*, Routledge, p.20
19. Forester, Thomas (1854), *The Chronicle of Florence of Worcester*, Henry G Bohn
20. Koch, John (2005), *Celtic Culture: A Historical Encyclopedia* (five volumes), ABC-CLIO
21. Adams, Max (2014), *The King in the North: The Life and Times of Oswald of Northumbria*, Head of Zeus
22. Albert, Edoardo and Gething, Paul (2020), *Warrior: A life of war in Anglo Saxon Britian,* Granta Press, p.232
23. Pace, Edwin (2023), *Long War for Britannia*, Pen & Sword, p.131
24. Harper, Paul (2018), 'REVEALED: The mystery warrior who founded mighty kingdom that became England', 9 March, *Daily Star* online
25. Old English Translation of Gregory the Great's 'Cura Pastoralis' (890–97), Bodleian Library, University of Oxford
26. *Ceawlin, the Man Who Created England*, p.118
27. Ashley, Mike (2005), *Mammoth Book of King Arthur*, Mammoth, pp.80–81

28. Copley, Gordon (1954), *The Conquest of Wessex in the 6th Century*, Phoenix House, p.144
29. Harrison, K. (1976), *The Framework of Anglo-Saxon History to AD 900*, CUP
30. Dumville, David (1985), 'The West Saxon Genealogical Regnal List and the Chronology of Early Wessex', *Peritia,* Vol 4, pp.21–66
31. Retief, Francois Pieter and Cilliers, Louise (2010), 'Causes of death among the Caesars (27 BC–AD 476)', *Acta Theologica*, Vol. 26(2), pp.89–106
32. Crawford, O.G.S. (1931), 'Cerdic and The Cloven Way', *Antiquity Journal*, Vol. 5, pp.441–58
33. Elkwall, Eilert (1936*), The Concise Oxford Dictionary of England Place Names* (fourth edition), Clarendon Press, p.245
34. Jones, Graham (1998), Penda's Footprint? Place-Names Containing Personal Names Associated with those of Early Mercian Kings, *Nomina*, Vol. 21, pp.29–62
35. *The Concise Oxford Dictionary of England Place Names*, p.129
36. *The Concise Oxford Dictionary of England Place Names*, p.129, p.136
37. S 272, AD 825 (Criodantreow, 19 Aug.; Southampton, 26 Dec.). Egbert, king, to Old Minster, Winchester; grant of 15 hides (manentes) at Alton Priors, Wilts., formerly held by Burgheard, præfectus., Winchester, Old Minster
38. S 273, AD 825 (Creodantreow, 19 Aug.; Southampton, 26 Dec.). Egbert, king, to the minster of SS Peter and Paul (Winchester); grant of 5 hides (cassati) at (Martyr) Worthy, Hants, Winchester, Old Minster
39. Both Cynric's and Ceawlin's reigns are clearly questionable, but the evidence is contradictory. Cynric is given reign lengths of 26×3, 23 and 27 years in the Regnal List but only fought in two battles as king. Ceawlin's seven year kingship is also possible, but he was recorded as a *Bretwalda*, which meant overlordship of Anglo-Saxon kingdoms south of the Humber, in such a short timeframe. I'm certain Creoda ruled at some point in the later-sixth century but speculating on exact dates with so many conflicting issues, after much deliberation, is best avoided.
40. *Countryfile*, 23 August 2009. BBC One

Chapter 5–6: The Volcanic Winter and Justinian Plague

1. Harper, Kyle (2019), *Fate of Rome: Climate, Disease, and the End of an Empire*, Princeton University Press, p.279
2. Nicola Royan (18 May 2015), 'Eclipses and comets and portents (oh my)', University of Nottingham blog
3. Cesario, Marilina, 'Medieval recordings of comet sightings map, 676 to 1145', Queen University Belfast (British Academy website)
4. Cassiodorus (2006), *The Letters of Cassiodorus Being A Condensed Translation Of The Variae Epistolae Of Magnus Aurelius Cassiodorus Senator,* Project Gutenberg, translated by Thomas Hodgkin
5. Gibbons, Ann (2018) 'Why 536 was 'the worst year to be alive', *Science*, 15 November
6. Newfield, Timothy (2018), 'The Climate Downturn of 536–50', *The Palgrave Handbook of Climate History* Palgrave Macmillan, pp.447–93
7. Hamilton, F. J. and Brooks, E. W. (translators) (1899), *The Syriac Chronicle Known as that of Zachariah of Mitylene*, Methuen
8. The Chronicle of Marcellinus, Migne, Jacques (translator), *Patrologia Latina*, Vol. 51
9. 'The Climate Downturn of 536–50'
10. Sarris, Peter, 'Climate and Disease', in Hermans, Erik (editor), *A Companion to the Global Early Middle Ages, Arc Companions*, ARC Humanities Press, Chapter 18
11. Sarris, Peter, *Climate and Disease*
12. *Fate of Rome*, p.224
13. Little, Lester (2007), *Plague and the End of Antiquity: The Pandemic of 541–750*, Cambridge University Press
14. Procopius (1914), *History of the Wars* (seven volumes), translated by H. B. Dewing, Loeb Library of the Greek and Roman Classics, Harvard University Press, Vol. I, pp.451–73
15. Sarris, Peter (2022), 'Viewpoint New Approaches to the "Plague of Justinian", *Past & Present*, Vol. 254, Issue 1, February, pp.315–46
16. *Fate of Rome*, p.223
17. Sarris, Peter, *Climate and Disease*
18. Figure from contemporary historian John of Ephesus (Plague in the Ancient World: A Study from Thucydides to Justinian by Christine A.

Smith. *The Student History Journal*, 1996–1997, Vol. XXVIII, Loyola University, New Orleans, History Department)

19. Sarris, Peter, 'Viewpoint New Approaches to the "Plague of Justinian"'
20. *Fate of Rome*, p.226, p.236
21. *Fate of Rome*, p.262
22. *Fate of Rome*, p.278
23. Wagner, D. M., Klunk, J. and Harbeck, M. (2014), 'Yersinia pestis and the Plague of Justinian 541–543 AD: a genomic analysis', *Lancet Infectious Diseases*
24. *Fate of Rome*, p.210 (Mapping risk of plague in Qinghai-Tibetan Plateau, China, *BCM Infectious Diseases*, 2014)
25. 'The Climate Downturn of 536–50'
26. Sigl, M. et al (2015), 'Timing and climate forcing of volcanic eruptions for the past 2,500 years', *Nature*, Vol. 523, pp.543–49
27. Gibbons, Ann (2018), 'Why 536 was 'the worst year to be alive', *Science*, 15 November
28. 'The Climate Downturn of 536–50'
29. El Chichon eruption implicated in Maya upheaval, BBC News, 20 April 2016
30. Toohey, Matthew et al (2016), 'Climatic and societal impacts of a volcanic double event at the dawn of the Middle Ages', *Climatic Change*, Vol. 136, pp.401–12
31. Keller, M. et al (2019), 'Ancient *Yersinia pestis* genomes from across Western Europe reveal early diversification during the First Pandemic (541–750)', *PNAS*, Vol. 116 (25), pp. 12363–72
32. 'Generating the genomes of ancient plague' (7 April 2019), (www.Archaeology.co.uk)
33. Email correspondence (10 March 2023)
34. *Age of Arthur*, pp.222–23
35. *Fate of Rome*, p.225
36. Thomas, Charles (1993), *Tintagel: Arthur and Archaeology*, Batsford/English Heritage
37. Pryor, Frances (2004), *Britain AD: a Quest for Arthur, England and the Anglo-Saxons*, Harper Perennial, p.183
38. Sarris, Peter, Viewpoint New Approaches to the 'Plague of Justinian'
39. Fleming, Robin, *Britain after Rome: The Fall and Rise, 400–1070*, Penguin History of Britain, pp.32–35

40. Historic England website, 'Large multivallate hillfort and associated earthworks at South Cadbury' (https://historicengland.org.uk/listing/the-list/list-entry/1011980)
41. Adams, Max (2021), *The First Kingdom, Britain In the Age of Arthur*, Head of Zeus, pp.92–94
42. Pryor, Francis (2004), *Britain AD, A Quest for Arthur, England and the Anglo Saxons*, Harper Perennial, pp.167–72
43. English Heritage website (www.english-heritage.org.uk/visit/places/silchester-roman-city-walls-and-amphitheatre/history)
44. Gräslund, Bo and Price, Neil (2012), 'Twilight of the gods? The "dust veil event" of AD 536 in critical perspective', *Antiquity*, Vol. 86, Issue 332, June, pp.428–43
45. Löwenborg, Daniel (2012). 'An Iron Age Shock Doctrine – Did the AD 536-7 event trigger large-scale social changes in the Mälaren valley area?', *Journal of Archaeology and Ancient History*, No. 4
46. Gräslund, B. (2007), *Fimbulvintern, Ragnarök och klimatkrisen år 536–537 e. Kr*, Saga & Sed, pp.93–123
47. *Fate of Rome*, pp.100–101
48. Breeze, Andrew (2020), *British Battles 493–937: Mount Badon to Brunanburh*, Anthem Press, p.7
49. Lloyd, Scott and Blake, Steve (2002), *Pendragon, The Definitive Account of the Origins of Arthur*, Rider Books, p.169–73
50. *Pendragon*, p.148
51. Grigg, Erik (2018), *Warfare, Raiding and Defence*, Robert Hale, pp.113–18
52. Oosthuizen, Susan (2019), *The Emergence of the English (Past Imperfect)*, Arc Humanities Press, p.78
53. Maddicott, John (2012), 'Plague in Seventh-Century England' in Little, Lester K. (editor) *Plague and the End of Antiquity The Pandemic of 541–750*, CUP, pp.171–214

Chapters 7–8: The Solent and New Forest

1. Alexander, Michael J. (translator) (1996), *The Early English Poems*, Penguin Classic
2. New Forest National Park website (www.newforestnpa.gov.uk/things-to-do/walking/new-forest-walks/lepe-to-fawley)

3. Clarke, Arthur (2003), 'The Roman road on the eastern fringe of the New Forest, from Shorn Hill to Lepe', *Proceedings of the Hampshire Field Club*, Vol. 58, pp.33–58
4. Hampshire HERs 29936, Roman Road Margary Rr42
5. Crawford, Osbert G. S. (1952), 'Cerdic's Landing Place', *Antiquity*, Vol. 26(104), pp.193–200
6. Hampshire HERs 29940, Roman Ring
7. Hampshire HERs 29942, Bronze Roman Coins
8. Hampshire HERs 70361, Roman Coins
9. Hampshire HERs 29933, Roman Amulet
10. 'The Roman road on the eastern fringe of the New Forest, from Shorn Hill to Lepe'
11. Nicolle, David and McBride, Angus (1984), *Arthur and the Anglo-Saxon Wars*, Osprey Military
12. Williams, Rupert (2012), *Ceawlin, The Man who Created England*, Pen & Sword, pp.131–33
13. Fixing an exact date of battles in Cerdic's revised reign has been avoided as the New Year was calculated differently by chroniclers with some starting the year in March, 25 December or 1 January. With the clear pattern of dating, entries should be forwarded by nineteen years, but this could be from one or two specific years, which could also be a year out given differing original dates for the landing and taking over the kingdom, making 'late 530s' etc. more appropriate.
14. Copley, Gordon (1954), *The Conquest of Wessex in the 6th Century*, Phoenix House, p.150
15. Pace, Edwin (2021), *The Long War for Britannia*, Pen & Sword, p.103
16. Southampton Archaeology Unit Report 1035, 'Archaeological desk-based assessment of Bitterne Manor Park, Southampton'. PR Cottrell BA 2011
17. Englefield, H. (1805), *A Walk Through Southampton* (second edition), Baker and Fletcher
18. Wessex Archaeology website (www.wessexarch.co.uk/our-work/southampton-st-marys-stadium)
19. Davies, Sue, Walker, Karen and Coleman, Linda (1998), *The New Forest Historical Landscape*, Wessex Archaeology, p.13
20. *Cerdic's Landing Place*
21. SU3501, linear earthwork on Beaulieu Heath, New Forest (www.geograph.org.uk/photo/458651)

22. *S 229. Cenwalh, king of Wessex, to the church of SS Peter and Paul, Winchester (Old Minster); grant of 100 hides (mansae) at Downton, Wilts, Winchester, Old Minster*
23. Hill, A. du Boulay (1910), 'The Saxon Boundaries of Downton, Wilts.' *Wiltshire Archaeological Magazine*, Vol. 36, pp.50–56
24. Crawford, Osbert (1931), 'Cerdic and the Cloven Way', *Antiquity*, Vol. V, December
25. Wiltshire HERs, SU21NW610, SU21NE605, MWI6453
26. Hampshire HERs 54141, Searchfield Deer Park
27. Hampshire HERs 29666, Flint Scatter
28. *Ceawlin, The Man who Created England*, p.135
29. Wrathmell, S., Roberts, B. (2003), *Region and Place: A Study of English Rural Settlement*, English Heritage
30. Albany, F. Major (1913), *The Early Wars of Wessex*, Cambridge University Press
31. Hampshire HERs 21748, Bowl Barrow
32. Hampshire HERs 56858, Long Barrow 600 yards (550m) SE of Vanity
33. Wiltshire HERs SU12SW629, Five Barrows, North East of Grims Ditch Angle With W Fork
34. Elkwall, Eilert (1936), *The Concise Oxford Dictionary of England Place Names* (fourth edition), Clarendon Press, p.338
35. Breeze, Andrew (2000), 'Netley Marsh, Hampshire', in Coates, Richard and Breeze, Andrew with Horovitz, David (editors), *Celtic Voices, English Places*, Shaun Tyas, pp.97–99
36. New Forest National Park website (www.newforestnpa.gov.uk)
37. *The Concise Oxford Dictionary of England Place Names*, p.336
38. Downton Moot website (downtonmoot.co.uk/moot-history)
39. Sarah Nash, 'Downton Moot: A Norman Castle Under 18th Century Gardens' (archaeology-travel.com/england/downton-moot)
40. *Early Wars of Wessex (The Moot and its Traditions, EP Squarey, 1906)*
41. 'Downton Moot: A Norman Castle Under 18th Century Gardens'
42. Rockbourne Roman Villa, Hampshire Cultural Trust website (www.hampshireculture.org.uk)
43. Wiltshire HERs, SU12SE402, SU12SE301, SU12SE400
44. Keys, David (2020), 'Sixth century warrior set to shed new light on Dark Ages', *Independent*, 5/10/2020 (rdg.ac/marlowwarlord)
45. 'Anglo Saxon Beasts', History Extra website, 3 January 2019 (www.historyextra.com)

46. Hampshire Archaeology website (hampshirearchaeology.wordpress.com/2015/09/21/buried-in-time-the-breamore-bucket)
47. Hinton, David and Worrell, Sally (2017) 'An Early Anglo-Saxon Cemetery and Archaeological Survey at Breamore, Hampshire, 1999–2006', *Archaeological Journal*, Vol. 174, Issue 1, pp.68–145
48. *Cerdic's Landing Place*
49. *The Concise Oxford Dictionary of England Place Names*
50. Lipscomb, George (1847), *The History and Antiquities of the County of Buckingham* (Volume 4), J. & W. Robins
51. www.dot-domesday.me.uk/wessex.htm (Frank Stenton, *Anglo-Saxon England,* Oxford University Press, 1971)
52. Eagles, Bruce (2001), 'Anglo Saxon Presence and Culture in Wiltshire c. AD450–c. AD677', Bournemouth University
53. Eagles, Bruce, Algar David and Saunders, Peter, with a contribution by Kirsten Egging Dinwiddy (2014) 'Two graves near Old Sarum: further insight into early Anglo-Saxon settlement around Salisbury', *Wiltshire Archaeological & Natural History Magazine*, Vol. 107, pp.77–90
54. 'Anglo Saxon Presence and Culture in Wiltshire'

Chapter 9: Elegy for Geraint

1. Camden, William (1607) *Britannia,* George Bishop
2. Lloyd, Scott and Blake, Steve (2002), *Pendragon, The Definitive Account of the Origins of Arthur*, Rider Books, p.49
3. *Portchester Castle*, English Heritage Guidebooks
4. Cotterill, John (1993), 'Saxon Raiding and the Role of the Late Roman Coastal Forts of Britain, Britannia', *Society for the Promotion of Roman Studies,* Vol. 24, pp.227–39.
5. Pearson, Andrew (2002), *The Roman Shore Forts, Coastal Defences of Southern Britain*, Tempus Publishing, pp.137–38
6. Hawkins, Jill (2020), 'Swords and Swords: People and Power along the Solent in the 5th Century' in Langlands, Alexander and Lavelle, Ryan (editors), *The Land of the English Kin: Studies in Wessex and Anglo-Saxon England in Honour of Professor Barbara Yorke*, Brill, pp.50–69

7. Email correspondence (9 January 2023). Dr Hawkins said: 'I know forts such as Portchester did have such sites nearby because they were protected by walls, and boats couldn't get inside. However, the general use of *wic* to signify an emporium happened, I believe, later on, with the sites I mentioned before, and others, and including for example *Quentovic* near the mouth of the Canche across the Channel. But, as we know, *wic* has a variety of significances and was used in the developing English language in various ways, such as its early usage in all the places called *wicham.'*
8. Probert, Duncan (2010), 'New light on Aldhelm's letter to King Gerent of Dumnonia', in Barker, Katherine and Brooks, Nicholas (editors), *Aldhelm and Sherborne: Essays to Commemorate the Founding of the Bishopric*, Oxbow, pp.110–28
9. Morris, John (1973), *The Age of Arthur, A History of the British Isles from 350 to 650,* Phoenix Press
10. Cunliffe, Barry, *Excavations of Portchester Castle* (five volumes) The Society of Antiquaries of London
11. Cunliffe, Barry (1993), *Wessex to AD 1000*, Longman, p.72
12. Elkwall, Eilert (1936), *The Concise Oxford Dictionary of England Place Names* (fourth edition), Clarendon Press, p.34
13. *The Concise Oxford Dictionary of England Place Names*, p.42
14. *The Concise Oxford Dictionary of England Place Names*, p.96
15. Porthscatho and Gerrans Bay walk, South West Coast Path website (www.southwestcoastpath.org.uk/print-walk/653/)
16. *Portchester Castle*, English Heritage Guidebooks
17. Pace, Edwin (2021), *Long War for Britannia, Arthur and the History of Post Roman Britain*, Pen and Sword, p.197
18. Bartrum, Peter (1993), *A Welsh Classical Dictionary* (first edition), National Library of Wales pp.496–506
19. https://en.wikipedia.org/wiki/Glynarthen
20. Ceredigion Bay HERs 25473, 40420, 23235
21. Dyfed Archaeological HERs 56969, Beddgeraint, nr Newcastle Emlyn, Carmarthenshire
22. https://coflein.gov.uk/en/site/103703
23. Fleming, Robin (2011), *Britain After Rome: The Fall and Rise, 400 to 1070*, Penguin History of Britain, p.97
24. Lloyd, Scott and Blake, Steve (2002), *Pendragon, The Definitive Account of the Origins of Arthur*, Rider Books p.114–15

Chapter 10: Isle of Wight

1. Alexander, Michael J. (translator) (1996), *The Early English Poems*, Penguin Classic
2. Snow, Dan (2015), *Armada: 12 Days to Save England*, BBC Two
3. Carisbrooke Castle display, English Heritage
4. Waller, Ruth (2006), Archaeological Resource Assessment of the Isle of Wight: Early Medieval Period, Isle of Wight History Centre
5. Copley, Gordon (1954), *The Conquest of Wessex in the 6th Century*, Phoenix House, p.150
6. Yorke, Barbara (1995), *Wessex in the Early Middle Ages*, Leicester University Press, p.37
7. Harrington, Sue (2020), 'A Well-Married Landscape: Networks of Association and 6th-Century Communities on the Isle of Wight' in Langlands, Alexander and Lavelle, Ryan (editors), *The Land of the English Kin: Studies in Wessex and Anglo-Saxon England in Honour of Professor Barbara Yorke*, Brill, pp.95–111; Arnold, C. J. (1982), *The Anglo-Saxon Cemeteries of the Isle of Wight*, British Museum Press
8. O'Brien, Elizabeth (1996), 'Post Roman Britain to Anglo-Saxon England: The Burial Evidence Reviewed', thesis, Corpus Christi College, University of Oxford
9. *A Well-Married Landscape*
10. *A Well-Married Landscape*
11. Historic England website: 'Two bowl barrows 460m NNW of Longstone Cottage: part of a round barrow cemetery on Mottistone Down' (https://historicengland.org.uk/listing/the-list/list-entry/1007797)
12. *A Well-Married Landscape*
13. *Wessex in the Early Middle Ages*, p.37
14. https://brewminate.com/anglo-saxon-england-and-decoding-anglo-saxon-art/
15. Stedman, M. (1998), 'Three early Anglo-Saxon metalwork finds from the Isle of Wight, 1993–6', *Proceedings of the Hampshire Field Club*, Vol. 53, pp.109–19
16. Crawford, Osbert (1931), 'Cerdic and the Cloven Way', *Antiquity*, Vol. 5, pp.441–58
17. Carisbrooke Castle, English Heritage guidebook
18. Mills, A. D. (1998), *Dictionary of English Place-Names* (second edition)

19. Stoodley, N. and Stedman, M. (2001), 'Excavations at Shavards Farm, Meonstoke: the Anglo-Saxon cemetery', *Proceedings of the Hampshire Field Club* , Vol. 56, 129–69
20. Hawkins, Jill (2020), 'Swords and Swords: People and Power along the Solent in the 5th Century', in Langlands, Alexander and Lavelle, Ryan, *The Land of the English Kin: Studies in Wessex and Anglo-Saxon England in Honour of Professor Barbara Yorke*, Brill
21. Aldsworth, F. G. (1975), 'The pagan Saxon cemetery at Droxford', *Hampshire Archaeology and Local History Newsletter*, No. 2, pp.105–7
22. Dickinson, Tania, Morris, Elaine (2002), 'Early Saxon graves and grave goods', in Young, C. J. (editor), *Excavations at Carisbrooke Castle, Isle of Wight, 1921–1996*, Wessex Archaeology (Salisbury), pp. 86–96
23. Young, C. J. (editor) (2000), *Excavations at Carisbrooke Castle, Isle of Wight, 1921–1996*, Wessex Archaeology
24. *Carisbrooke Castle*, English Heritage guidebook
25. 'Early Saxon graves and grave goods'
26. *Carisbrooke Castle*, English Heritage guidebook
27. Rigold, S. E. (1975), 'Coins and museums', *British Numismatic Journal*, Vol. 45, pp.119–26
28. *A Well-Married Landscape*
29. Copley, Gordon (1954), *The Conquest of Wessex in the 6th Century*, Phoenix House p.148
30. https://unaparolaalgiorno.it/amp/significato/consobrino
31. *The Conquest of Wessex in the 6th Century*, p.149

Chapter 11: The Gewisse and the Upper Thames

1. Austin, Matthew (2017), 'Anglo-Saxon Great Hall Complexes' Elite Residences and Landscapes of Power in Early England, c. AD 550–700', PhD, University of Reading School of Archaeology, Geography and Environmental Sciences (SAGES), p.6
2. 'Anglo-Saxon Great Hall Complexes' (Drauschke, J. (2010), 'The Search for Central Places in the Merovingian Kingdom, in Ludowici, B. et al (editors) (2010), *Trade and Communication Networks of the First Millennium Ad in the Northern Part of Central Europe: Central Places, Beach Markets, Landing Places and Trading*

Centres, Neue Studien zur Sachsenforschung 1, Niedersächsisches Landesmuseum)

3. Sawyer, P. (1983), 'The Royal Tun in Pre-Conquest England' in Wormald, P., Bullough, D. and Collins, R. (editors), *Ideal and Reality in Frankish and Anglo-Saxon Society*, Blackwell, pp.273–97
4. Hamerow, H., Ferguson, C. and Naylor, J. (2013), 'The Origins of Wessex Pilot Project', *Oxoniensia*, Vol. 78, pp.49–69
5. Kirk, J. and Leeds, E.T. (1952), 'Three Early Saxon Graves from Dorchester, Oxon.', *Oxoniensia*, Vol. 17–18, pp.63–76
6. Kirk, J. and Leeds, E.T. (1952), 'Three Early Saxon Graves from Dorchester, Oxon.', *Oxoniensia*, Vol. 17–18, pp. 75–76)
7. 'The Origins of Wessex Pilot Project' (Booth, P. (2014), *A Late Roman Military Burial from the Dyke Hills, Dorchester on Thames, Oxfordshire*, Cambridge University Press')
8. 'The Origins of Wessex Pilot Project'
9. Clarke, Giles (1979), *Pre-Roman and Roman Winchester, Part II: The Roman cemetery at Lankhills* (Winchester Studies III), Oxford University Press, pp.288–89
10. Härke, H. (2011), 'Anglo-Saxon immigration and ethnogenesis', *Medieval Archaeology*, Vol. 55, pp.1–28. Based on figures from Budd, P., Millard, A. and Chenery, C. (2004) 'Investigating population movement by stable isotope analysis: a report from Britain', *Antiquity*, Vol. 78, pp.127–41 and Montgomery, J., Evans, J. A. and Powlesland, D. (2005), 'Continuity or colonization in Anglo Saxon England?', *American Journal of Physical Anthropology*, Vol. 126(2), pp.123–38 Harke notes: 'The proportion of 17% of first-generation(s) immigrants is not stated as such in their texts, but has to be calculated from the presented data.'
11. 'Anglo-Saxon immigration and ethnogenesis'
12. 'Anglo-Saxon immigration and ethnogenesis' (Sayer, D. (2007), 'Community, Kinship and Household: An Analysis of Patterns in early Anglo-Saxon Inhumation Cemeteries', University of Reading. Sayer has suggested a slightly different cemetery organisation at Berinsfield, but he also inferred the existence of three contemporaneous cemetery plots)
13. Email correspondence (17 March 2022)
14. Clay, John-Henry (2013), 'Adventus, warfare and the Britons in the development of West Saxon identity'. In Pohl, W. and Heydemann, G.

(editors), *Post-Roman transitions: Christian and Barbarian identities in the Early Medieval West*, Brepols, pp.169–213

15. Baring-Gould, John Fisher (1907), *The Lives of the British Saints The Saints of Wales and Cornwall and Such Irish Saints as Have dedications in Britain*, Vol. 1, p.44
16. www.livius.org/articles/legion/legio-ii-augusta
17. Email correspondence (11 January 2023)
18. Coates, Richard (1989–90), 'On some controversy surrounding Gewissae/Gewissei, Cerdic and Ceawlin', *Nomina*, Vol. 13, pp.1–11.
19. Email correspondence (26 January 2023)
20. Coates, Richard (2013), 'The name of the Hwicce: A discussion', *Anglo-Saxon England*, Vol. 42, pp.51–61.
21. King, Anthony (2020), 'Venta Belgarum: What Is in the Name for Roman Winchester?' in Langlands, Alexander and Lavelle, Ryan (editors), *The Land of the English Kin: Studies in Wessex and Anglo-Saxon England in Honour of Professor Barbara Yorke*, Brill, pp.13–25
22. Chambers, R. A. (1987), 'The late- and sub-Roman cemetery at Queenford Farm, Dorchesteron-Thames, Oxon', *Oxoniensia*, Vol. 52, pp.35–69
23. Fleming, Robin (2010), *Britain After Rome, The Fall and Rise*, Allen Lane, pp.53–54
24. Hughes, Susan S. et al. (2014), 'Anglo-Saxon origins investigated by isotopic analysis of burials from Berinsfield, Oxfordshire', *Journal of Archaeological Science*, Vol. 42, February, pp.81–92
25. 'Anglo-Saxon immigration and ethnogenesis'
26. Pace, Edwin, *Long War for Britannia*, Pen & Sword, p.163
27. Jones, Graham (1998), 'Penda's Footprint? Place-Names Containing Personal Names Associated with those of Early Mercian Kings', *Nomina*, Vol. 21, pp.29–62
28. 'The Origins of Wessex Pilot Project'
29. Akerman, John (1861), 'Report on Researches in an Anglo-Saxon Cemetery at Long Wittenham, Berkshire, in 1859', *Archaeologia*, Vol. 38, No. 2, pp.327–352
30. 'The Origins of Wessex Pilot Project'
31. 'The Origins of Wessex Pilot Project'
32. Austin, Matthew (2017), 'Anglo-Saxon Great Hall Complexes' Elite Residences and Landscapes of Power in Early England, c.

AD 550–700, PhD, University of Reading School of Archaeology, Geography and Environmental Sciences (SAGES), p.142
33. Millett, M. and James, S. (1983), 'Excavations at Cowdery's Down, Basingstoke, Hampshire, 1978–81', *Archaeological Journal*, Vol. 140, pp.151–279
34. Anglo-Saxon Great Hall Complexes', p.31
35. Halsall, Guy (2013), *Worlds of Arthur: Facts and Fictions of the Dark Ages*, Oxford University Press, p.105
36. Pryor, Francis (2004), *Britain AD, A Quest for Arthur, England and the Anglo Saxons*, Harper Perennial, p.208

Chapter 12: Monmouth, Caradoc and Arthur

1. Ogden, Daniel (1999), 'Binding Spells: Curse Tablets and Voodoo Dolls in the Greek and Roman Worlds' in Ankarloo, Bengt and Clark, Stuart (editors), *Witchcraft and Magic in Europe, Volume 2: Ancient Greece and Rome*. pp.1–90
2. Gager, John G. (1999), *Curse Tablets and Binding Spells from the Ancient World*, OUP
3. Thorpe, Lewis (1973), *The History of the Kings of Britain*, Penguin Classics, p.17
4. Lloyd, Scott and Blake, Steve (2002), *Pendragon, The Definitive Account of the Origins of Arthur*, Rider Books, p.14
5. Russell, Miles (2017), *Arthur and the Kings of Britain: The Historical Truth Behind the Myth*, Amberley, p.290–93
6. Pace, Edwin (2016), 'Athelstan, "Twist-Beard", and Arthur's Tenth-Century Breton Origins for the "Historia Regum Britanniae" (Zenker, Rudolf (1896), *Das Epos von Isembard und Gormund*, Niemeyer, pp.81–83)
7. *Arthur and the Kings of Britain*, p.297, p.298
8. Email correspondence (11 May 2020)
9. Pace, Edwin (2021), *Long War for Britannia, Arthur and the History of Post Roman Britain*, Pen and Sword, pp.323–25
10. Breeze, Andrew (2002), 'Elaphus the Briton, St Germanus, and Bede', *The Journal of Theological Studies*, Vol. 53, Issue 2, 1 October, pp.554–57
11. Email correspondence (11 January 2023)

12. Pace, Edwin (2021), *Long War for Britannia, Arthur and the History of Post Roman Britain*, Pen and Sword, p.64
13. Bartrum, Peter (1993), *A Welsh Classical Dictionary* (first edition), National Library of Wales, p.276
14. Olsen, Brandon (2011), 'The Dedication of Roman Weapons and Armor in Water as a Religious Ritual', *Popular Archaeology*, 27 May
15. Keys, David (1990), 'The Sword that had to Die', *New Scientist*, 17 March
16. Bartrum, Peter (1993), 'Life of St Tatheus' in *A Welsh Classical Dictionary* (first edition), National Library of Wales, p.113
17. Caerwent Church, Early British Kingdoms website (www.earlybritishkingdoms.com/archaeology/caerwentch.html)
18. *A Welsh Classical Dictionary*
19. Baring-Gould, Sabine and Fisher, John (1990), 'Lives of the British Saints', Vol. 4. p.375, Llanerch Press (Hafod MS 19 (1536), p.141)
20. Email Correspondence (26 January 2023)
21. Philips, Graham (2016), *The Lost Tomb of King Arthur*, Bear & Company, p.200
22. Rudmin, John C. and Rudmin, Joseph, W. (1993), 'Arthur, Cerdic, and the Formation of Wessex', James Madison University
23. Harper, Paul (2018), 'REVEALED: The mystery warrior who founded mighty kingdom that became England', 9 March, *Daily Star* online
24. Williams, Thomas (2022), *Lost Realms, Histories of Britain from the Romans to the Vikings*, William Collins, pp.233–324

Chapters 13–16: Cerdic's Barrow

1. Orwell, George (1941), 'England Your England' essay, *The Lion and the Unicorn: Socialism and the English Genius*, Secker & Warburg
2. Historic England (2018), Prehistoric Barrows and Burial Mounds, Introductions to Heritage Assets, Historic England (https://historicengland.org.uk/images-books/publications/iha-prehistoric-barrows-burial-mounds)
3. Myres, John (1989), *The English Settlements*, Oxford History of England, p.155
4. S 359, AD 900 (Winchester), King Edward to the familia of Winchester Cathedral; grant of 10 hides (manentes) at Stoke by Hurstbourne,

Hants., in exchange for land at Chisledon, and Sparcells in Lydiard Millicent, Wilts. Incorporating a record, in English, of services and dues rendered at Hurstbourne, Winchester, Old Minster

5. Grundy, George (1927), 'The Saxon Land Charters of Hampshire with Notes on Place and Field Names', *The Archaeological Journal*, Vol. 84, pp.160–340
6. www.hampshire-history.com/weyhill-fair/
7. Lewis, Samuel (1848), 'Andover–Anston', *A Topographical Dictionary of England*, S Lewis and Co., pp.58–62 (www.british-history.ac.uk/topographical-dict/england/pp58-62)
8. www.purple-emperor.co.uk/harewood-forest
9. William of Malmesbury's 'Regesta Regum Anglorum' (Deeds of the English Kings)
10. Spaul, John (2004), *Andover 950–1974*, Aluric Press, pp.176–77
11. Department of Plant Science, University of Oxford. The Ancient Oaks of England, Deer Parks (www.herbaria.plants.ox.ac.uk)
12. Hooke, D. (1998), *The Landscape of Anglo-Saxon England*, University of Leicester Press, p.154
13. Gedye, Sharon (2022), 'The Bucks of Buckfast: a venerable tale of venery and venison', *A Walk in English Weather Dartmoor, Devon, and Beyond* (https://awalkinenglishweather.com)
14. Stamper, P. (2008), 'Deer parks and hunting', *Parks and Gardens* (www.parksandgardens.org)
15. Halili, Jonah (2021), 'A Study of Hunting Scenes and Virtus in Roman Art, Third to Sixth Centuries', thesis McMaster University
16. 'A Study of Hunting Scenes and Virtus in Roman Art'
17. Allen, Martyn, 'Hunting in the Roman world: anthropology, animal bones and ancient literature', University of Reading (https://notjustdormice.wordpress.com/)
18. Sykes, N. J., White, J., Hayes, T. and Palmer, M. (2006), 'Tracking animals using strontium isotopes in teeth: the role of fallow deer (Dama dama) in Roman Britain', *Antiquity*, Vol. 80, pp.948–59
19. Cunliffe, Barry (1983), *Danebury: Anatomy of an Iron Age Hillfort*, Batsford
20. Historic England, scheduled monument, Bury Hill camp (https://historicengland.org.uk/listing/the-list/list-entry/1001951)
21. Davies, S. M. (1979), Excavations at Old Down farm, Andover. Part I: Saxon, *Proceedings of Hampshire Field Club*, Vol. 36, pp. 161–80

22. Hampshire HERs 29056, Saxon and Roman find spots, Finkley Down
23. Hawkes, Sonia and Grainger, Guy (2003), The Anglo-Saxon Cemetery at Worthy Park, Kingsworthy, near Winchester, Hampshire, *Oxford University School of Archaeology Monographs*, University of Oxford
24. 'Buried in time – Portway East Saxon cemetery, Andover', 20/4/2015 (https://hampshirearchaeology.wordpress.com/) (Cook, Alastair and Dacre, Maxwell (1985), 'Excavations at Portway, Andover 1973–75', Oxford University Committee for Archaeology)
25. 'Weyhill, Andover – an Anglo-Norman execution cemetery' (20/11/2017), Cotswold Archaeology (www.cotswoldarchaeology.co.uk)
26. Email correspondence (13 April 2023)
27. Apsley Farms website (www.apsleyfarms.com/about-us/about-apsley-farms/)
28. Hampshire HERs 17667, Bowl Barrow
29. Email correspondence (25 February 2022)
30. Email correspondence (8, 10 March 2022)
31. Hampshire HERs 17664, Ashtree Barrow, W of Apsley Farms
32. Gunter, James and Roberts, Vaughan (2005), Geophysical surveys Ashtree and Cerdic's Barrows Andover, Hampshire, University of Bristol
33. Hampshire Geophysical Surveys, Cerdicesbeorg, Stoke and Hurtsbourne, 23/1/2015, Wiltshire Archaeology Field Group
34. Dumville, David (1985), The West Saxon Genealogical Regnal List and the Chronology of Early Wessex
35. Email correspondence (21 February 2022)
36. Email correspondence (17 March 2022)
37. Williams, Howard (1997), Ancient Landscapes and the Dead: The Reuse of Prehistoric and Roman Monuments as Early Anglo-Saxon Burial Sites, *Medieval Archaeology*, Vol. 41 (1), pp.1–32
38. Fleming, Robin (2011), *Britain After Rome, The Fall and Rise, 400 to 1070*, Penguin
39. Dinwiddy, K. E. (2011), *An Anglo-Saxon cemetery at Twyford*, Winchester, Hampshire Field Club & Archaeological Society
40. Historic England Research Records, 867123, Devils Ditch ('Devil's Ditch + Andyke in Hampshire - Map Mysteries', Paul and Rebecca Whitewick, YouTube)
41. Williams-Freeman, J.P. (1933), *The Belgae Hampshire*, Hampshire Field Club & Archaeological Society, Vol. 12, pp.99–126

42. Hampshire HERs 30569, Devil's Ditch Within Pepper Hill Firs
43. Wiltshire and Swindon HERs, SU35NW619, Undated Linear Ditch, Little Down to Conholt Hill
44. Hampshire HERs 61319, Devil's Ditch
45. Hampshire HERs 66620, Devil's Ditch
46. Grigg, Erik (2015), 'Early medieval dykes (400 to 850 AD)', thesis, University of Manchester
47. Lennon, Ben (2010), 'The Relationship between Wansdyke and Bedwyn Dykes', *Wiltshire Archaeological and Natural History Magazine*, pp.269–88
48. Myres, John (1989), *The English Settlements*, Oxford History of England, OUP
49. Fowler, Peter (2001), 'Wansdyke in the Woods: An unfinished Roman military earthwork for a non-event' in Ellis, Peter (editor), *Roman Wiltshire and After: Papers in Honour of Ken Annable*, Wiltshire Archaeological and Natural History Society, pp179–98
50. Elkwall, Eilert (1936), *The Concise Oxford Dictionary of England Place* Names (fourth edition), Clarendon Press, p.21
51. Wansdyke Project 21, Vortigern Studies website (http://www.wansdyke21.org.uk)
52. Jones, Graham (1998), 'Penda's Footprint? Place-Names Containing Personal Names Associated with those of Early Mercian Kings', *Nomina*, Vol. 21, pp.29–62
53. Pitt-Rivers (1892), *Excavations in Bokerley Dyke and Wansdyke Dorset and Wilts*, Folk-Lore, Volume 4
54. Malim, Tim (2020), Grim's Ditch, Wansdyke, and the Ancient Highways of England: Linear Monuments and Political Control, *Offa's Dyke Journa*, Vol. 2, pp.160–99
55. O.G.S. Crawford (1931) 'Cerdic and The Cloven Way'. An original article from *Antiquity*
56. Hampshire HERs 21362, Bowl Barrow E of Smannell (B)
57. Email correspondence (7 November 2022)
58. Hampshire HERs, 23143, Roman Villa, Near Finkley Manor Farm
59. Email correspondence (5 December 2022)
60. Trees for Cities website (www.treesforcities.org)
61. Chisholm, Hugh (editor) (1911), 'Bourne', *Encyclopædia Britannica* (11th edition), Vol. 4, Cambridge University Press, pp.332–33
62. Hampshire HERs 23082, Bowl Barrow NW of Devil's Dyke

63. Crummy, Philip (1997), *City of Victory: The story of Colchester – Britain's first Roman town*, Colchester Archaeological Trust, p.22
64. www.isleofwight.com/our-ancient-island-barrows-and-burial-mounds
65. British Apples and Pears website (www.britishapplesandpears.co.uk/history-of-pears)
66. Lewis, Charlton T. and Short, Charles (1879), *A Latin Dictionary*, Clarendon Press
67. Gunter, James and Roberts, Vaughan (2005), 'Geophysical surveys Ashtree and Cerdic's Barrows Andover, Hampshire', University of Bristol
68. Hampshire HERs 55386, Iron Age, Roman Field System, Tinkers Hill
69. Brayley, Edward (1850), *A topographical history of Surrey*, Vol. 4, G Willis. p.218
70. Grinsell, Leslie (1958), *The Archaeology of Wessex*, Methuen. p.298
71. Langlands, Alexander (2019), *The Ancient Ways of Wessex: Travel and Communication in an Early Medieval Landscape*, Windgather Press
72. Hampshire HERs 223739, Devil's Ditch
73. Historic England, scheduled monument, 1015434, Devil's ditch: boundary earthwork (https://historicengland.org.uk/listing/the-list/list-entry/1015434?section=official-list-entry)
74. Elkwall, Eilert (1936), *The Concise Oxford Dictionary of England Place Names* (fourth edition), Clarendon Press, p.106
75. Ekblom, Laurentius Einar (2018), *The Place-names of Wiltshire, Their Origin and History*, Franklin Classics
76. History of Flowerdown Barrows, English Heritage website

Index